NSX-T Logical Routing

Fortify Your Understanding to Amplify
Your Success

Shashank Mohan

Apress®

NSX-T Logical Routing: Fortify Your Understanding to Amplify Your Success

Shashank Mohan
ACT, Australia

ISBN-13 (pbk): 978-1-4842-7457-6
https://doi.org/10.1007/978-1-4842-7458-3

ISBN-13 (electronic): 978-1-4842-7458-3

Managing Director, Apress Media LLC: Welmoed Spahr
Acquisitions Editor: Aditee Mirashi
Development Editor: Laura Berendson
Coordinating Editor: Shrikant Vishwakarma

Cover designed by eStudioCalamar

Cover image designed by Pexels

Distributed to the book trade worldwide by Springer Science+Business Media LLC, 1 New York Plaza, Suite 4600, New York, NY 10004. Phone 1-800-SPRINGER, fax (201) 348-4505, e-mail orders-ny@springer-sbm. com, or visit www.springeronline.com. Apress Media, LLC is a California LLC and the sole member (owner) is Springer Science + Business Media Finance Inc (SSBM Finance Inc). SSBM Finance Inc is a **Delaware** corporation.

For information on translations, please e-mail booktranslations@springernature.com; for reprint, paperback, or audio rights, please e-mail bookpermissions@springernature.com, or visit http://www.apress. com/rights-permissions.

Apress titles may be purchased in bulk for academic, corporate, or promotional use. eBook versions and licenses are also available for most titles. For more information, reference our Print and eBook Bulk Sales web page at http://www.apress.com/bulk-sales.

Any source code or other supplementary material referenced by the author in this book is available to readers on GitHub via the book's product page, located at www.apress.com/978-1-4842-7457-6. For more detailed information, please visit http://www.apress.com/source-code.

Printed on acid-free paper

"Dogs' lives are too short. Their only fault, really."
—Agnes Turnbull

This book is dedicated to my German shepherd, Sara,
who touched my life in ways that words cannot describe.
You will always be loved. Rest in peace.

Table of Contents

About the Author

Shashank Mohan (Shank) is the ANZ Professional Services practice lead for networking at VMware. He brings over a decade of experience in IT infrastructure and architecture, with a specialization in networking, virtual cloud networking (VCN), and VMware Cloud Foundation (VCF).

Shank is a VMware Advanced Professional in Network Virtualization, a vExpert in NSX, Security, and NSX Advanced Load Balancer (AVI), to name a few VMware certifications. He is also CISCO and AWS certified.

Shank was born and raised in Sydney, Australia, but now prefers the calm and cold capital city, Canberra. Between firmware upgrades and breaking his home lab, he makes time for weight lifting, gardening, and, most importantly, his family.

While Shank is a first-time author, he is a serial blogger. If you'd like to get in touch or continue to learn about virtualization, look up `www.lab2prod.com.au/`.

About the Technical Reviewers

Iwan Hoogendoorn (MSc) started his IT career in 1999 as a helpdesk agent.

Soon after this, Iwan started to learn Microsoft products that resulted in his MCP, MCSA, MCDBA, and MCSE certification.

While working as a Microsoft Systems engineer, Iwan gained an excellent basis to develop additional skills and knowledge in computer networking. Networking became a passion in his life. This passion resulted in learning networking with Cisco products and achieving his CCIE number on six different tracks.

Iwan is currently a staff consultant at VMware and is working on private and public clouds and the related products that VMware developed to build the Software-Defined Data Center (SDDC). He is certified on multiple VMware products, including NSX, and he is actively working together with VMware certification to develop network-related exams for VMware. Next to his VMware certifications, Iwan is also AWS and TOGAF certified.

Iwan is also the author of the two books that teach the basics of NSX-T:

1. *Getting Started with NSX-T: Logical Routing and Switching*

2. *Multi-Site Network and Security Services with NSX-T*

From high-school network administration through to enterprise IT with global companies, **Doug Scobie**'s career has spanned three decades.

For the last 10 years, he has been working for IT vendors, specializing in datacenter technologies, cloud computing, and software solutions for transforming customers.

Outside of work, Doug has a busy outdoor-focused lifestyle with his wife and two daughters. He has a strong affinity for the ocean, bush, and nature.

Luke Flemming is a veteran with over 15 years of IT experience. Luke has been working at VMware for six years, initially joining as a senior consultant in professional services and currently as a technical account manager. Prior to life at VMware, Luke worked for various managed service providers within a number of federal government departments. Upon first being introduced to VMware technologies, he was amazed at the technology potential and value that could be realized and went about specializing in all things VMware.

Outside of work, Luke enjoys playing golf, watching sports (golf, basketball, and rugby league), barbecuing and/or smoking meat, and spending time with his wife and dog.

Acknowledgments

To my best friend and wife, Nikki, thank you for taking care of everything so I could focus on writing this book. Your optimism and belief in what I can achieve is invaluable. You motivate me to keep learning, think outside the box, and be the best version of myself. I am also very thankful for your creative influence on this book.

To my reviewers, Luke, Iwan, and Doug, thank you for sharing your time so generously. Your brutal honesty and willingness to put up with my grammar will not be forgotten. Iwan, I am also very grateful for your mentoring and friendship when I needed it the most.

To my family, both Mohans and Iyers, thank you for your willingness to help in any way you could, whether it was a hot meal on a cold day or uplifting virtual encouragement (#lifeinlockdown). I deeply appreciate having each one of you in my corner.

To my friends, extended family, colleagues, and associates around the world, thank you for encouraging me, inspiring me, and forgiving long periods of silence from me.

Finally, I am grateful to the team at Apress Publishing for reaching out, taking a chance on me, and converting a messy Word document into the book you now have.

Introduction

Have you ever felt like you can't respond to a curveball question from a coworker or client? Have you ever lacked confidence or conviction in your responses? Have you not really understood how or why something functions the way it does?

I have. As a newbie to NSX-T, even with a relatively strong "traditional" networking experience, I found myself constantly seeking help online and reaching out to colleagues. I spent hours trying to find solutions that matched the exact situations that I was in, but two situations are rarely the same.

Despite having spent countless hours on various aspects of the product, I still did not have the answers on hand, and this irked me. I got frustrated with always being on the back foot and decided to take some action to change that.

First, I invested in a home lab. This has been, without a doubt, one of the best investments I have ever made. If you'd like, you can read about my "home lab" (`www.lab2prod.com.au/the-lab`).

Second, I started to replicate customer environments, situations, and issues in my home lab. My lab is constantly evolving (and breaking), but this gave me a safe platform to test possible solutions and start to unpack how things work and develop a deep understanding of NSX-T.

Third, I started to document and share my experiences, as well as connect with peers around the world to learn from their experiences.

As a result of these actions, I am now able to confidently vocalize my opinions, repeatedly demonstrate my expertise in NSX-T, and maintain a strong reputation with my clients and peers.

The purpose of this book is to save you hours of research by giving you everything you need in one spot. It will equip you to figure out solutions to unique situations you find yourself in every day and amplify your confidence and success!

Are you wondering why you should trust me or follow my advice?

As a NSX-T lead at VMware, I have custom-designed NSX-T to be integrated into complex and bespoke client environments, deployed NSX-T in greenfield environments, and advised IT infrastructure teams on networking and NSX-T best practices. These solutions have been provided to multibillion-dollar organizations across defense, technology, telecommunication, education, and public sector industries.

I have been involved with networks for a long time, and it's more than just work to me. It's also something I have an insatiable curiosity for. This continued when I was working as a lead engineer, where I often found myself exploring Software-Defined Networking (SDN) solutions. As a result, I made the decision to join VMware and get in-depth experience designing and deploying NSX-T solutions for some of the largest organizations in Australia and New Zealand.

I am also deeply driven by a passion to help people learn and succeed. As the VMware ANZ practice lead for networking, one of the main focuses of my job is people enablement. I have conducted trainings, acted as a mentor and sounding board, and offered my home lab as a sandbox.

As a vExpert, I have demonstrated my resolve to sharing knowledge and contributing back to the community, beyond my day job. Some of the ways I have done so include publishing blogs, participating in VMware communities, posting video blogs, staying active on online tech forums, and, most recently, publishing this book.

The buck doesn't stop here; you can get in touch with me or continue to learn and explore virtualization through my blog (`www.lab2prod.com.au/`).

Now, let's get down to business.

What is covered in this book?

Chapter 1: The book begins by exploring Software-Defined Data Centers and how NSX-T is incorporated within them. It introduces the basics of NSX-T, including the management, control, data plane, and the various components that these constructs are made up of.

Chapter 2: This chapter explores the difference between underlays and overlays. It then dives deep into tunnel endpoints including configuration practices, tunnel endpoint communication, and tunnel endpoint failure behavior.

Chapter 3: This chapter briefly discusses remote tunnel endpoints, their uses, configuration, and cross-site communication using NSX-T Federation.

Chapter 4: The focus of this book is Logical Routing, and this chapter defines all components that are utilized in the NSX-T fabric. It covers differences between single and multi-tiered Logical Routing. It displays packet walks covering different scenarios and illustrates how packets are routed through the NSX-T data plane.

Chapter 5: This chapter demonstrates how NSX-T handles failures at various layers and provides high availability. This is a critical subject and one that all adopters of NSX-T should be familiar with. The chapter concludes with an introduction to equal cost multipathing and how it is utilized at various layers in NSX-T.

Chapter 6: The final chapter explores NSX-T integration with the datacenter network. It covers NSX-T's implementation of dynamic and static routing and how it operates with the physical network. The chapter also introduces deterministic peering and BFD with the physical network. The book concludes with an explanation of unicast reverse path forwarding behavior in NSX-T in various scenarios.

CHAPTER 1

Introduction

 The aim of this chapter is to provide a basic understanding of:

- Software in the modern data center

- How VMware NSX-T provides a Software-Defined Networking (SDN) solution to make the Software-Defined Data Center (SDDC) possible

The Modern-Day Software-Defined Data Center

In the last decade or so, there has been a major shift in the way organizations manage their IT infrastructure systems. Datacenter functions and services have largely been virtualized to run as "software on commodity compute" platforms to disaggregate services from bespoke hardware devices. Companies such as VMware have made large investments in software-defining the IT infrastructure space.

One of the benefits of software-defining the data center is that organizations can now automate operations to more efficiently, reliably, and securely manage their infrastructure.

You may be asking yourself, what a Software-Defined Data Center is?

A Software-Defined Data Center (SDDC) takes commodity hardware and adds a layer of virtualization to allow efficient use of its resources while providing services through software features. Operations are streamlined through the use of SDDC, via the centralization of compute, networking, and storage management. However, this does increase the responsibility of the traditional virtual infrastructure (VI) admin to encompass networking and storage disciplines.

© Shashank Mohan 2022
S. Mohan, *NSX-T Logical Routing*, https://doi.org/10.1007/978-1-4842-7458-3_1

The benefits organizations realize from SDDC's include the ability to be more agile with their infrastructure and scale up on demand without dependence on hardware device features. When software is leveraged for features and services rather than hardware appliances; upgrades, feature enhancements, and hardware contestability become more easily achievable. When operating a traditional three-tier architecture, each component must be designed considering High Availability (HA) and fault tolerance:

- Compute must be N+1.

- Networking must be redundant and available.

- Storage arrays must be configured in HA configuration.

To achieve this, you require physical servers for each function, storage servers, switches, routers, firewalls, and intrusion detection and prevention systems. SDDCs and Hyperconverged Infrastructure (HCI) simplify compute and storage availability designs as both are collocated in the HCI "node" and have a cluster of hypervisors to create virtual machines on demand.

For organizations running a traditional data center, scaling up infrastructure is a challenging activity requiring large capital investment. It usually involves procuring new hardware, ensuring they have enough physical space for storage, and considering additional power consumption.

Software-Defined Datacenter Architecture

There are different ways of designing and deploying a SDDC. Each organization/vendor/ community that has developed such an offering has standard principles and architecture that they recommend. Underneath the covers they have their own methods of presenting a single pane for storage, compute, networking, and management to simplify operations.

VMware has developed a framework for deploying and maintaining the SDDC.

VMware's framework classifies types of workload into "domains": Management Domain and Workload Domain. These domains consist of a number of certified HCI nodes that are clustered to provide a shared pool of resources.

VMware's preferred method for SDDC automated deployment is to utilize VMware Cloud Foundation (VCF). There are two validated deployment models recommended: Consolidated SDDC and Standard SDDC.

VMware Cloud Foundation consists of the same suite of software-defined products with two additional orchestration appliances. These appliances make it possible to automate the build of the environment and build it to VMware best practices.

Regardless of which deployment model you choose, they both will consist of the following components:

- ESXi

- vSAN

- NSX-T Manager appliances, Edge Transport Nodes, Host Transport Nodes

- vCenter server

- VMware Identity Manager

- SDDC Manager and Cloud Builder – if you are deploying VMware Cloud Foundation (VCF)

The following components are optional add-ons that can be deployed:

- VMware Identity Manager – to support cross-region applications

- vRealize Suite Lifecycle Manager

- vRealize Operations Manager

- vRealize Log Insight

- vRealize Automation

- VMware Horizon

The next section will describe the Consolidated SDDC and the Standard SDDC models.

Consolidated Software-Defined Datacenter Architecture

This deployment model consists of a single domain design, which does not separate the Management Domain and the Workload Domain. This architecture is generally utilized when there are limited hardware resources available or for proof of concept deployments.

Figure 1-1 depicts the foundation of the Consolidated architecture.

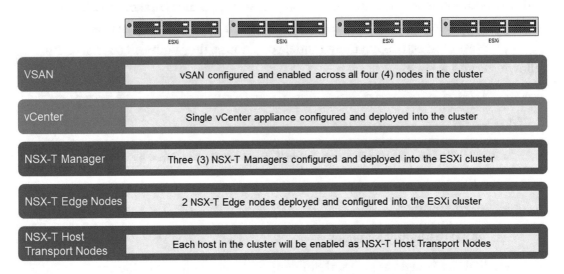

Figure 1-1. *Consolidated Software-Defined Datacenter architecture*

This cluster will host all the management appliances to provide services such as storage, compute, networking, identity, and management.

Regardless of whether you chose to build this manually or use VCF, the earlier list of components will still be required.

vSphere Distributed Resource Scheduler (DRS) is enabled and configured on the cluster. This is to ensure the cluster's resources are adequately balanced, to keep critical management appliances separated, and to avoid complete failure if one host was to go offline.

DRS anti-affinity rules are configured to ensure applications such as the NSX-T Managers are separated; therefore, if a host fails, it will not have the potential to fail two of the three (or all three) NSX-T Managers with it.

Similarly, DRS rules are created for the NSX-T Edge Nodes in order to keep them separated. VMware's published best practices stipulates the recommended configuration for vSphere DRS.

vSphere High Availability (HA) is enabled and configured to protect virtual machines (VM) in the cluster, in the event of an ESXi host failure. If an ESXi host in the cluster fails, vSphere HA restarts the VMs that were on that host on another host in the cluster. Admission control should also be configured in order to ensure there are adequate resources always available to accommodate host failures or to reserve a percentage of resources for failure. The operation of vSphere HA is out of scope for this book; however, details surrounding its functionality can be found on the VMware website.

Once all the management infrastructure is provisioned, workload virtual machines can be either provisioned directly on the cluster or migrated onto it from an existing environment.

Standard Software-Defined Datacenter Architecture

Figure 1-2 depicts the Standard VMware SDDC deployed with VCF, consisting of a four-node Management Domain and minimum three-node Workload Domain.

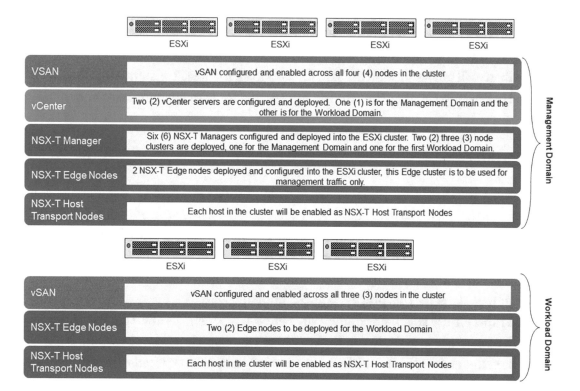

Figure 1-2. *Standard Software-Defined Datacenter architecture*

Management Domain

The Standard SDDC model has a Management Domain and, at minimum, one Workload Domain. The Management Domain will host all the same management appliances as the Consolidated model; however, there will be no workload virtual machines in the Management Domain. This domain is reserved for all management appliances. This domain can also host customer management virtual machines such as image repositories and Active Directory.

As with the Consolidated design, vSphere HA and vSphere DRS should be configured. In the case of a VCF deployment, they will be enabled and configured automatically.

Additional appliances, such as the second vCenter server and NSX-T Manager cluster, are not required to be deployed until the first Workload Domain is going to be deployed; once again this is automated with VCF.

As there will be a dedicated domain for workload, the NSX-T instance that had been created in the Management Domain will be reserved for management hosts and traffic only.

Workload Domain

Each time a Workload Domain is created, a vCenter server is created in the Management Domain and linked to the existing vCenter servers in the same Single Sign On (SSO) domain. The hosts that are being added to this Workload Domain are also added into a data center and cluster in this new vCenter server.

The NSX-T Managers for the Workload Domain should be deployed into the Management Domain. This process is also automated with VCF.

You must ensure adequate connectivity between the managers and the ESXi hosts that will be configured for NSX-T in the Workload Domain. The VMware website is a valuable resource for specific details on connectivity and port requirements; the required ports can be found here: https://ports.vmware.com/home/NSX-T-Data-Center.

All hosts in all Workload Domains will be prepared for NSX-T, which then allows them to participate in NSX-T.

Edge Transport Nodes should be provisioned for North-South traffic routing and other stateful services that may be required. Depending on how you wish you structure your environment, you may wish to build an NSX-T Edge cluster per Workload Domain or utilize one Edge cluster for multiple workload domains.

VMware NSX-T: SDDC Networking

NSX-T is a Software-Defined Networking (SDN) solution by VMware:

- It utilizes software to provide networking and security in the SDDC. Doing so avoids single points of failure and allows you to perform traditional network functions in a distributed manner.

- It integrates with the rest of the VMware suite of products to provide a seamless experience to the system administrator or individual designing, deploying, and maintaining the platform.

- It is not limited to a single data center and is able to accommodate geographically dispersed sites.

- It is also capable of extending its reach to cloud platforms, such as AWS, Azure, Google Cloud, etc.

In contrast, with traditional network infrastructure, it is extremely difficult to dynamically connect, secure, and automate networking for applications.

The Basics of NSX-T

This section will act as a precursor for the rest of the book – it will describe the NSX-T platform and start diving deeper into how it functions. In the coming chapters, this book will focus purely on how NSX-T communicates and logically routes data.

NSX-T has three distinct planes for functionality. They are:

- The management plane

- The control plane

- The data plane

Figure 1-3 shows how these components are logically structured.

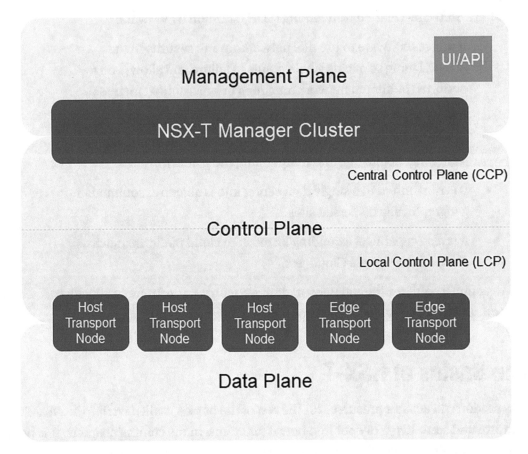

Figure 1-3. *NSX-T logical component overview*

Management Plane

NSX-T Manager Cluster Availability

The NSX-T management plane is made up of the NSX-T Manager cluster. A three-node cluster is recommended to avoid split brain, and to ensure you do not lose access to your management plane as a result of a single manager going offline.

With the release of NSX-T 3.1, administrators have the option to deploy a single manager in production. However, the same caveats apply, and they must be taken into consideration.

There could be several reasons as to why one may lose an NSX-T Manager; a few of those reasons are listed here:

- Host failure

- Datastore failure

- Host isolation

- Appliance corruption

Table 1-1 highlights filesystem access to the NSX-T Manager when there has been a varying number of nodes lost.

Table 1-1. *NSX-T Management Plane Availability*

	Three (3) available	Two (2) available	One (1) available
Three-node manager cluster	Full read and write	Full read and write	Read only
Single manager			Full read and write

 If only a single NSX-T Manager node was deployed and the cluster was never scaled out, the single manager will have full read and write access.

If you do lose access to your NSX-T Manager cluster or it is in read-only mode, the data plane will continue to function. It is, however, in your best interest to restore access to the management plane as quickly as possible.

Management Plane Functionality

The management plane provides an entry point for users to be able to consume NSX-T. NSX-T can be consumed either via the user interface (UI) or its application programming interface (API).

Common configuration tasks are performed at the management plane layer, regardless of whether the UI or API was used.

The following is a list of common configuration objects that are stored in the database:

- Uplink profiles

- Transport node profiles

- Host configuration

- Host status

- Segments

- Tier-1 gateways

- Tier-0 gateways

The list of configuration tasks that can be done at this layer is quite extensive, and not all of them are listed here.

Once a configuration change has been made, the management plane validates the configuration, stores a copy in its database, and then replicates it to the remaining manager nodes. Finally, the configuration is pushed to the central control plane (CCP).

Each node (Host Transport Node or Edge Node) has a management plane agent running on it. The management plane polls these agents to retrieve statistics that can be used for troubleshooting.

Policy and Manager Mode

In NSX-T 3.0 and above, there are two consumption models in the UI: Policy Mode and Manager Mode.

In previous versions, Policy Mode was called the *Simplified UI*. Policy Mode is the default UI mode and can be used to perform most tasks. As new versions of NSX-T are released, more functionalities will be added to Policy Mode. In saying this, there are some use cases that may require the use of Manager Mode. The reasons to use Manager Mode are not covered in this book. However further information is available on the VMware website.

Control Plane

The control plane is broken up into two planes:

- The central control plane (CCP)

    It sits within the NSX-T Manager cluster, but its functionality is separate to that of the management plane.

- The local control plane (LCP)

The CCP receives configuration updates from the management plane, which is considered the source of truth for all configuration. Once the CCP receives the data, it disseminates the data to the LCP, which sits on every transport node. A transport node only receives configuration data if it requires it. The specifics of how the different planes communicate will not be covered in this book.

Data Plane

Transport Nodes

There are two different types of entities that live in the data plane: the Host Transport Nodes (ESXi hypervisors, KVM Hypervisors) and Edge Nodes (can either be a VM or a bare metal appliance).

An ESXi hypervisor does not become a Host Transport Node until it has been prepared for NSX-T. What this means is NSX-T Manager has to push the VIBs required for NSX-T onto the host and install it. Once that is successfully completed, the host appears in the NSX Manager UI with successful NSX configuration status and with a status of "Up."

Users may use the NSX-T Manager UI to deploy the Edge Node VM appliances, doing so will configure the VMs with the settings provided through the wizard. With this method the VMs are automatically joined to the management plane. Another method to deploy an Edge Node VM appliance is by manually deploying the OVF template. However, this method will require manual intervention so that the management plane sees the appliances.

The second type of Edge Node is the bare metal server. This is a physical server (or, most commonly, servers) dedicated to performing the edge functions. This type of Edge Node is used when there are specific requirements for it; generally most deployments should suffice with the Edge Node VM appliance.

Transport Zones

There are two types of Transport Zones: VLAN Transport Zones and Overlay Transport Zones.

The easiest way to think of a Transport Zone is like having a gym membership and having access to all its amenities (segments). Any one node host attached to a specific Transport Zone has access to and will see all segments that are created and attached to that Transport Node.

As an example, Figure 1-4 shows two Transport Zones, an Overlay and a VLAN Transport Zone. What should be discernible is that transport nodes 1 to 3 are attached to the Overlay Transport Zone and can see the overlay segments; however, they cannot see the VLAN segments. And on the other hand, transport nodes 4 and 5 are attached to the VLAN Transport Zone and cannot see the overlay segments.

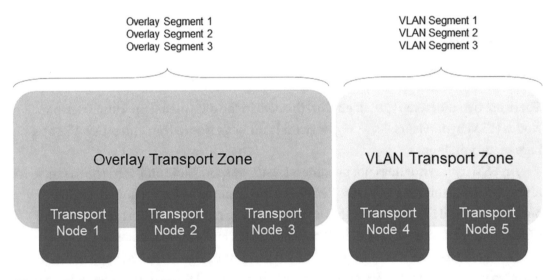

Figure 1-4. *Transport Zones*

 A transport node can be a member of two Overlay Transport Zones; however, it requires dedicated uplink interfaces (NICs) for each Overlay Transport it is a member of.

NSX-T can provision two types of networks, they are, VLAN-backed segments and overlay segments:

- **VLAN-backed segment:** This type of segment is straightforward; the easiest way to think of it is just a typical portgroup with a VLAN tag. Packet forwarding for a VLAN-backed segment can be thought of being the same as standard VLAN communication for ingress and egress to the hypervisor.

- **Overlay segment:** This type of segment is instantiated on each Host Transport Node that has been added to the Overlay Transport Zone. It utilizes GENEVE headers and does not rely on traditional VLANs. An overlay segment enables true East-West packet switching and routing in the NSX-T domain, which isn't possible with traditional networking.

This book will focus on how Logical Routing in NSX-T operates and will cover overlay segments and logical-switches in a little more detail in the coming chapters.

Tunnel Endpoints

NSX-T configures each of its transport nodes with a Tunnel Endpoint (TEP) address. That is, both the Host Transport Nodes and the Edge Nodes are configured with a minimum of one TEP address and, for redundancy and load balancing purposes, can be configured with two TEP interfaces. The number of TEP addresses and interfaces are determined by the amount of uplink interfaces the node has. That is, if there is a single uplink on a host, it will have a single TEP address; however, if there are two interfaces, it can be configured with two TEP addresses.

NSX-T transport nodes form GENEVE tunnels between TEP endpoints and utilize these tunnels for East-West communication. Tunnels are formed between each host TEP address, between the Edge TEPs, and from Host Transport Node TEP addresses to the Edge TEP addresses. One thing to keep in mind is the tunnel on a host will remain in a down state, unless there is active workload on a segment on a host.

An in-depth walkthrough of TEP communication between transport nodes will be covered in Chapter 2.

Summary

In this chapter, we introduced the benefits of the SDDC and discussed the VMware interpretation of it with VMware best practice and VMware Cloud Foundation. We then covered some of the fundamentals of NSX-T and how the components communicate. This provides enough of an overview into the platform before deep-diving into the technology and uncovering its true potential. In the next chapter, this book will cover topics such as the difference between underlay and overlay, VXLAN and GENEVE encapsulation, and how the transport nodes communicate.

CHAPTER 2

Tunnel Endpoints

 This chapter will delve deeper into overlay networking in contrast to traditional networking. By the end of this chapter, readers should understand the following:

- Overlay networking, specifically Generic Network Virtualization Encapsulation (GENEVE) encapsulation

- How NSX-T transport nodes communicate

- The prerequisites to configure tunnel endpoints and transport nodes

- How to configure tunnel endpoints on transport nodes

- How GENEVE packets flow between transport nodes

- Tunnel endpoint failure behavior

© Shashank Mohan 2022
S. Mohan, *NSX-T Logical Routing*, https://doi.org/10.1007/978-1-4842-7458-3_2

Overlay Networking

What Is a Network Overlay?

The concept of overlay networking is not new and has been around for close to two decades. Overlay networking abstracts traditional networking functions from the physical network fabric and performs them in software. This is achieved by encapsulating the data packet with an additional header. Technologies such as Virtual Extensible VLAN (VXLAN), Network Virtualization using Generic Routing Encapsulation (NVGRE), Stateless Transport Tunnelling (STT), and GENEVE were introduced to combat the limitations of traditional network and VLAN limitations.

VLANs

VLANs were developed and remain heavily utilized to provide network segregation for both security and to limit the broadcast domain. Due to the 12-bit 802.1Q field limitation, engineers and administrators are restricted to having a maximum of 4094 usable VLANs on their network. Previously this was sufficient for most, if not all, implementations; however, with the introduction of network automation and datacenter virtualization, this is no longer the case. Engineers and administrators quickly started reaching this limitation, and this was one of the major drivers for overlay encapsulation.

The following section will discuss the differences between VXLAN and GENEVE.

Differences Between VXLAN and GENEVE

VXLAN

VXLAN is currently one of the most used encapsulation protocols for network overlay. RFC7348, published by the IETF, is a highly detailed document that outlines VXLAN and its capabilities. This section will highlight the main use cases and benefits of the protocol; for further detail, please review RFC7348 published by the IETF.

- **VLAN exhaustion:** VXLAN overcomes the limitation of 4094 VLANs by inserting an 8-byte header into the ethernet frame. The VXLAN header is an 8-byte header that consists of a 24-bit VXLAN Network Identifier (VNID) and a few reserved bits. The VNID is used to identify layer 2 segments, like how a VLAN operates. This 8-byte header can support up to 16 million different layer 2 segments.

- **Multitenancy:** Multitenancy in the data center refers to the logical isolation of resources. Tenants or customers are provided compute, storage, and networking resources on shared physical hardware used by other tenants or customers; however, all data and traffic between tenants remain completely isolated from one another.

  While the networking component could be achieved with traditional layer 2 VLANs, this method is not scalable beyond 4094 VLANs. With the growing number of cloud providers and on-premises cloud computing, tenancies are becoming more common. VXLAN (and other encapsulation protocols) make it possible to scale out the data center to accommodate this requirement.

- **Layer 2 loop avoidance:** Traditional approach to stretching VLANs is to extend the layer 2 broadcast domain over physical fabric. In doing so, this could cause unintended issues with Spanning Tree Protocol (STP). If the design and implementation of the network has not been appropriately scoped, this could cause major issues, including but not limited to; datacenter outages and links being disabled.

  What VXLAN does is create layer 2 adjacencies over routed layer 3 links. As a layer 3 link is used, Spanning Tree Protocol is avoided. This allows maximum utilization of all physical network links.

  On the other hand, if a data center is designed with STP, careful consideration must be made to the design. If improperly or incorrectly configured, redundant links may be blocked, subpar performance may be encountered, and layer 2 loops may materialize.

GENEVE

A GENEVE encapsulated ethernet frame looks very similar to a VXLAN frame in that GENEVE also overcomes VLAN exhaustion, enables multitenancy, and avoids layer 2 loops. However, there are some key differences that set it apart:

- **Control plane data:** Unlike earlier encapsulation protocols, GENEVE does not carry any control plane data; for example, VXLAN must utilize a protocol for control plane learning, which may be either multicast, unicast or MP-BGP.

Most encapsulation protocols are structured similarly for data; the main difference between them is their control planes.

The GENEVE protocol utilizes a data only structure in that there is no control plane data in the header. This is to make GENEVE a pure tunnel format to work with all forms of control planes.

- **GENEVE header:** GENEVE has a flexible inner header; this inner header makes it possible to define the length, fields, and content based on the instruction given by the tunnel endpoint, which is the node encapsulating the frame. This flexible header also makes the GENEVE protocol flexible, allowing it to fulfill the needs of many control planes.

NSX-T utilizes the GENEVE protocol for tunnel endpoint communication. Further information on transport node communication within NSX-T will be discussed in the next section. If you would like more information on the GENEVE protocol, please review RFC8926 published by the IETF.

NSX-T Transport Node Communication

This section will explore tunnel endpoints (TEPs) in further detail; it will expand on what a TEP is, what purpose a TEP serves, the impact of poorly or misconfigured TEPs, how components in the data plane use TEPs to communicate, and different TEP failure scenarios.

Transport Node Types

Before looking into TEPs and transport VLANs, this section will expand a little more on NSX-T transport nodes. As briefly discussed in Chapter 1, the data plane consists of transport nodes. There are two types of transport nodes:

- **Host Transport Nodes:** These are the hypervisors participating in NSX-T. A hypervisor does not become a Host Transport Node until it has been prepared for NSX-T. This means it has had the NSX-T kernel modules installed on it.

The NSX-T kernel modules for an ESXi host are vSphere Installation Bundles (VIBs), and on KVM, depending on which type you are using, there are packages made for that type of operating system. This process can be done through the NSX-T Manager user interface or manually. The next section will show the configuration of a Host Transport Node.

This book will focus on ESXi; however, it will refer to KVM in various sections.

Ensure you check the software compatibility list for the version of NSX-T Data Center that you are installing. Failing to do so could result in undesirable behavior or render your environment in a nonworking state. VMware's Interoperability tool `https://interopmatrix.vmware.com/#/Interoperability` *will assist in checking software compatibility.*

Once a Host Transport Node has been successfully configured, the host is added into the NSX-T fabric and will have a host-switch configured on it. This is enabled at the kernel level and does not require any additional appliances or software to run at the guest layer. This step is essential for the transport node to be able to perform its packet forwarding functions.

- **Edge Transport Nodes:** These can be either a virtual machine sitting on a Host Transport Node or a bare metal server. Edge Transport Nodes are required to enable North-South connectivity between the NSX-T domain and the physical network.

  Aside from enabling connectivity to the physical network, Edge Transport Nodes can also provide stateful services, such as load balancing, DHCP, stateful firewall, VPN, and stateful NAT.

  Edge VMs can be deployed automatically through the NSX-T Manager UI or manually using the binaries found on the VMware website.

Bare Metal Edge Transport Nodes must be deployed with an ISO; this can be done automatically using a Preboot Execution Environment (PXE) or manually installing the ISO.

Like Host Transport Nodes, Edge Nodes that are deployed have a host-switch instantiated on them, which allows them to perform packet forwarding operations.

What Is a Tunnel Endpoint?

A tunnel endpoint (TEP) is an interface, or more commonly multiple interfaces, assigned to either a Host Transport Node or Edge Transport Node. These interfaces, as with any other interface on the host or edge, have an IP address and MAC address assigned to them. When transport nodes send and receive overlay traffic, they need to encapsulate and de-encapsulate GENEVE packets and use their TEP interfaces to do so.

The number of TEP interfaces assigned to a transport node is dependent on the number of interfaces they have enabled and configured to be used with NSX-T.

In Figure 2-1, the Host Transport Node has two physical network interfaces that are connected and configured for use with NSX-T.

Physical adapters

Device		Actual Speed		Configured Speed		Switch		MAC Address	
vmnic0		1 Gbit/s		Auto negotiate		mgmt-vds		24:6e:96:60:b0:a0	
vmnic1		1 Gbit/s		Auto negotiate		mgmt-vds		24:6e:96:60:b0:a1	
vmnic2		Down		Auto negotiate		--		24:6e:96:60:b0:a2	
vmnic3		Down		Auto negotiate		--		24:6e:96:60:b0:a3	

Figure 2-1. *Host Transport Node physical NICs*

Starting with NSX-T 3.x, the recommended way to configure ESXi Host Transport Nodes is to use a vSphere Distributed Switch (VDS) instead of an NSX-T Virtual Distributed Switch (N-VDS).

Figure 2-2 shows the switch visualization from the NSX-T Manager UI. The image shows the vmnics mapped to the VDS, as well as the uplinks tied to the VDS.

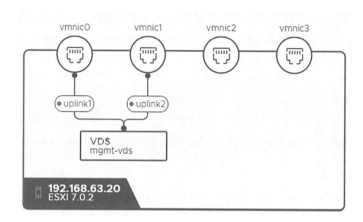

Figure 2-2. *NSX-T VDS Switch Visualization*

Once a host has been successfully prepared for NSX-T, it will have the NSX-T VIBs or packages installed on it, have a host-switch instantiated on it, and at minimum one, or in the example image (Figure 2-2) two, VMkernel interface configured on it for overlay communication. There is an additional interface which is configured as part of NSX-T and not visualized in Figure 2-2. This is the *vmk50* interface; this interface is the HyperBus interface and typically used with Tanzu Kubernetes Grid Integration.

Excluding vmk50, the amount of VMkernel ports created is dependent on the number of TEP interfaces being deployed and configured. This will be covered later in this chapter.

Figure 2-3 shows the two VMkernel interfaces created on the host; take note of the VMkernel interface number and the TCP/IP stack; these interface numbers will be consistent across all ESXi Host Transport Nodes, as will the TCP/IP stack.

vmk0	mgmt-vds	192.168.63.20	Default
vmk1	mgmt-vds	10.55.0.240	Default
vmk2	mgmt-vds	10.56.0.240	Default
vmk10	mgmt-vds	192.168.65.2	nsx-overlay
vmk11	mgmt-vds	192.168.65.3	nsx-overlay

Figure 2-3. *Host Transport Node physical interfaces*

Once transport nodes have been installed and configured, they form GENEVE tunnels between themselves. Figure 2-4 shows GENEVE tunnels being formed between the Host Transport Node and the Edge Nodes.

Tunnel Status: ALL   13 UP   8 DOWN   Filter by BFD Status: ALL

Source IP	Remote IP	Status	BFD Diagnostic Code	Remote Transport Node	Encap Interface	Encap	Tunnel Name
192.168.65.55	192.168.66.31	● Up	0 - No Diagnostic	en02	vmk11	GENEVE	geneve32322524...
192.168.65.54	192.168.66.32	● Up	0 - No Diagnostic	en01	vmk10	GENEVE	geneve32322524...
192.168.65.55	192.168.66.32	● Up	0 - No Diagnostic	en01	vmk11	GENEVE	geneve32322524...

Figure 2-4. *Host Transport Node GENEVE tunnel status*

If there are no active workloads on an NSX-T segment, the tunnel status on the transport node will be in a down state.

Tunnel Endpoint Communication

This section will focus on communication between transport nodes, will dive deeper into packet communication between endpoints, and will provide a packet walk to demonstrate the importance of TEP communication.

Figure 2-4 shows several GENEVE tunnels that have formed between the TEP interfaces of a Host Transport Node and two edge appliances. The following details can be gleaned from this image:

- **Source IP:** This is the originating TEP IP address from which the GENEVE tunnel is being initiated.

- **Remote IP:** This is the destination TEP IP address to which the GENEVE tunnel is being formed with.

- **Status:** The status will either be green to symbolize the tunnel being up or red to symbolize the tunnel being down.

- **BFD diagnostic code:** There are nine different diagnostic codes; "0 – No diagnostic" indicates the tunnel is up and there are no issues. Further details on these diagnostic codes can be found on the VMware website.

- **Remote transport node:** This indicates which transport node the tunnel has been formed with.

- **Encap interface:** This is the source interface from which the GENEVE tunnel was initiated from.

- **Encap:** This is the protocol used for encapsulation.

- **Tunnel name:** A unique identifying name is given to each tunnel.

For GENEVE tunnels to successfully form, there are requirements that must be met in your physical network; these can be seen in Table 2-1.

Table 2-1. *TEP Requirements*

Requirement	Specification
MTU	Minimum 1600 bytes.
GENEVE protocol	UDP port 6081 must be open.
Transport VLANs	VLANs used to transport TEP data between transport nodes.
Routing between transport VLANs	If multiple VLANs are being used to segregate host and Edge TEP addresses, these VLANs must be routable or else the tunnels will not form.

The minimum required MTU is 1600 bytes; to leave room for future expansion of features, it is best to configure an MTU of 9000 bytes in the physical network. NSX-T Federation recommends an MTU of 1700 bytes.

If the MTU is not set, the packets are fragmented and can cause varying issues in your deployment.

Routed Transport VLANs

So far, this chapter has introduced the concept of TEP interfaces and addresses, as well as what their function is between transport nodes.

This section will focus on transport VLANs and how they are used in conjunction with TEP interfaces.

For tunnel endpoints to communicate over a physical network, the physical ports and networking fabric must be configured to support them. This is where the physical networking design plays a major role in the successful deployment of NSX-T. Network design is out of scope for this book; however, details on these requirements can be found on the VMware website.

In simple terms, tunnel endpoints are just an endpoint, like a client on a network. For them to be able to ingress and egress over the network, they either need to be switched or routed through a top of rack switch or gateway.

This is where transport VLANs are used. In simple terms, they are the VLAN that carry TEP traffic between transport nodes. In versions preceding NSX-T 3.1, it was typical to have two transport VLANs, one for Host Transport Nodes and one for Edge Transport Nodes. In version 3.1 a feature called inter-TEP traffic was added. This allows the use of a single VLAN to transport both host and Edge TEP traffic. This will be covered later in this chapter.

Overlay Communication on 2 pNIC Hosts

Separate VLANs are required on hosts that have two physical network interfaces. The reason the two transport VLANs are required is that the Host Transport Nodes TEP can only send and receive GENEVE traffic on a physical network interface configured with a TEP address. The traffic between Host Transport Nodes and Edge VMs needs to be routed externally and then ingress into the physical NIC of the Host Transport Node. If both are configured with the same transport VLAN, the packets are sent directly between the TEP interfaces of the edge and host transport node and subsequently dropped. This means the GENEVE tunnels will not form and therefore will result in no North-South communication. Tunnels between Host Transport Nodes will still be instantiated as the packets will ingress and egress their physical NICs.

Figure 2-5 depicts the issue of having a single TEP VLAN on a 2 pNIC host.

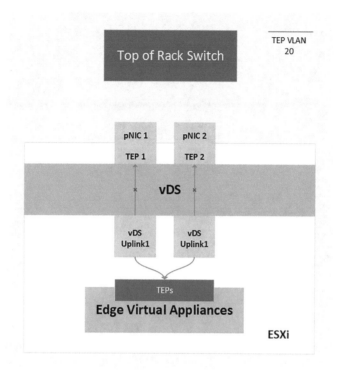

Figure 2-5. *2 pNIC host with a single TEP VLAN*

In Figure 2-5, we can see that there is a single VLAN (20), for both host and Edge TEPs. The issue here is, as both the edge and host TEP interfaces are on the same VLAN, the TEP traffic is sent directly between the interfaces. The traffic is dropped when it is received on the TEP address of the host; this is because GENEVE traffic is only accepted on the physical interface of the host.

Figure 2-6 shows the typical data path for TEP traffic on a 2 pNIC host.

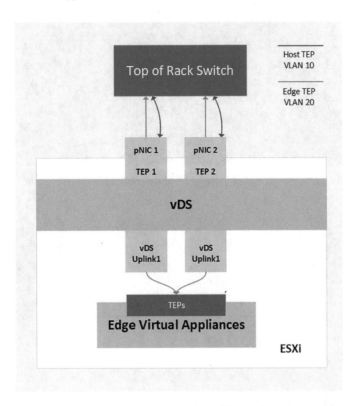

Figure 2-6. *2 pNIC host with separate edge and host TEP VLANs*

Figure 2-6 highlights working TEP configuration for a 2 pNIC host. As the Edge TEP VLAN is in a different subnet to the host TEPs, the data is routed externally and sent back to the physical interfaces of the host. Once the data is received, it is sent to the TEP interface on the Host Transport Node. Having two separate VLANs for edge and host overlay aligns with VMware best practices.

Overlay Communication on 4 pNIC Hosts

If the host has four physical network interfaces, the same transport VLAN may be used. A host with four physical network interfaces typically has two VDS. The first switch should handle all management traffic, such as management, vMotion, vSAN, and other services you may enable. The second VDS (N-VDS in previous versions) would handle the overlay and VLAN traffic from NSX-T. In this case, the Edge VM would be plumbed into VDS 1. TEP traffic originating from the Host Transport Node egresses either pNIC 3 or pNIC 4 from the

Host Transport Node and ingresses into one of the physical uplinks of VDS 1. The same applies for traffic from the edge back to the Host Transport Node; it leaves either pNIC 1 or pNIC 2, is switched by the top of rack switch, and then ingresses into pNIC 3 or pNIC 4.

Figure 2-7 shows typical edge and Host Transport Node configuration with 4 pNICs, where the edge appliance resides on the Host Transport Node.

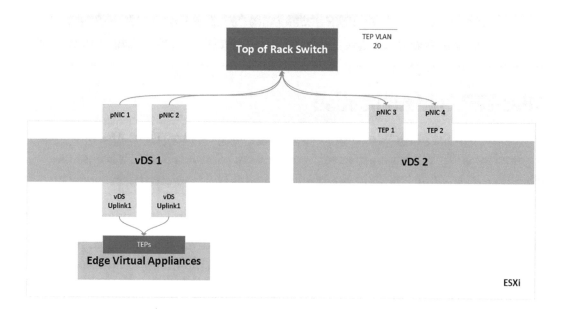

Figure 2-7. *4 pNIC host with 1 TEP VLAN*

Figure 2-7 shows a valid approach to configuring a multi-VDS NSX-T environment. Notice a single TEP VLAN being used here. It is also possible to use the two VLAN approach with this deployment architecture. If this is part of a VCF deployment, it is currently a requirement to have two separate VLANs for edge and host overlay. It is also possible to have a single VDS with 4 pNICs, and if this is the case, two VLANs will still be required, as you will see similar behavior to the two pNIC approach.

The preceding examples show 2 and 4 pNIC hosts; however, more pNICs may be used with hosts. The same principles of edge wiring and tunnel endpoints should be used.

As this book's focus is on NSX-T, the physical network is displayed as a single entity. It should be noted as best practice, for redundancy, two top of rack switches should be deployed as part of the solution. They may be used as the layer 2 and layer 3 termination point and have routing enabled on them, or routing may be done at the aggregation or core layer. This is dependent on the network architecture being deployed. More details on recommended physical network design can be found on VMware's website.

Inter-TEP Communication

As described in the previous section, in certain topologies, two TEP VLANs were required for GENEVE tunnels to form. In the current release of NSX-T, it is possible to utilize a single VLAN for TEP communication; this is also referred to as inter-TEP communication.

Inter-TEP communication enables the use of a single transport VLAN for both the host and edge. The only difference in configuration is that you must use a VLAN-backed segment created in NSX-T for the edge appliances uplink interfaces, as opposed to a standard VDS portgroup. Whichever method chosen to deploy the environment is valid and supported.

Prior to looking at TEP packet flow, an overview for configuring TEP interfaces will be provided in the following section.

Tunnel Endpoint Configuration

Most of the time, tunnel endpoints are created on a Host Transport Node as they are being prepared for NSX-T. The only time they are not is when there is an issue with the IP pool, DHCP server, or if they are prepared for VLAN microsegmentation only. In the last instance they do not require a TEP IP address.

Edge TEP addresses are configured during the deployment of the Edge Transport Node if you use the wizard to deploy the appliances. If you have manually deployed the edge using the OVA, there are additional steps to have the Edge Transport Nodes ready for data transport, including adding them to the management plane and configuring NSX on the Edge Transport Node.

Before preparing a Host Transport Node for NSX-T, a few steps need to be taken so they can be prepared. The next section will cover these prerequisites.

Tunnel Endpoint Configuration Prerequisites

This section briefly covers the prerequisites required to successfully deploy transport nodes. It is not a comprehensive list of all NSX-T prerequisites, as this chapter focuses on tunnel endpoint configuration.

Add a Compute Manager

One of the first steps after deploying NSX-T and assigning a license is that you are required to add a compute manager. A compute manager is an appliance that manages hosts and virtual machines and is generally vCenter.

Without a compute manager, NSX-T will not see any of the hosts that will be prepared and used in the NSX-T domain.

Add Hosts to VDS

To be able to prepare the host using the VDS option, the host must first be added to a VDS. This book assumes the following exist:

- Hosts with no NSX-T VIBs installed

- vCenter with a VDS of version 7.0 or later and hosts for NSX-T added to it

- VLANs required for host and Edge TEPs trunked to the hosts

- Minimum 1600 MTU configured in the network, where NSX-T transport nodes will be communicating

Figure 2-8 displays expected behavior when attempting to prepare a host that has not been added to a VDS in vCenter. Notice the "Name" drop-down list is empty. This list is enumerated based on VDSs configured in vCenter. If there is no VDS configured, and the host is not attached to the VDS, this list will be empty.

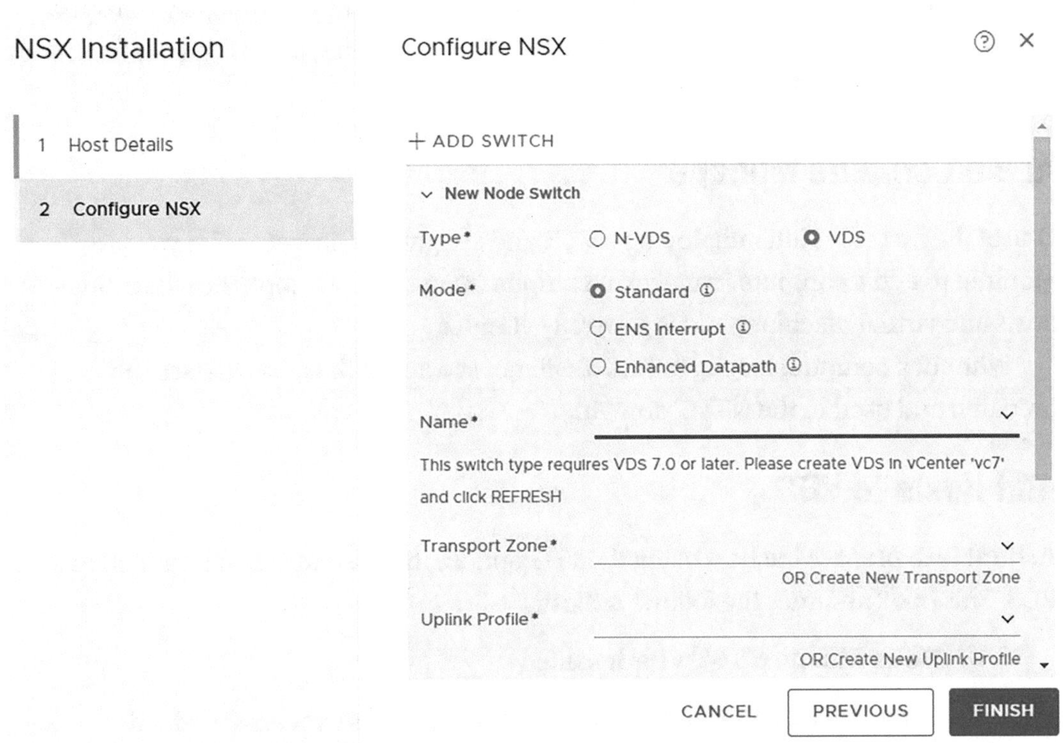

Figure 2-8. *Preparing a host with no VDS in vCenter*

Figure 2-9 displays the same wizard after the host has been attached to a VDS in vCenter.

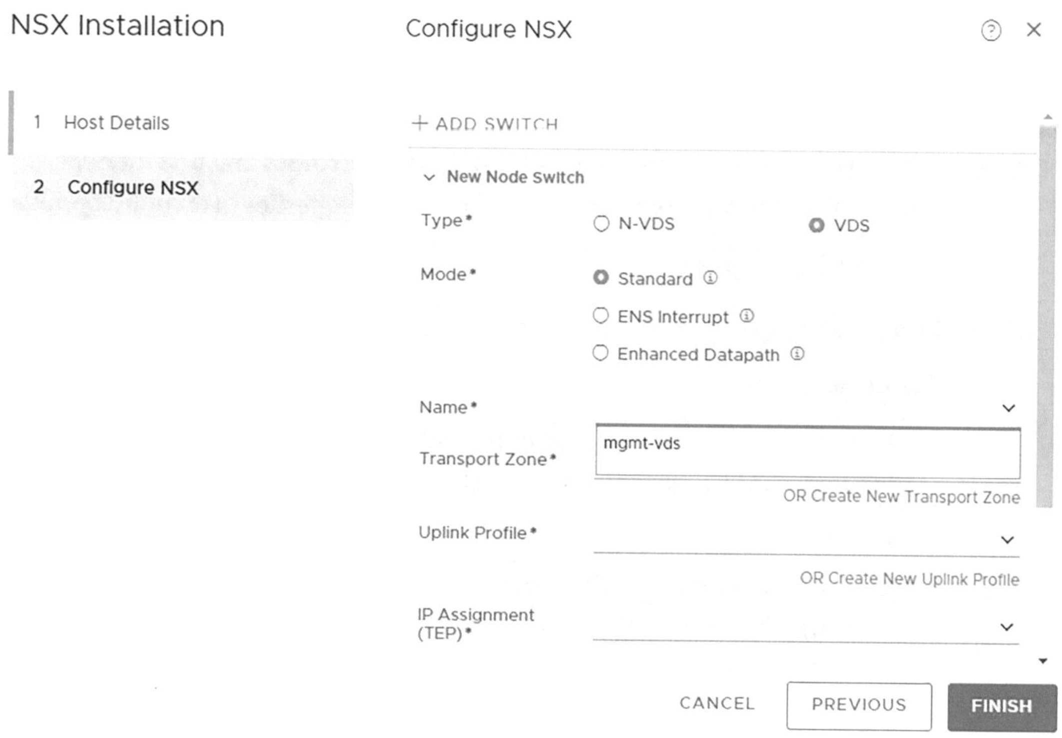

NSX Installation

Configure NSX

1   Host Details

2   Configure NSX

+ ADD SWITCH

⌄ New Node Switch

Type *   ○ N-VDS   ● VDS

Mode *   ● Standard ⓘ
                ○ ENS Interrupt ⓘ
                ○ Enhanced Datapath ⓘ

Name *

Transport Zone *   mgmt-vds

                    OR Create New Transport Zone

Uplink Profile *

                    OR Create New Uplink Profile

IP Assignment
(TEP) *

CANCEL   PREVIOUS   FINISH

Figure 2-9. *Preparing a host that is attached to a VDS*

Creating a Transport Zone

Chapter 1 described a Transport Zone's function and how they can be used. As part of host preparation, the hosts must be added to a Transport Zone. Depending on the design requirements, a host may be prepared with just a VLAN Transport Zone or an Overlay Transport Zone. The transport node can also be attached to both an Overlay Transport Zone and a VLAN Transport Zone at the same time; this will give administrators the ability to utilize both overlay segments and VLAN-backed segments. Two default Transport Zones exist in NSX-T after deploying the managers – one for overlay and one for VLAN. These can be utilized if administrators wish to do so.

It is common to configure an additional VLAN Transport Zone. This Transport Zone is attached to the Edge Transport Nodes, instead of attaching the VLAN Transport Zone that is linked to the hosts. This is done so all VLAN-backed segments presented to the hosts are not also presented to the edges. From a functional perspective, you may use a single VLAN Transport Zone; however, when attaching segments to uplink interfaces on the Tier-0 gateway, a separate VLAN Transport Zone for the edges makes this process simpler.

Create Uplink Profiles

An uplink profile is an important component of transport node preparation. It is common to have two uplink profiles, one for Host Transport Nodes and one for Edge Transport Nodes. Administrators can define the following properties in an uplink profile:

- Name and description

- LAGs

- Teamings policy:

  - **Failover order** – Single active uplink, with a standby uplink for failover. KVM hosts can only be configured with this teaming policy.

  - **Load balance source** – Enables two or more active uplinks and multi-TEP load balancing. Load is balanced based on source port ID.

  - **Load balance source MAC** – Best used if configuring guest VLAN tagging. It is useful when multiple MAC addresses are coming from the same port ID.

- **Transport VLAN** – Define the VLAN to be used for overlay transport.

- **MTU** – If using VDS, MTU settings are taken from VDS settings, else this can be configured.

It is generally not recommended to use LAGs, but this is dependent on individual use cases. Both load balancing methods require more than one physical NIC and VDS uplink. There are some default uplink profiles that are created as part of the initial NSX-T deployment; however, they will not reflect the environment requirements.

Create IP Pool

IP pools can be created to allocate TEP addresses to host and Edge Transport Nodes within NSX-T. IP pools are not mandatory; Host Transport Nodes can use DHCP or have their addresses manually assigned during node preparation.

Edge Transport Nodes have the options of either using IP pools or static assignment.

Transport Node Profiles

Transport node profiles are handy when configuring multiple hosts. Without a transport node profile, each individual host needs to be configured separately. Transport node profiles can be attached to a cluster to prepare the entire cluster at a time.

Properties that can be defined in a transport node profile include

- Name and description
- N-VDS or VDS
- Mode
  - Standard
  - ENS interrupt
  - Enhanced data path
- Name – name of the host-switch used for packet forwarding on the host
- Transport Zone
- NIOC Profile
- Uplink Profile
- LLDP Profile – optional
- IP Assignment (TEPs) – choice of DHCP or IP pool
- Teaming Policy Uplink Mapping

Host Transport Node and TEP Configuration

This section provides an overview of the steps required to configure a Host Transport Node. The prerequisites in the previous section must be met prior to completing this section.

Deployment and Configuration Process

1. Log in to NSX-T Manager, navigate to System → Fabric → Nodes, and then select the *Host Transport Nodes* tab.

2. In the *Managed by* drop-down menu, select the compute manager you added in as part of the prerequisites. After the compute manager is selected, the cluster and hosts added in vCenter should appear in the UI.

3. If you are assigning a transport node profile, click the check box next to the cluster, select configure NSX, and then select the transport node profile that you created. Finally click apply – this will apply the configuration set in the profile to all hosts in the cluster. Figure 2-10 is an example of applying a transport node profile.

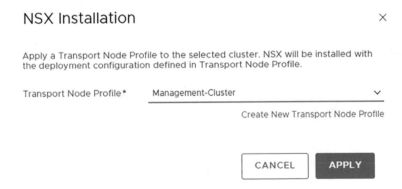

Figure 2-10. *Applying transport node profiles*

4. If you are configuring individual hosts, select the check box next to the host you want to configure, and then select *configure NSX*.

5. On the first page, you enter the hostname and description; once done click *next*.

6. Here you configure:

a. **Switch type:** N-VDS or VDS.

b. **Mode:** Standard, ENS Interrupt, Enhanced Datapath.

c. **Name:** Either enter the N-VDS name or, if using VDS, select the VDS applicable to the host.

d. **Transport Zone:** Select the Transport Zones you wish the host to be part of.

e. **Uplink profile:** Select the appropriate uplink profile for the host.

A separate uplink profile will be required for KVM hosts if you are configuring a teaming method other than failover order on Host Transport Nodes.

---

f. **IP Assignment (TEP):** Select DHCP, IP pool, or static IP list.

g. **Teaming Policy Uplink Mapping:** The number of uplinks that are configured here is dependent on the uplinks configured in the uplink profile. Map the uplinks to the correct VDS uplinks for external communication.

Multiple switches can be added to Host Transport Nodes; this instantiates additional host-switches on the transport node. Each host-switch requires an uplink; keep this in mind if additional switches are added. It is also recommended to have at least two uplinks per host-switch for redundancy.

Figure 2-11 is an example of the configuration required to prepare a Host Transport Node, without using a transport node profile.

Figure 2-11. *Host Transport Node configuration*

7. Once all the fields are populated, click Finish. The host will be prepared with all the details provided. The progress and status of the configuration can be monitored in the NSX Manager UI. Log files on the host can also be checked for more detailed information of the process; they can be found in /var/logs. The nsx-syslog.log and nsxcli.log files will provide you with additional insight.

Based on the example configuration provided in Figure 2-11, this host should have two TEP interfaces assigned. This can be confirmed by checking the NSX-T Manager UI or using command line on the host directly.

Figure 2-12 shows the additional VMkernel interfaces assigned to the Host Transport Node. The TEP interfaces are vmk10 and vmk11; vmk50 is also created but is not used as a TEP interface. The command to check the interfaces on the host is *esxcfg-vmknic -l*.

```
[root@mgmt-esxi:~] esxcfg-vmknic -l
Interface  Port Group/DVPort/Opaque Network     IP Family IP Address           Broadcast           MTU   NetStack
vmk0       65                                   IPv4     192.168.63.20          192.168.63.255      9000  defaultTcpipStack
vmk0       65                                   IPv6     fe80::266e:96ff:fe60:b0a0                    9000  defaultTcpipStack
vmk10      183e1903-a2a0-4774-b3fb-a325a77e9e87 IPv4     192.168.65.58          192.168.65.255      9000  vxlan
vmk10      183e1903-a2a0-4774-b3fb-a325a77e9e87 IPv6     fe80::250:56ff:fe64:e744                     9000  vxlan
vmk11      8e0cdfe2-5102-4094-a745-c08b48e98392 IPv4     192.168.65.59          192.168.65.255      9000  vxlan
vmk11      8e0cdfe2-5102-4094-a745-c08b48e98392 IPv6     fe80::250:56ff:fe6b:338f                     9000  vxlan
vmk50      f32bd5a3-ec09-411f-8009-528cc1b9cd4a IPv4     169.254.1.1            169.254.255.255     9000  hyperbus
vmk50      f32bd5a3-ec09-411f-8009-528cc1b9cd4a IPv6     fe80::250:56ff:fe69:c734                     9000  hyperbus
```

Figure 2-12. *Host TEP interfaces*

 Some details have been omitted for readability; details relevant to TEPs have been captured in the output.

The number of TEP interfaces assigned to a Host Transport Node is dependent on the number of uplink interfaces the host-switch has. If multiple host-switches are being configured, there will be a TEP interface for each uplink across each host-switch. Keep in mind, if deploying multiple host-switches, the TEP interfaces for the additional host-switches can reside in different subnets. Support for this was brought in the latest release of NSX-T

Edge Transport Node and TEP Configuration

The process of deploying and configuring an Edge Transport Node varies to a Host Transport Node. This section will focus on deploying an Edge Transport Node using the NSX-T Manager UI.

Before you can deploy an Edge Transport Node, there are additional prerequisites that must be met; these are in addition to the requirements in the previous section:

- **vSphere cluster:** A vSphere cluster in vCenter must be created.

- **Management portgroup:** This must be created in vCenter to be used for management traffic on the Edge Node. The portgroup used here can be the same management portgroup used by other appliances in the environment.

- **Uplink portgroups:** These can either be created in NSX-T as VLAN-backed segments or VDS portgroups. These will be attached to the edge appliance and will be used to communicate with the physical network. These should be configured as trunking portgroups.

Deployment and Configuration Process

1. Log in to NSX-T Manager. Navigate to System ➤ Fabric ➤ Nodes, and then select the *Edge Transport Nodes* tab.

2. Select *Add Edge Node*; on the Name and Description page, enter the name, FQDN, and description, and select the form factor you wish to deploy. You also have the option of modifying the resource reservations associated with the appliance. This is not mandatory and default reservations are recommended.

3. On the second page Credentials, enter the desired password for each account, and enable "Allow SSH Login" if that is a requirement. Not enabled is default for security reasons.

4. The third page Configure Deployment is for the placement of the appliance; fill in the details accordingly for your environment.

5. The fourth page Configure Node Settings is configuring the appliances management settings. Enter the details as required for the environment.

6. The final page of the Edge Node deployment is where you add in the NSX-T specific configuration details.

   a. **Edge Switch Name:** This field is relevant to the Edge Node; it does not need to match that of the Transport Zone or Host Transport Node in the latest release of NSX-T.

   b. **Transport Zone:** Attach the Edge Node to the required Transport Zones. To be able to participate in North-South traffic routing for the overlay segments, the Edge Nodes must be attached to the same Overlay Transport Zone as the Host Transport Nodes for which it will provide North-South communication for.

The second Transport Zone an Edge Transport Node *should* be attached to is a VLAN Transport Zone used specifically for Edge uplinks. This allows the Edges to have visibility over VLAN-backed segments created for physical network connectivity. These segments are used as uplink interfaces on Tier-0 gateways and are assigned a VLAN tag.

   c. Uplink Profile

   d. TEP IP Assignment

   e. Teaming Policy Uplink Mapping

Figure 2-13 is an example of an Edge Node deployment.

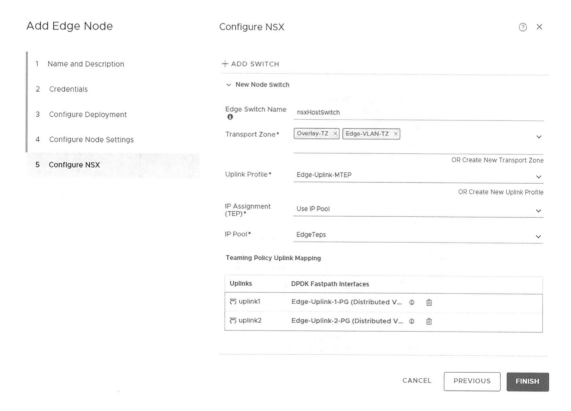

Figure 2-13. *Edge Node deployment*

7. Click *finish* and complete the deployment wizard. Upon completion, the Edge Node will start to deploy in vCenter.

The Edge virtual appliance is not supported on KVM.

As with Host Transport Nodes, verifying the TEP interfaces of an Edge Node can be done either by the NSX-T Manager user interface or Command Line Interface (CLI).

Figure 2-14 utilizes the CLI to discover the TEP addresses assigned to the Edge Transport Node. To replicate this, the administrator will need an SSH client, such as PuTTy. Connect to the Edge Transport Node, and issue the command *get logical-router interfaces.*

```
en1> get logical-router interfaces

interface  : 947b4aaa-9897-51ff-81da-78634f50478f
ifuid      : 260
VRF        : 736a80e3-23f6-5a2d-81d6-bbefb2786666
name       :
Fwd-mode   : IPV4_ONLY
mode       : lif
port-type  : uplink
IP/Mask    : 192.168.66.6/24
MAC        : 00:50:56:86:80:10
VLAN       : 66
LS port    : 04a25aca-f65e-56c5-884b-0a59a98d3055
urpf-mode  : PORT_CHECK
admin      : up
op_state   : up
MTU        : 1600
arp_proxy  :

interface  : 15b25658-0ed1-5330-b7b6-46b010be31f0
ifuid      : 262
VRF        : 736a80e3-23f6-5a2d-81d6-bbefb2786666
name       :
Fwd-mode   : IPV4_ONLY
mode       : lif
port-type  : uplink
IP/Mask    : 192.168.66.7/24
MAC        : 00:50:56:86:94:7f
VLAN       : 66
LS port    : 45ccce1b-a2ce-5757-a78b-25ba7c43486e
urpf-mode  : PORT_CHECK
admin      : up
op_state   : up
MTU        : 1600
```

***Figure 2-14.** Edge TEP interfaces*

Multiple interfaces can be seen in the output of Figure 2-14. However, there are only two TEP interfaces; notice they are both marked as uplinks and have IP and MAC addresses assigned to them.

Now that the transport nodes have been prepared, it is possible to look at GENEVE packet flow between them. The next section will display both East-West and North-South packet walks.

Tunnel Endpoint Packet Walk

This section will demonstrate tunnel endpoint communication. A packet tracer and a SSH client are all that are required to reproduce the data found in this section.

East-West Communication

East-West communication is communication between workload on Host Transport Nodes in an NSX-T domain. Generally, most communication in NSX-T is East-West; a few examples of East-West traffic could be:

- A web server communicating with a database server within the same data center on two separate segments

- Application servers communicating with each other across different segments

- Two virtual machines on the same segment communicating with each other

There are numerous possibilities of East-West communication; this book does not cover all of them.

The packet flow discussed in this section will show communication between two Host Transport Nodes. Figure 2-15 provides a visual representation of how the Host Transport Nodes are connected and provides interface details for each device.

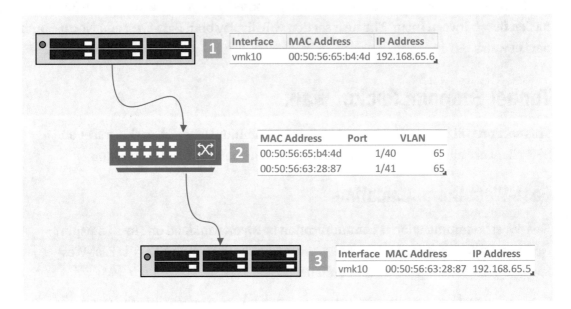

Interface	MAC Address	IP Address
vmk10	00:50:56:65:b4:4d	192.168.65.6

MAC Address	Port	VLAN
00:50:56:65:b4:4d	1/40	65
00:50:56:63:28:87	1/41	65

Interface	MAC Address	IP Address
vmk10	00:50:56:63:28:87	192.168.65.5

Figure 2-15. *East-West dataflow*

Step 1: Power on workload on both Host Transport Nodes. Without active workload, no GENEVE packets will be sent. Ensure workload is attached to an overlay segment.

If workload is only active on one host, no tunnels will be instantiated and no GENEVE traffic will pass. The Host Transport Node tunnel status will be down, and the node status will be red and shown as down. The Host Transport Node with no workload on it will have a tunnel status of not available, with a node status of green and up.

Transport node 1 encapsulates a packet; the source MAC address is the TEPs MAC, and the destination is the MAC address of the destination TEP address. If the TEPs were on different subnets, the destination MAC address would have been the gateway of node 1's TEP interface.

Figure 2-16 is a capture that shows Host Transport Node 1 sending a GENEVE packet to Host Transport Node 2. There is quite a bit of information in the output; however, pay close attention to the highlighted sections.

```
> Frame 146: 116 bytes on wire (928 bits), 116 bytes captured (928 bits)
∨ Ethernet II, Src: VMware_65:b4:4d (00:50:56:65:b4:4d), Dst: VMware_63:28:87 (00:50:56:63:28:87)
   > Destination: VMware_63:28:87 (00:50:56:63:28:87)
   > Source: VMware_65:b4:4d (00:50:56:65:b4:4d)
     Type: IPv4 (0x0800)
∨ Internet Protocol Version 4, Src: 192.168.65.6, Dst: 192.168.65.5
     0100 .... = Version: 4
     .... 0101 = Header Length: 20 bytes (5)
   > Differentiated Services Field: 0x00 (DSCP: CS0, ECN: Not-ECT)
     Total Length: 102
     Identification: 0x0000 (0)
   > Flags: 0x40, Don't fragment
     Fragment Offset: 0
     Time to Live: 64
     Protocol: UDP (17)
     Header Checksum: 0x372b [validation disabled]
     [Header checksum status: Unverified]
     Source Address: 192.168.65.6
     Destination Address: 192.168.65.5
> User Datagram Protocol, Src Port: 50503, Dst Port: 6081
> Generic Network Virtualization Encapsulation, VNI: 0x000000, OAM
∨ Ethernet II, Src: VMware_65:b4:4d (00:50:56:65:b4:4d), Dst: VMware_63:28:87 (00:50:56:63:28:87)
   > Destination: VMware_63:28:87 (00:50:56:63:28:87)
   > Source: VMware_65:b4:4d (00:50:56:65:b4:4d)
     Type: IPv4 (0x0800)
> Internet Protocol Version 4, Src: 192.168.65.6, Dst: 192.168.65.5
> User Datagram Protocol, Src Port: 49175, Dst Port: 3784
∨ BFD Control message
     001. .... = Protocol Version: 1
     ...0 0000 = Diagnostic Code: No Diagnostic (0x00)
     11.. .... = Session State: Up (0x3)
   > Message Flags: 0xc0
     Detect Time Multiplier: 3 (= 300 ms Detection time)
     Message Length: 24 bytes
     My Discriminator: 0x6e1b349d
     Your Discriminator: 0x800d1d9b
     Desired Min TX Interval:  100 ms (100000 us)
     Required Min RX Interval: 1000 ms (1000000 us)
     Required Min Echo Interval:   0 ms (0 us)
```

Figure 2-16. *Host East-West communication*

- **Source** and **destination:** They show that the source is Host Transport Node 1 and the destination is Host Transport Node 2.

- **Fragmentation:** Packets are set to not be fragmented. Therefore, MTU configuration is crucial to a successful NSX-T deployment.

- **DST port:** UDP 6081, which is used by the GENEVE protocol.

- **GENEVE header:** The GENEVE packet header has been inserted into the frame.

- **BFD control message:** Different diagnostic codes are available for troubleshooting and are part of the packet. 0x00 is a No Diagnostic code and indicates there are no issues with communication. Further information on diagnostic codes can be found on the VMware website.

Step 2: The packet is sent to the physical networking infrastructure. From here the packets are either switched or routed; this depends on whether the TEPs are in the same subnet or separate subnets; both methods are supported for Host Transport Nodes. This example displays East-West communication with the Host Transport Nodes in the same TEP VLAN.

The top of rack switch has populated its MAC address table with the MAC addresses of the Host Transport Node TEP interfaces. Once it receives the frame from Host Transport Node 1, it inspects the ethernet frame header to find the destination MAC and forwards the packet out the correct interface. Figure 2-17 is the MAC address table of the top of rack switch. Notice the source and destination entries match those of the previous packet capture's source and destination MAC addresses.

```
SSH@Leaf-1#show mac-address
MAC-Address        Port    Type        Index    VLAN
0050.5663.2887     1/41    Dynamic     44640    65
0050.5665.b44d     1/40    Dynamic     38252    65
```

Figure 2-17. *Top of rack switch MAC table*

Step 3: The destination Host Transport Node receives the packet, de-encapsulates the frame, and sends it to the destination TEP interface. Once received, the VNI header is inspected and the packet sent to the destination logical port. This process will be expanded on in Chapter 4.

North-South Communication

North-South communication refers to communication that is sourced from within the NSX-T domain to a destination that exists outside of the NSX-T domain. In other words, packets will traverse between a Host Transport Node and the Edge Transport Node and then egress the edge appliances uplink interface.

Like the previous section, we will start with a high-level diagram to better visualize the scenario. Following this, we will break down the steps and have a look at the packets moving between the transport nodes.

Figure 2-18 is a visual representation of the communication path that will be discussed.

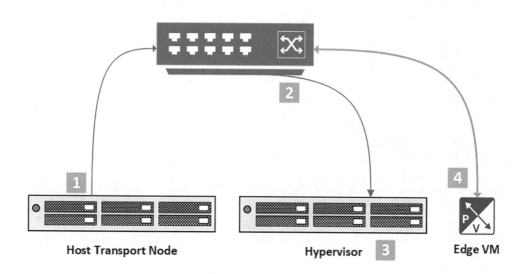

Figure 2-18. *North-South dataflow*

 If there are no active workloads on the Host Transport Node, no tunnels are formed between individual Host Transport Nodes and Edge Transport Nodes.

Step 1: Once workload is connected to an overlay segment and powered on, the host initiates a tunnel to the Edge Transport Node.

As the host TEP addresses and Edge TEP addresses are in different subnets, the packets between the two of them need to be routed. The host encapsulates the packet with a destination MAC address of its gateway and sends it to the gateway.

Aside from this difference, the remainder of the fields in the packet are like the fields shown in Figure 2-19.

```
> Frame 1105: 116 bytes on wire (928 bits), 116 bytes captured (928 bits)
v Ethernet II, Src: VMware_65:b4:4d (00:50:56:65:b4:4d), Dst: BrocadeC_b7:bd:14 (cc:4e:24:b7:bd:14)
   > Destination: BrocadeC_b7:bd:14 (cc:4e:24:b7:bd:14)
   > Source: VMware_65:b4:4d (00:50:56:65:b4:4d)
     Type: IPv4 (0x0800)
v Internet Protocol Version 4, Src: 192.168.65.6, Dst: 192.168.66.62
     0100 .... = Version: 4
     .... 0101 = Header Length: 20 bytes (5)
   > Differentiated Services Field: 0x00 (DSCP: CS0, ECN: Not-ECT)
     Total Length: 102
     Identification: 0x0000 (0)
   > Flags: 0x40, Don't fragment
     Fragment Offset: 0
     Time to Live: 64
     Protocol: UDP (17)
     Header Checksum: 0x35f2 [validation disabled]
     [Header checksum status: Unverified]
     Source Address: 192.168.65.6
     Destination Address: 192.168.66.62
> User Datagram Protocol, Src Port: 62550, Dst Port: 6081
> Generic Network Virtualization Encapsulation, VNI: 0x000000, OAM
v Ethernet II, Src: VMware_65:b4:4d (00:50:56:65:b4:4d), Dst: BrocadeC_b7:bd:14 (cc:4e:24:b7:bd:14)
   > Destination: BrocadeC_b7:bd:14 (cc:4e:24:b7:bd:14)
   > Source: VMware_65:b4:4d (00:50:56:65:b4:4d)
     Type: IPv4 (0x0800)
> Internet Protocol Version 4, Src: 192.168.65.6, Dst: 192.168.66.62
> User Datagram Protocol, Src Port: 49173, Dst Port: 3784
v BFD Control message
     001. .... = Protocol Version: 1
     ...0 0000 = Diagnostic Code: No Diagnostic (0x00)
     11.. .... = Session State: Up (0x3)
   > Message Flags: 0xc0
     Detect Time Multiplier: 3 (= 300 ms Detection time)
     Message Length: 24 bytes
     My Discriminator: 0x8954de3f
     Your Discriminator: 0x4373df1e
     Desired Min TX Interval:  100 ms (100000 us)
     Required Min RX Interval: 1000 ms (1000000 us)
     Required Min Echo Interval:   0 ms (0 us)
```

Figure 2-19. *Host North-South communication*

Step 2: Once the gateway receives the packet, standard packet routing mechanisms apply. The gateway inspects the ethernet frame, ensures it is not corrupt, de-encapsulates the packet, and checks the IP header to ensure it is not corrupt. It then looks at the destination IP address and checks it against its routing table. It then forwards the packet out of the correct interface. This is a summary of the process that the gateway runs through to route a packet; for further information on this, refer to Cisco's website. Also note, if you are using a layer 3 switch and have inter-VLAN routing configured, this process is slightly different.

Step 3: The host where the edge resides receives an 802.1q tagged frame. This tag will be the VLAN of the Edge TEPs. The host removes the header, inspects destination IP address, and sends the packet to the destination virtual machine, which is one of the Edge VM's TEP interfaces. Once the packets are received, a tunnel between the two transport nodes is initiated.

This process is simplified when using a bare metal host, because the ESXi layer is removed. The tagged frame is sent to the physical network interface of the Bare Metal Edge, the packet is de-encapsulated and processed, and the tunnel is initiated.

Step 4: Once the edge appliance receives the packet, it processes the packet and determines the destination. It performs a route lookup and forwards the packet out of one of its uplink interfaces.

 The steps described play a major role in the Logical Routing process which will be covered in Chapter 4 in more detail.

Tunnel Endpoint Failure

To conclude this chapter, this section will focus on TEP failure scenarios. The teaming policy chosen during uplink profile creation has a direct impact on TEP interface utilization and failure behavior. This section will start with demonstrating host TEP failure scenarios and will then look at Edge TEP failure.

Host TEP Failure

Failover Order

As mentioned earlier in this chapter, this teaming policy has one active uplink, with one standby.

Figure 2-20 shows TEP configuration on a host configured with an uplink policy that sets the teaming policy to failover order.

Notice, there is only one VMkernel interface instantiated, and vmk10 is the only VMkernel port enabled and has an IP address associated with it.

[root@mgmt-esxi:~] esxcfg-vmknic -l							
Interface	Port Group/DVPort/Opaque Network	IP Family	IP Address	Netmask	MAC Address	MTU	NetStack
vmk0	65	IPv4	192.168.63.20	255.255.255.0	00:1b:21:85:c8:20	9000	defaultTcpipStack
vmk0	65	IPv6	fe80::266e:96ff:fe60:b0a0	64	00:1b:21:85:c8:20	9000	defaultTcpipStack
vmk10	183e1903-a2a0-4774-b3fb-a325a77e9e87	IPv4	192.168.65.58	255.255.255.0	**00:50:56:61:d8:ae**	9000	vxlan
vmk10	183e1903-a2a0-4774-b3fb-a325a77e9e87	IPv6	fe80::250:56ff:fe64:e744	64	00:50:56:61:d8:ae	9000	vxlan
vmk50	f32bd5a3-ec09-411f-8009-528cc1b9cd4a	IPv4	169.254.1.1	255.255.0.0	00:50:56:63:b9:05	9000	hyperbus

Figure 2-20. *Host TEP configuration – failover order*

The output in Figure 2-20 also does not make it easy to determine which physical interface or vmnic vmk10 is attached to. The MAC address is a virtual MAC address assigned to the interface. To identify which vmnic the TEP interface is using, the CLI can be used. Issue the command *esxtop* and then press *n*; this displays network information for the host. Figure 2-21 is a snippet of the esxtop output for the host in Figure 2-20.

PORT-ID USED-BY		TEAM-PNIC	DNAME	PKTTX/s	MbTX/s	PSZTX	PKTRX/s	MbRX/s	PSZRX	%DRPTX	%DRPRX
67108874	Management	n/a	DvsPortset-0	0.00	0.00	0.00	0.00	0.00	0.00	0.00	0.00
67108879	vmk0	vmnic5	DvsPortset-0	251.94	9.35	4862.00	626.46	4.35	910.00	0.00	0.00
67108880	vmk1	vmnic5	DvsPortset-0	0.00	0.00	0.00	0.00	0.00	0.00	0.00	0.00
67108881	vmk2	vmnic5	DvsPortset-0	549.99	1.27	303.00	544.91	19.93	4795.00	0.00	0.00
67108882	**vmk10**	**vmnic4**	DvsPortset-0	0.00	0.00	0.00	1.70	0.00	60.00	0.00	0.00
67108883	vmk50	void	DvsPortset-0	0.00	0.00	0.00	0.00	0.00	0.00	0.00	0.00

Figure 2-21. *Host TEP – failover order – vmnic mapping*

From this output we can see which vmnic the TEP interface vmk10 is attached to – vmnic4. It's also important to note that while this is the vmnic the TEP interface is using to communicate with the network, GENEVE packets are being encapsulated, and using the virtual MAC of the TEP interface as the source, in this example, the MAC address is 00:50:56:61:d8:ae.

For vmk10 to move to vmnic5, a failure needs to occur on the physical interface. This could either be a switch or switch port failure or even a NIC failure on the host.

In Figure 2-22, a switch port failure has occurred, and we can see vmk10 has moved to vmnic5.

PORT-ID USED-BY		TEAM-PNIC DNAME		PKTTX/s	MbTX/s	PSZTX	PKTRX/s	MbRX/s	PSZRX	%DRPTX	%DRPRX
67108874	Management	n/a	DvsPortset-0	0.00	0.00	0.00	0.00	0.00	0.00	0.00	0.00
67108879	vmk0	vmnic5	DvsPortset-0	151.94	9.35	4442	4.46	3.35	710.00	0.00	0.00
67108880	vmk1	vmnic5	DvsPortset-0	0.00	0.00	0.00	0.00	0.00	0.00	0.00	0.00
67108881	vmk2	vmnic5	DvsPortset-0	649.99	2.27	203.00	144.91	19.93	5795.00	0.00	0.00
67108882	**vmk10**	**vmnic5**	DvsPortset-0	0.00	0.00	0.00	1.70	0.00	60.00	0.00	0.00
67108883	vmk50	void	DvsPortset-0	0.00	0.00	0.00	0.00	0.00	0.00	0.00	0.00

Figure 2-22. *Host TEP failover order with vmnic4 failed*

The TEP interface is also pre-emptive, that is, once vmnic4 is active again, vmk10 will move back to vmnic4.

The behavior displayed previously can also be expected on KVM, as it will be configured with failover order.

Load Balance Source and Load Balance Source MAC

Both load balancing teaming policies behave the same in the event of vmnic or TEP failure. Therefore, the behavior demonstrated in this section applies to both policies.

Figure 2-23 shows the host has two TEP interfaces configured, as the teaming policy has been changed to load balance source.

```
[root@mgmt-esxi:~] esxcfg-vmknic -l
Interface Port Group/DVPort/Opaque Network    IP Family IP Address       Netmask       MAC Address       MTU   NetStack
vmk0      65                                   IPv4    192.168.63.20      255.255.255.0 00:1b:21:85:c8:20 9000  defaultTcpipStack
vmk0      65                                   IPv6    fe80::266e:96ff:fe60:b0a0  64               00:1b:21:85:c8:20 9000  defaultTcpipStack
vmk10     3ba6b085-4a7d-436e-a7bc-944dfd721ac6 IPv4    192.168.65.56      255.255.255.0 00:50:56:61:d8:ae 9000  vxlan
vmk10     3ba6b085-4a7d-436e-a7bc-944dfd721ac6 IPv6    fe80::250:56ff:fe61:d8ae  64               00:50:56:61:d8:ae 9000  vxlan
vmk11     398642e3-03ae-4bcf-81e0-dd30cc990399 IPv4    192.168.65.57      255.255.255.0 00:50:56:6d:7e:38 9000  vxlan
vmk11     398642e3-03ae-4bcf-81e0-dd30cc990399 IPv6    fe80::250:56ff:fe6d:7e38  64               00:50:56:6d:7e:38 9000  vxlan
vmk50     f32bd5a3-ec09-411f-8009-528cc1b9cd4a IPv4    169.254.1.1        255.255.0.0   00:50:56:63:b9:05 9000  hyperbus
vmk50     f32bd5a3-ec09-411f-8009-528cc1b9cd4a IPv6    fe80::250:56ff:fe69:c734  64                                 9000  hyperbus
```

Figure 2-23. *Host TEP load balance source*

To ensure this is the case, use esxtop again to check the vmk to vmnic mapping.

PORT-ID	USED-BY	TEAM-PNIC	DNAME	PKTTX/s	MbTX/s	PSZTX	PKTRX/s	MbRX/s	PSZRX	%DRPTX	%DRPRX
67108874	Management	n/a	DvsPortset-0	2.65	0.00	75.00	0.00	0.00	0.00	0.00	0.00
67108879	vmk0	vmnic5	DvsPortset-0	237.51	8.33	4596.00	618.64	4.27	904.00	0.00	0.00
67108880	vmk1	vmnic5	DvsPortset-0	0.17	0.00	90.00	0.33	0.00	75.00	0.00	0.00
67108881	vmk2	vmnic5	DvsPortset-0	820.82	1.61	257.00	799.59	33.50	5491.00	0.00	0.00
67108882	**vmk10**	**vmnic5**	DvsPortset-0	0.17	0.00	90.00	0.17	0.00	60.00	0.00	0.00
67108883	vmk50	void	DvsPortset-0	0.00	0.00	0.00	0.00	0.00	0.00	0.00	0.00
67108885	vdr-vdrPort	vmnic4	DvsPortset-0	0.00	0.00	0.00	0.00	0.00	0.00	0.00	0.00
67108947	**vmk11**	**vmnic4**	DvsPortset-0	0.17	0.00	90.00	0.17	0.00	60.00	0.00	0.00

Figure 2-24. *Host TEP load balance source vmnic mapping*

From the output in Figure 2-24, vmk10 is attached to vmnic5 and vmk11 is attached to vmnic4. To determine failure behavior, the switch ports attached to these vmnics will be failed again.

Figure 2-25 shows the behavior of the interfaces after a link failure is simulated on vmnic4.

PORT-ID	USED-BY	TEAM-PNIC	DNAME	PKTTX/s	MbTX/s	PSZTX	PKTRX/s	MbRX/s	PSZRX	%DRPTX	%DRPRX
67108874	Management	n/a	DvsPortset-0	2.65	0.00	75.00	0.00	0.00	0.00	0.00	0.00
67108879	vmk0	vmnic5	DvsPortset-0	237.51	8.33	4596.00	618.64	4.27	904.00	0.00	0.00
67108880	vmk1	vmnic5	DvsPortset-0	0.17	0.00	90.00	0.33	0.00	75.00	0.00	0.00
67108881	vmk2	vmnic5	DvsPortset-0	820.82	1.61	257.00	799.59	33.50	5491.00	0.00	0.00
67108882	**vmk10**	**vmnic5**	DvsPortset-0	0.17	0.00	90.00	0.17	0.00	60.00	0.00	0.00
67108883	vmk50	void	DvsPortset-0	0.00	0.00	0.00	0.00	0.00	0.00	0.00	0.00
67108885	vdr-vdrPort	vmnic4	DvsPortset-0	0.00	0.00	0.00	0.00	0.00	0.00	0.00	0.00
67108947	**vmk11**	**vmnic5**	DvsPortset-0	0.17	0.00	90.00	0.17	0.00	60.00	0.00	0.00

Figure 2-25. *Host TEP load balance source vmnic4 failed*

Figure 2-25 shows that once the switch port or vmnic has failed, vmk11 failed to vmnic5 from vminc4. This shows us that if a physical NIC has failed, all the workload attached to that TEP interface will not suffer a complete outage. The workload sitting behind the TEP interface being failed over may have minor packet loss as the interface is failed over. This behavior will be the same for all TEP interfaces on the host.

Edge TEP Failure

The edge virtual appliance usually resides on an ESXi hypervisor. Its network interfaces are virtual and attached to the virtual machine; therefore, the way its interfaces fail is slightly different to that of a Host Transport Node. Chapter 5 will cover virtual port group configuration in more detail.

The edge vNics of the edge appliance attach themselves to a vmnic on the host. For an Edge TEP interface to fail, the hosts vmnic must go offline, like the behavior of a Host Transport Node.

In this section we will discuss TEP interface failure for both failover and load balance source teaming policies. It should also be noted that these are the only two teaming policies the edge supports.

Failover Order

The difference between the Edge Nodes and Host Transport Nodes is, with the failover order teaming policy, the Edge Nodes do not support a standby uplink. This is because the vNic of the edge can failover to another vmnic of the physical host. The reason the Host Transport Nodes support multiple uplinks is because the uplinks are mapped to a vmnic or physical NIC interface.

Figure 2-26 shows a single TEP interface on the Edge virtual machine; this is after changing the teaming policy to failover order.

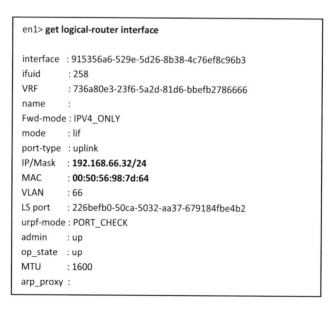

```
en1> get logical-router interface

interface  : 915356a6-529e-5d26-8b38-4c76ef8c96b3
ifuid      : 258
VRF        : 736a80e3-23f6-5a2d-81d6-bbefb2786666
name       :
Fwd-mode : IPV4_ONLY
mode       : lif
port-type  : uplink
IP/Mask    : 192.168.66.32/24
MAC        : 00:50:56:98:7d:64
VLAN       : 66
LS port    : 226befb0-50ca-5032-aa37-679184fbe4b2
urpf-mode : PORT_CHECK
admin      : up
op_state   : up
MTU        : 1600
arp_proxy :
```

Figure 2-26. *Single Edge TEP interface using failover order*

The MAC address shown in Figure 2-26 is the same as the MAC address assigned to the network interface of the virtual machine in vCenter. This can be confirmed by editing the virtual machine in vCenter and expanding the network interface to show the MAC address.

The vNic to vmnic mapping can be seen by using esxtop on the Host Transport Node where the Edge virtual machine resides. Figure 2-27 displays this mapping.

PORT-ID USED-BY	TEAM-PNIC DNAME	PKTTX/s	MbTX/s	PSZTX	PKTRX/s	MbRX/s	PSZRX	%DRPTX
67109143 27156562:**en01.eth1**	vmnic4 DvsPortset-0	15.99	0.02	163.00	31.97	0.03	112.00	0.00
67109144 27156562:en01.eth0	vmnic4 DvsPortset-0	5.63	0.01	289.00	5.27	0.01	200.00	0.00

Figure 2-27. *Edge VM vNic to vmnic*

We can see here that en01.eth1 is the interface the TEP resides on and is attached to vmnic4. A switch port failure or vmnic failure will result in the link going offline and en01.eth1 moving to vmnic5. This can be seen in Figure 2-28.

PORT-ID USED-BY	TEAM-PNIC DNAME	PKTTX/s	MbTX/s	PSZTX	PKTRX/s	MbRX/s	PSZRX	%DRPTX	
67109143 27156562:**en01.eth1**	vmnic5 DvsPortset-0	15.99	0.02	163.00	31.97	0.03	112.00	0.00	0.00
67109144 27156562:en01.eth0	vmnic5 DvsPortset-0	5.63	0.01	289.00	5.27	0.01	200.00	0.00	0.00

Figure 2-28. *Edge TEP interface failure using failover order*

En1.eth1 will move back to vmnic4 once the link becomes active.

Load Balance Source

Refer to Figure 2-29 for the TEP interface assignments for the edge; there are two interfaces listed, each with their own IP address and MAC address.

```
en1> get logical-router interface
interface  : 9fd3c667-32db-5921-aaad-7a88c80b5e9f
ifuid      : 257
VRF        : 736a80e3-23f6-5a2d-81d6-bbefb2786666
mode       : blackhole
port-type  : blackhole

interface  : 915356a6-529e-5d26-8b38-4c76ef8c96b3
ifuid      : 258
VRF        : 736a80e3-23f6-5a2d-81d6-bbefb2786666
name       :
Fwd-mode : IPV4_ONLY
mode       : lif
port-type  : uplink
IP/Mask    : 192.168.66.32/24
MAC        : 00:50:56:98:7d:64
VLAN       : 66
LS port    : 226befb0-50ca-5032-aa37-679184fbe4b2
urpf-mode : PORT_CHECK
admin      : up
op_state   : up
MTU        : 9000
interface  : b55b26d4-a82d-5e5f-a1d0-c4f64c356c62
ifuid      : 355
VRF        : 736a80e3-23f6-5a2d-81d6-bbefb2786666
name       :
Fwd-mode : IPV4_ONLY
mode       : lif
port-type  : uplink
IP/Mask    : 192.168.66.33/24
MAC        : 00:50:56:98:2c:b1
VLAN       : 66
LS port    : 1d4aecac-2f91-59c0-8486-bb7edc00010a
urpf-mode : PORT_CHECK
admin      : up
op_state   : up
MTU        : 9000
```

Figure 2-29. *Edge Node with two TEP interfaces*

The vNic to vmnic mapping can be seen by using *esxtop*; refer to Figure 2-30 to see the mapping prior to a link failure.

PORT-ID USED-BY	TEAM-PNIC DNAME	PKTTX/s	MbTX/s	PSZTX	PKTRX/s	MbRX/s	PSZRX	%DRPTX
67109143 27156562:**en01.eth1**	vmnic4 DvsPortset-0	15.99	0.02	163.00	31.97	0.03	112.00	0.00
67109144 27156562:en01.eth0	vmnic5 DvsPortset-0	5.63	0.01	289.00	5.27	0.01	200.00	0.00
67109156 27156562:**en01.eth2**	vmnic5 DvsPortset-0	16.99	0.07	263.00	41.97	0.04	117.00	0.00

Figure 2-30. *Edge Node TEP interface mapping*

In Figure 2-30, we can see three interfaces on en01: eth0, which is its management interface, and eth1 and eth2, which are the two interfaces identified earlier that are being used for TEP interfaces and packet forwarding.

The first TEP interface for the Edge Node is 192.168.66.32 with a MAC address of 00:50:56:98:7d:64; this is attached to en01.eth1. From Figure 2-30 we can see the interface is attached to vmnic4; to test failover here, either vmnic4 or the switch port must fail. A switch port failure will be simulated in this demonstration.

Figure 2-31 shows en01.eth1 has failed over to vmnic5 from vmnic4; once that link becomes active again, en01.eth1 will move back to vmnic4. This behavior will be seen across both vNics and TEP interfaces, that is, both will fail to the remaining interface if a physical link were to go offline. The same behavior can be seen if a link failure on en01.eth2 is simulated.

PORT-ID USED-BY	TEAM-PNIC DNAME	PKTTX/s	MbTX/s	PSZTX	PKTRX/s	MbRX/s	PSZRX	%DRPTX
67109143 27156562:**en01.eth1**	**vmnic5** DvsPortset-0	15.99	0.02	163.00	31.97	0.03	112.00	0.00
67109144 27156562:en01.eth0	vmnic5 DvsPortset-0	5.63	0.01	289.00	5.27	0.01	200.00	0.00
67109156 27156562:**en01.eth2**	vmnic5 DvsPortset-0	16.99	0.07	263.00	41.97	0.04	117.00	0.00

Figure 2-31. *Edge Node load balance source TEP failure testing*

A Bare Metal Edge Node will have the same failure results as that of a Host Transport Node. This is because they are not virtualized and have direct access to the physical network interfaces.

Summary

In this chapter we covered the differences between VXLAN and GENEVE encapsulation, how overlay networking works, and how NSX-T TEP interfaces operate. In the next chapter, we will cover Remote Tunnel Endpoints (RTEPs), what they are, and how they are utilized in NSX-T.

Chapter 5 covers the various VDS portgroup configurations and their impacts on data plane availability for Edge nodes.

CHAPTER 3

Remote Tunnel Endpoints

 This chapter will briefly cover NSX-T Federation and Remote Tunnel Endpoints (RTEPs). By the end of this chapter, readers should be able to:

- Describe NSX-T Federation

- Describe Remote Tunnel Endpoints

- Identify the requirements for Federation

- Configure and verify Remote Tunnel Endpoints

A Solution for Multiple Sites

NSX-T offers various deployment models for environments that span multiple sites. However, in versions prior to NSX-T 3.1, these options are limited to the use of a single instance of NSX-T.

Multisite architecture in NSX-T versions prior to 3.1 meant the management, control, and data plane needed to be failed to a secondary site in the event of a datacenter outage. This restriction has been alleviated with NSX-T Federation.

NSX-T Federation enables the ability to extend Logical Routers, segments, and security policies across sites without having to stretch the underlay. This allows multiple independent instances of NSX-T to be deployed at each site.

© Shashank Mohan 2022
S. Mohan, *NSX-T Logical Routing*, https://doi.org/10.1007/978-1-4842-7458-3_3

For NSX-T Federation to function, Remote Tunnel Endpoints (RTEPs), like TEPs, are configured on the Edge Nodes at each site. This chapter will cover RTEPs and how they are utilized for cross-site communication. This book does not cover NSX-T Federation in depth. For more information, refer to *Multi-Site Network and Security Services with NSX-T*.

NSX-T Federation Components

NSX-T Federation brings its own set of components and requirements. Figure 3-1 provides a logical representation of the components required by NSX-T Federation.

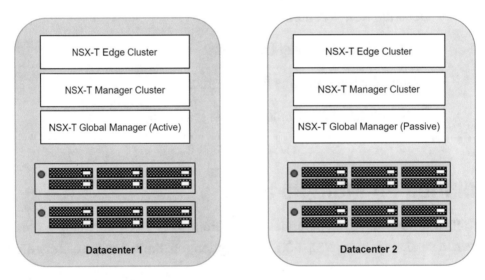

Figure 3-1. *Logical diagram of NSX-T Federation components*

The following list provides a description of each component in Figure 3-1:

- **Global Manager cluster:** A cluster of appliances like the NSX-T Manager; this is deployed in addition to the Local Manager appliances. The Global Manager federates multiple sites and supports an active-standby configuration.

- **Local Manager cluster:** An existing NSX-T Manager cluster instance, in charge of networking and security components for a particular site.

- **Spanned network object:** A network object created from Global Manager can either be local or spanned across multiple sites.

- **Regions:** There are multiple classifications for a region.

  - **Location based:** Each location added to the Global Manager is considered a region; this is generally a data center or an instance of NSX-T.

  - **Global:** All locations added into the Global Manager.

  - **Custom Regions:** A logical construct and works as a form of grouping. If multiple on-locations have been added to the Global Manager, they can be further grouped into regions, which allows configuration to be pushed to the region specifically. It is important to note, each local manager is considered its own region, and currently local managers can only belong to one additional region.

- **RTEPs:** Encapsulation interface for inter-site traffic; RTEPs are not shown in Figure 3-1. The next section discusses RTEPs in more detail.

What Are Remote Tunnel Endpoints?

Each NSX-T Edge Node that will be participating in NSX-T Federation requires an RTEP interface. These interfaces behave similarly to TEP interfaces in that they form GENEVE tunnels between each other. There are some differences in the way the RTEP interfaces operate when compared to TEP interfaces:

- RTEP GENEVE tunnels only form across sites. Edges within the same site do not form a tunnel between each other using their RTEP interfaces.

- Fragmentation is supported; it is however recommended to have at least an MTU of 1500 between sites.

- A separate VRF instance is instantiated on each Edge Node; this VRF is specifically used for RTEP configuration.

- Edge RTEP VLANs at each location must be routable and must be able to communicate on port 6081.

- Once a GENEVE tunnel is formed between Edge RTEP interfaces, they form an iBGP session between each other. A full mesh topology is configured between each peer.

Figure 3-2 depicts the logical NSX-T Federation RTEP topology.

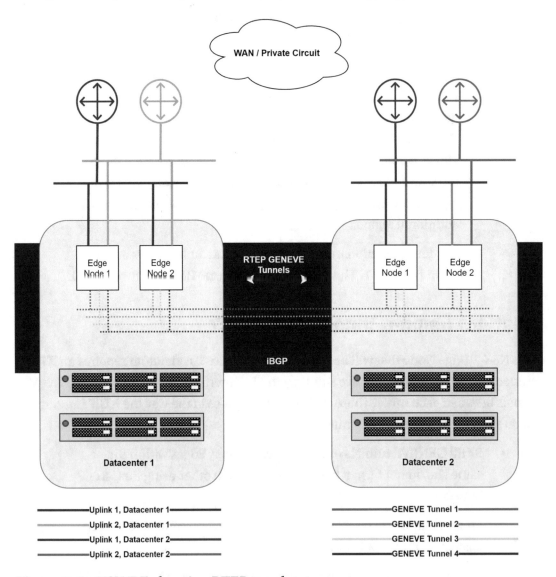

Figure 3-2. *NSX-T Federation RTEP topology*

Figure 3-2 highlights that:

- Each data center has two NSX-T Edge Nodes, deployed and configured for Federation.

- Each Edge Node has two uplink interfaces, which provide uplink redundancy to both ToR switches or gateways.

- Each edge RTEP interface has a GENEVE tunnel formed with the remote RTEP interface. Tunnels are not formed between RTEP interfaces within a location.

- Within the GENEVE tunnel, there is an iBGP peering between endpoints.

- There is cross-site connectivity, that is, packets on RTEP VLANs between each site are routable and port 6081 is open between Edge Nodes.

NSX-T Federation Prerequisites

This section briefly outlines the requirements for NSX-T Federation to operate correctly between sites.

The following list provides an overview of NSX-T Federations requirements:

- Global Manager appliances deployed and configured

- Site connectivity

  - A routable VLAN for RTEPs at each site.

  - Edge Node RTEP interfaces must have connectivity, that is, the RTEP VLANs at all sites must have connectivity between them. If there are firewalls between the sites, ensure they can communicate on port 6081. To achieve full communication between sites, the detailed list of firewall ports available at `www.ports.vmware.com/home/NSX-T-Data-Center` must be opened.

- The Global Manager must have connectivity to the Local Managers.

- The Local Manager instances at each site must have connectivity among each other.

- The Global and Local Managers must have a maximum round-trip time of 150ms. If either the Global or Local Managers of the same cluster are placed in different locations, the round-trip time must be 10ms or less.

- NSX-T datacenter 3.1.0 or later must be installed with an Enterprise Plus license key. All other versions do not allow the use of Federation.

Further details on the requirements for NSX-T Federation are available on VMware's website.

Configuring RTEPs and NSX-T Federation

This section covers the configuration of RTEP interfaces on the Edge Nodes participating in NSX-T Federation. It does not cover the configuration of other required components, such as uplink interfaces, TEPs, Logical Routers, and segments.

1. Log in to the NSX-T Global Manager; in the drop-down next to the NSX-T logo, select the first site that you will be configuring.

2. Navigate to **Networking ➤ IP Address Pools**, and then select **add IP Address Pool**.

3. Create a new address pool; this pool will be used for the RTEP interfaces for the site being configured. Ensure you configure a gateway that resides on the physical network, as the interfaces will utilize this gateway to route between sites.

Figure 3-3. *IP pool for RTEP interfaces*

4. Once this is complete, **select a Location from the drop-down menu ➤ System ➤ Quick Start**, and then select **Configure Remote Tunnel Endpoint**.

5. This will take you to a new screen; on this screen select the Edge cluster that will be used to configure the RTEP interfaces. Here you are required to specify the following information:

   a. **Edge Switch:** This drop-down will list all host-switches available on the edge appliances that were selected. The RTEP interface will be configured on the selected host-switch.

   b. **Teaming Policy Name:** This is not a mandatory field; however, if you have created a teaming policy for use, it can be selected here.

   c. **RTEP VLAN:** Specify the VLAN ID associated with the subnet configured for RTEPs.

   d. **IP Pool for all Nodes:** Select the IP pool to be used for RTEP configuration.

   e. **Inter Location MTU:** This setting is not configurable here; if the setting needs to be changed, this must be done from **System ➤ Fabric ➤ Settings ➤ Remote Tunnel Endpoint**.

Once all fields have been populated, it should look like Figure 3-4.

Remote Tunnel Endpoint Configuration

Edge Switch *	netName-overlay ⌄
Teaming Policy Name	Select Teaming Policy ⌄
RTEP VLAN *	81
IP Pool for all Nodes *	DC2-RTEPS ⌄
Inter Location MTU	1700 ⓘ

SAVE

Figure 3-4. *Edge appliance RTEP configuration*

6.   Once complete, a green banner should appear stating that the
Edge Nodes have been configured successfully. Refer to Figure 3-5.

Configure Edge Nodes for Stretch Networking ⓘ

Remote tunnel endpoints are the source IP address used by the Edge Nodes to communicate through tunnels with remote location. **All Edges in the Cluster must be configured.**

Select Edge Cluster   DC2-FED ⌄

⊘ All Edge Nodes has been configured successfully. Edit can be done under "System > Fabric > Nodes > Edge Transport Nodes > Tunnels". Go to Edge Transport Nodes page   ✕

Select Edge Node

SELECT ALL

☐ en05
  10.0.0.62 • Configured

☐ en06
  10.0.0.63 • Configured

Figure 3-5. *Edge Node RTEP configuration*

Verifying RTEP Interface Configuration

This section will walk through verifying RTEP configuration using the command line. However, if you would like to verify using the user interface, this can be done by navigating to **System ➤ Fabric ➤ Nodes ➤ Edge Transport Nodes**. Select **Edge**

Transport Node, and then click **Tunnels**. If the configuration process in the previous section was complete for the remote site as well, you should see active tunnels with a green status symbol. Refer to Figure 3-6 for an example of established tunnels.

Remote Tunnel Endpoint	EDIT	CLEAR CONFIGURATION						

Edge Switch Name	nsxHostSwitch	RTEP VLAN	81
Teaming Policy Name	Default	RTEP IP Address Method	IP Pool
IP Pool	DC2-RTEPS		

■ Data Sent   ■ Data Received

Source IP	Remote IP	Location	Data Received	Data Sent	Dropped Packets IN	Dropped Packets OUT	Status
192.168.81.2	192.168.80.2	DC1	0	0	0	0	● Established
192.168.81.2	192.168.80.3	DC1	0	0	0	0	● Established

C REFRESH   1 - 2 of 2 Record(s)

Figure 3-6. *RTEP tunnels established*

If both sites have been configured and the tunnels have a red status, refer to the previous prerequisites section as there may be a communication issue between sites.

Using Command Line to Verify RTEP Configuration

Verification of RTEP interfaces using the command line is like verifying TEP interfaces.

1. Use any preferred client to SSH onto the Edge Node; log in using the admin account.

2. Issue the command *get logical-routers*; you should see a screen similar to Figure 3-7.

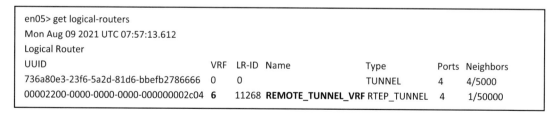

```
en05> get logical-routers
Mon Aug 09 2021 UTC 07:57:13.612
Logical Router
UUID                                      VRF  LR-ID  Name                    Type          Ports  Neighbors
736a80e3-23f6-5a2d-81d6-bbefb2786666   0    0                              TUNNEL        4      4/5000
00002200-0000-0000-0000-000000002c04   6    11268  REMOTE_TUNNEL_VRF RTEP_TUNNEL   4      1/50000
```

Figure 3-7. *Edge Node Logical Routers*

3. Notice here we can see a VRF specifically created for RTEPS, called REMOTE_TUNNEL_VRF. Take note of the number in the VRF column.

4. Type in vrf <number>, and enter the number listed in the output for your environment. In this case it would be vrf 6.

5. At prompt, now type *get interfaces*; you should see an output like Figure 3-8.

```
Interface         : 908dcc7b-90a6-4622-92dd-abfdf3270b05
Ifuid             : 330
Name              : remote-tunnel-endpoint
Fwd-mode          : IPV4_ONLY
Internal name     : uplink-330
Mode              : lif
Port-type         : uplink
IP/Mask           : 192.168.81.2/24;fe80::250:56ff:fe98:8d9b/64(NA)
MAC               : 00:50:56:98:8d:9b
VLAN              : 81
Access-VLAN       : untagged
LS port           : 1CDUU878-9213-4d00-52fe-0b3010793c03
Urpf-mode         : STRICT_MODE
DAD-mode          : LOOSE
RA-mode           : RA_INVALID
Admin             : up
Op_state          : up
MTU               : 1700
arp_proxy         :
```

Figure 3-8. *Edge Node get interfaces*

6. From the output in Figure 3-8, we can see the following settings:

    a. **RTEP interface IP address:** 192.168.81.2/24

    b. **RTEP VLAN ID:** 81

    c. **MTU:** 1700

There is a lot more detail in the output; however, the three preceding fields are relevant to the configuration process that was followed in the previous section. We can see that based on the configuration that was applied, the RTEP interfaces have been configured accordingly.

Summary

In this chapter you have learned what NSX-T Federation is and why an organization may be required to deploy it. You have learned what a Remote Tunnel Endpoint is and what additional requirements are needed to be configured or made available in the environment to deploy NSX-T Federation. Finally, you should be able to configure RTEP interfaces and verify that they were deployed to the Edge Nodes correctly.

In Chapter 4, we take the knowledge learned thus far and expand on it. Chapter 4 will first shed light on Logical Routing and how it operates and then will dive deep into the technology and provide some packet walks in various scenarios.

CHAPTER 4

Logical Routing

The previous chapters of this book covered the foundational topics of NSX-T. Readers should now recognize the importance of NSX-T within a Software-Defined Data Center and how transport nodes communicate.

 This chapter will focus on one of the most fundamental features of NSX-T: Logical Routing. By the end of this chapter, readers should have an in-depth understanding of:

- What Logical Routing is and how it is different to traditional IP routing

- The various components NSX-T uses for Logical Routing

- Logical Routing architecture

- Packet flow within the NSX-T fabric

What Is Logical Routing?

As more emphasis is put on automation and Infrastructure as a Service (IaaS), consumption of these services continues to soar. As infrastructure services become more readily available to end users, infrastructure administrators must also ensure there are adequate resources to satisfy the increasing demand.

© Shashank Mohan 2022
S. Mohan, *NSX-T Logical Routing*, https://doi.org/10.1007/978-1-4842-7458-3_4

As the infrastructure grows, the network must also be able to cope with this expansion. It is common to see environments that have resource contention issues purchase hardware to overcome these contention issues. However, this is not a sustainable or adequate solution, and quite often, the underlying network is disregarded.

What Is an Optimally Configured Network?

The definition of an optimally configured network changes over time. This book won't cover the various iterations of network design, from inception to the present day. However, it will cover the differences between IP routing in the physical network and how that has changed with NSX-T. This will give readers an understanding as to why NSX-T plays an enormous role in Software-Defined Data Centers.

The following diagram shows a collapsed network architecture. The layer 2 and layer 3 boundary sits on the top of rack (ToR) switch; in other words, it is the routing point for VLANs sitting on the hypervisor.

A summary of the routing process between the VMs in the blue and green networks in Figure 4-1 is outlined below.

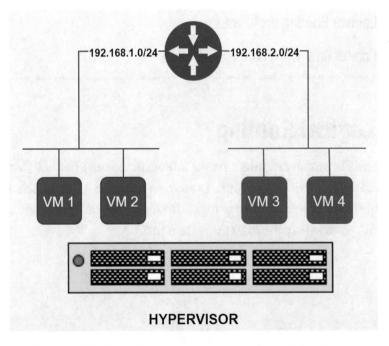

Figure 4-1. *Traditional IP-based routing for virtual workloads*

This is an overview of the routing process; it will not include detailed steps of the entire routing process.

1. VM 1 in the 192.168.1.0/24 blue subnet needs to communicate with VM 3 in the 192.168.2.0/24 green subnet. It looks at its own IP address, subnet mask, and the IP address of the destination VM.

2. VM 1 determines that VM 3 is in a different subnet and is not local. It encapsulates the IP packet in a frame; the source MAC address is the VM 1 MAC address, and the destination MAC address is the VM 1 default gateway MAC address. If VM 1 does not have the MAC address of its default gateway, it will send out an ARP request for its default gateway. The ToR switch receives the request and sends a response to VM 1, and VM 1 updates its ARP table and then sends the frame to its gateway.

3. The router or switch checks the frame, ensures it is not corrupt, and de-encapsulates the packet to determine the destination.

4. The router or layer 3 switch checks its routing table to identify the prefix. If the prefix is learned via another hop, it will do a second route lookup to ensure it has a path to the next hop. In this example, the gateway is aware of the 192.168.2.0/24 prefix as it is directly connected.

5. The router or switch checks its ARP table to ensure it has VM 3 MAC and IP address in its ARP table. If it doesn't exist, an ARP request is sent to all devices on the LAN to glean this information. Once the router or switch has this information, the IP packet is encapsulated into a frame. The source MAC address is set to the router or switch interface that is connected to the hypervisor, and the destination MAC address is the VM 3 MAC address. The packet is forwarded.

6. The host receives the frame and forwards it to VM 3. VM 3 de-encapsulates the packet and processes the IP packet.

7. This process is repeated for any return communication that may be required from VM 3 to VM 1.

> *Once the required ARP entries are resolved, clients will not send additional ARP requests. However, ARP entries can become stale and removed. This book will not cover this process.*

The preceding example highlights the communication process required between two VMs. This process has worked well in the last few decades, at a time when there was less emphasis on cloud and automation.

Software-Defined Data Centers place large emphasis on automation tools such as vRealize Automation, and other vendor automation products, which make it extremely easy to provision workloads on demand.

With this functionality comes increased East-West communication, that is, VM-to-VM connectivity, within a data center. With this increased demand on East-West communication and the ability to easily provision new workloads, the process highlighted previously does not scale well and therefore is not an optimal solution for the modern-day data center.

A Software-Defined Networking solution such as NSX-T removes the requirement of having to route all East-West traffic through a physical gateway. Once deployed and configured, NSX-T enables functionality called distributed routing. Each hypervisor participating in NSX-T instantiates a Logical Router within its kernel. This Logical Router is configured with a virtual interface, the virtual interface consists of a virtual MAC address, this virtual MAC address will be the same across all Host Transport Nodes. The interface will also have the gateway IP address applied to it, this is configured by the administrator where as the virtual MAC address is assigned automatically.

Figure 4-2 is a direct comparison to the routing process displayed in Figure 4-1. It shows how NSX-T logically routes traffic between two subnets without having to leave the transport node, and this is just one example of the power of NSX-T. The remainder of this chapter will elaborate on NSX-T Logical Routing functionality.

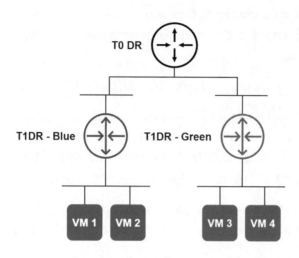

TRANSPORT NODE

Figure 4-2. *NSX-T Logical Routing within a single hypervisor*

An overview of the process that is followed to logically route packets within a single transport node is listed below:

1. VM 1 in the blue segment (192.168.1.0/24) needs to communicate with VM 3 in the green segment (192.168.2.0/24). It looks at its own IP address, subnet mask, and IP address of the destination VM.

2. VM 1 determines that VM 3 is in a different subnet and is not local. It encapsulates the IP packet in a frame; the source MAC address is the VM 1 MAC address, and the destination MAC address is the VM 1 default gateway MAC address. This gateway MAC address is the virtual MAC address of T1DR Blue downlink interface for the segment.

    If VM 1 does not have the gateway MAC address in its ARP table, it will send out an ARP request to glean this information. Once the gateway MAC address has been populated in VM 1 ARP table, it encapsulates the IP packet into a frame and sends it to T1DR Blue.

3. T1DR Blue de-encapsulates the frame and identifies that the prefix of the green segment (192.168.2.0/24) does not exist in its forwarding table. T1DR Blue has a default route pointing to its next hop of T0DR. T1DR Blue encapsulates the packet and sends T0DR.

4. T0DR receives the frame, de-encapsulates it and identifies the destination prefix, checks its forwarding table, and finds an entry for this prefix connected to its downlink port which is connected to T1DR Green.

5. T0DR encapsulates the packet and sends it to T1DR Green through its downlink interface.

6. T1DR Green de-encapsulates the frame and inspects the packet, identifies the destination IP address, and forwards the packet locally on the Host Transport Node to the destination VM.

7. VM 3 receives the packet and processes it accordingly; similarly if any return traffic is required, this process is repeated in reverse.

 The encapsulation and de-encapsulation process defined in this example is not referring to GENEVE encapsulation. A packet is only encapsulated in a GENEVE header when it must be sent to a destination transport node across a GENEVE tunnel.

As can be seen in the example in Figure 4-2, the packets did not have to leave the transport node to route between each endpoint, even though they are in different subnets. This is a high-level example to show a simple yet major difference between NSX-T and physically routing packets.

The process of logically routing packets in NSX-T is a lot more in depth than what was depicted in this example. The next section will detail the logical components that NSX-T uses for Logical Routing. This will provide readers with a better understanding of the components that are referred to in this and later chapters.

NSX-T Logical Components

The diagram in Figure 4-3 provides a visual representation to better understand how the different components of NSX-T fit together. This section will provide an explanation of NSX-T logical components. The components and abbreviations listed in this section will be used throughout this book.

Figure 4-3 is a diagram of the logical constructs that are used in NSX-T. The placement of these constructs in the diagram represents the actual placement of these components in an NSX-T environment.

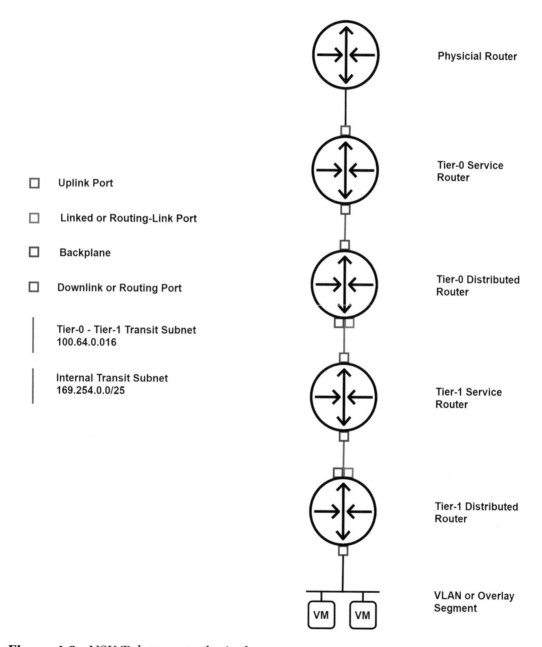

Figure 4-3. *NSX-T datacenter logical components*

- **Tier-0 Gateway:** A Logical Router construct which can be used in single or multi-tiered routing topologies. The Tier-0 gateway is made up of two logical constructs.

    – **Tier-0 Service Router (SR):** The Tier-0 SR is instantiated on an Edge VM once uplink interfaces are created on the Tier-0 gateway.

    – **Tier-0 Distributed Router (DR):** The Tier-0 DR performs the routing and forwarding of packets between separate Tier-1 gateways or segments. The Tier-0 DR also forwards traffic from segments or Tier-1 gateways to the Tier-0 SR if traffic needs to egress outside of NSX-T.

- **Tier-1 Gateway:** Typically considered the tenant gateway, the Tier-1 is plumbed into the Tier-0 gateway for egress to the external network. The Tier-1 gateway is also made up of two logical constructs:

    – **Tier-1 Service Router (SR):** The Tier-1 SR is instantiated on an Edge VM when a Tier-1 gateway is configured with an Edge cluster and stateful services.

    – **Tier-1 Distributed Router (DR):** The Tier-1 DR performs distributed Logical Routing and forwarding. If the Tier-1 DR does not have the required destination prefix, it uses an auto-plumbed default route which points to either a Tier-1 SR or Tier-0 DR.

- **Segments:** Once created, these appear as portgroups in vCenter; there are two types of segments that can be created:

    – **Overlay segments:** An overlay segment is an NSX-T construct. When used, it utilizes NSX-T Logical Routing and switching functionality.

    – **VLAN-backed segments:** These segments are a standard layer 2 portgroup. They can either be trunked or tagged portgroups, which allow administrators to continue to use VLANs in their environment.

- **Port types:** There are various logical port types used in NSX-T; the following are ports that will be referred to in this book:

- **Uplink port:** A logical port used for transit; this port is generally instantiated on the Tier-0 SR for egress to the physical network. This type of port also exists on Tier-1 SRs and Tier-1 DRs and connects to the linked port on the Tier-0 gateway.

- **Blackhole:** A port used to discard ingress or egress packets. This type of port can be found on all types of gateways on the edge appliances.

- **Linked or routing link:** This logical port provides connectivity between the Tier-1 DR Logical Router and the Tier-0 DR Logical Router.

- **Backplane:** A port used between the DR and SR Logical Routing components for communication.

- **Internal-routing:** A port used for inter-SR communication between edge appliances.

- **Downlink or routing:** A port connecting Tier-0 and Tier-1 gateways.

- **VIF:** A unique virtual interface assigned to each workload attached to a segment.

- **Tier-0–Tier-1 transit subnet:** A subnet that is auto-plumbed and used for communication between the Tier-0 and Tier-1 gateways. The default range used is 100.64.0.0/16.

- **Internal Transit Subnet:** A subnet that is auto-plumbed between the DR and SR components of a Logical Router. The default range used for these logical-switches are 169.254.0.0/25. This range is also used for inter-SR routing capabilities.

NSX-T Logical Routing Fundamentals

NSX-T has two types of gateways that are configurable:

- Tier-0 gateways

- Tier-1 gateways

Tier-0 Gateways

The Tier-0 gateway can be thought of as a provider gateway, that is, it provides routing between tenancies within NSX-T. The Tier-0 gateway is generally maintained by the provider, which could be an ISP or any team that has overarching responsibility for the environment.

The Tier-0 gateway provides North-South connectivity from the physical network into NSX-T and vice versa. This is where uplink interfaces, dynamic or static routing protocols, route filtering, stateful services, and many other features can be configured.

Tier-0 gateways have two Logical Routing components; they are:

- Tier-0 Service Router

- Tier-0 Distributed Router

The Tier-0 Service Router (T0SR) is instantiated the moment uplink interfaces are configured on a Tier-0 gateway; this is because uplink interfaces cannot be distributed.

The T0SR handles all ingress and egress traffic into the NSX-T environment. Administrators can configure stateful services on the Tier-0 gateway; however, it is vital to be aware of the impacts of doing so. This is covered later in this chapter.

The Tier-0 Distributed Router (T0DR) performs Logical Routing functions between Tier-1 gateways and works in conjunction with the T0SR to handle traffic into and out of NSX-T.

The T0SR and DR components are logically linked by a transit segment called the Internal Transit Subnet; by default logical interfaces performing these functions are assigned an IP address in the 169.254.0.0/25 range.

T0DR routers are linked to Tier-1 gateways using a logical segment called the Tier-0–Tier-1 transit subnet; by default these segments use the 100.64.0.0/16 address space.

As gateways are configured and linked to each other, these logical links and addresses are auto-plumbed, and no manual intervention is required from the administrator.

It is also possible to directly connect segments into Tier-0 gateways, bypassing the Tier-1 gateway. This will be explained later in this chapter.

Tier-1 Gateways

Tier-1 gateways are considered the tenant Logical Router. In these scenarios, providers manage the Tier-0 gateways and tenants have administrative access to their own Tier-1 gateway. This allows them the flexibility to configure services and availability modes suited to their environment.

Generally, Tier-1 gateways are plumbed into a Tier-0 gateway to enable North-South connectivity; however, they do not have to be linked to a Tier-0 gateway.

Tier-1 gateways have two Logical Routing components; they are:

- Tier-1 Service Router (T1SR)

- Tier-1 Distributed Router (T1DR)

T1SR are only instantiated once a stateful service is configured. Due to the nature of stateful services, they cannot be distributed among all transport nodes. The T1SR component is configured on an edge appliance, and all traffic that needs to route through the gateway is pinned to the edge appliance where the SR is active. The packet flows shown later in this chapter display this behavior.

T1DR are instantiated on all transport nodes, that is, each Host Transport Node and Edge Transport Node. It is for this reason that packets can be routed between T1DR and segments within a transport node and do not need to be routed or switched across hosts. An example of this can be seen in Figure 4-2. This behavior is expanded on in the next section.

Stateful Services

A stateful service is a service that cannot be distributed. This is because the states need to be maintained and monitored, which means they cannot be load-balanced across multiple nodes. Therefore, configuring stateful services on a Tier-0 or Tier-1 gateway forces the availability mode into Active-Standby. Examples of stateful services currently configurable in NSX-T are:

- Source NAT

- Destination NAT

- Load balancing

- Tier-1 firewall

- IPSEC VPN

- L2 VPN

 As of NSX-T version 3.1, when stateful services are configured on a gateway, they must be in Active-Standby high-availability mode.

Further details on the impact of configuring stateful services can be seen in the packet flows.

NSX-T Routing Principles

This section highlights the basic principles that adopters of NSX-T should be aware of:

- **Packets are routed locally:** In most circumstances, transport nodes make routing decisions locally. That is, if a packet needs to be routed between segments or gateways, all routing decisions are made on the source transport node. This behavior changes when stateful services are configured. This change in behavior is displayed later in this chapter.

- **No dynamic routing protocols:** Any segment, address, or gateway configured in NSX-T is known throughout NSX-T. This means that no dynamic routing protocol is used to propagate segment or prefix details between gateways. All subnets are auto-plumbed and learned automatically; NSX-T uses proprietary mechanisms to achieve this.

- **GENEVE encapsulation:** Packets sent between transport nodes are encapsulated in a GENEVE header. Packets that egress the edge appliances to the physical network are not encapsulated.

Logical Routing Architecture

NSX-T Logical Routing can be deployed in two different architectural models:

- Single-tiered Logical Routing

- Multi-tiered Logical Routing

The following section describes these topologies and the differences between them.

Single-tiered Routing

Not all environments require the use of multi-tiered routing architecture. It is possible to configure just the Tier-0 gateway and attach segments to it directly. This bypasses the additional hop of the Tier-1 gateways; transport nodes will have the T0DR instantiated, their downlink interfaces will have the segments attached, and the T0DR's uplink will be directly plumbed to the T0SR, which will be instantiated on the edge appliances.

The downside to this: if you configure stateful services on the Tier-0, you must use the Active-Standby availability mode. You will not have any tenant isolation for routing or permissions, and firewall rules must be placed at either the segment, workload, or Tier-0 gateway level.

If you wish to convert the topology to multi-tiered architecture at a later stage, it is possible, though it will require plumbing the segments into a Tier-1 gateway and linking that gateway to the Tier-0. Performing these actions will cause a minor outage to any workload sitting on segments that are being moved from the Tier-0 to the Tier-1 gateway.

Multi-tiered Routing

Multi-tiered routing architecture requires the deployment and configuration of both Tier-0 and Tier-1 gateways. This is a common consumption model; it provides flexibility in the environment for both tenants and providers.

The Tier-1 gateways are linked to the Tier-0 gateways using either the transit or Internal Transit Subnet. The subnet used is dependent on whether the Tier-1 gateway has stateful services configured.

The Tier-0 gateway can be considered an aggregation point for all Tier-1 gateways connected to it. With this deployment model, administrators can completely isolate tenants from one another, from both a routing and permissions perspective.

Tenant administrators are then able to configure their tenancies as they see fit; all segments are created and attached to tenant-specific Tier-1 gateways.

The multi-tiered deployment model is a common approach to deploying NSX-T.

Packet Flow Within the NSX-T Fabric

The details provided in the following sections are to highlight NSX-T's Logical Routing functionality. It will not provide in-depth details on physical network packet routing and switching, though will include an overview of the process where required.

East-West Logical Routing

East-West Logical Routing is communication between Host Transport Nodes in the NSX-T domain. This section will focus on demonstrating NSX-T East-West Logical Routing capabilities. It will provide the reader with logical diagrams and packet walks to further solidify the concepts discussed earlier in this chapter.

This section will cover two scenarios:

- East-West Logical Routing without stateful services

- East-West Logical Routing with stateful services

East-West Logical Routing Without Stateful Services

This example will demonstrate how packets are forwarded between workloads sitting on different Host Transport Nodes. This example will display how East-West communication works in NSX-T.

Figure 4-4 is a logical diagram of the example that will be covered in this section.

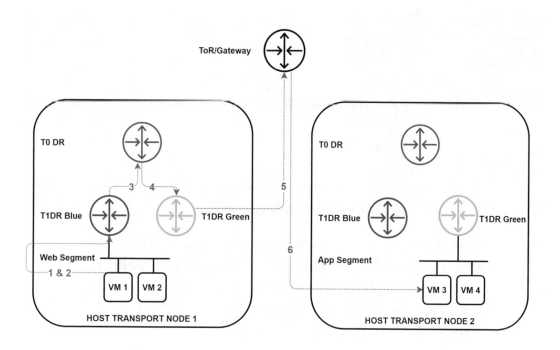

Figure 4-4. *NSX-T Logical Routing between two Host Transport Nodes*

 A diagram highlighting the TEP interfaces and segments is provided at the end of the packet walk.

To demonstrate East-West traffic, this example will show VM 1 connected to the Web Segment on Host Transport Node 1, communicating with VM 3 which is connected to the App Segment on Host Transport Node 2.

1. VM 1 needs to send a packet to VM 3. Because VM 3 is in a different subnet, VM 1 sends the packet to its default gateway. VM 1 default gateway is a downlink or routing port on T1DR Blue. The IP and MAC addresses assigned to this downlink port exist on all transport nodes and are identical. Figure 4-5 displays the downlink port on a Host Transport Node.

```
HOST TRANSPORT NODE 1> get logical-router b9ba5b04-9055-42cb-897e-0242307393c2 interfaces
LIF UUID              : 5f14f9ca-84bb-4cc9-b380-1280af909de4
Mode                 : [b'Routing']
Overlay VNI          : 27528
IP/Mask              : 192.168.190.1/24
Mac                  : 02:50:56:56:44:52
Connected DVS        : vds01
Control plane enable : True
Replication Mode     : 0.0.0.1
Multicast Routing    : [b'Enabled', b'Oper Down']
State                : [b'Enabled']
Flags                : 0x00388
DHCP relay           : Not enable
DAD-mode             : ['LOOSE']
RA-mode              : ['UNKNOWN']
```

Figure 4-5. *T1DR Blue downlink port for the Web Segment*

2. T1DR Blue receives the packet on its interface, removes the
   header, and checks the destination. T1DR Blue does not have the
   prefix in its forwarding table – it does have a default route with
   a next hop of the T0DR; this default route is auto-plumbed.
   Figure 4-6 is the T1DR Blue forwarding table.

```
HOST TRANSPORT NODE 1> get logical-router b9ba5b04-9055-42cb-897e-0242307393c2 forwarding

                    Logical Routers Forwarding Table
-----------------------------------------------------------------------------------------
Flags Legend: [U: Up], [G: Gateway], [C: Connected], [I: Interface]
[H: Host], [R: Reject], [B: Blackhole], [F: Soft Flush], [E: ECMP]


         Network                Gateway         Type      Interface UUID
=========================================================================================
0.0.0.0/0                      100.64.64.0       UG    d7b61332-7441-4bee-8b4b-e29816af65c0
100.64.16.2/31                 0.0.0.0           UCI   d7b61332-7441-4bee-8b4b-e29816af65c0
192.168.190.0/24               0.0.0.0           UCI   5f14f9ca-84bb-4cc9-b380-1280af909de4
::/0                           fcac:3a7b:d100:4001::1   UG    d7b61332-7441-4bee-8b4b-e29816af65c0
fcbf:9ce6:3dc7:7800::/64       ::                UCI   d7b61332-7441-4bee-8b4b-e29816af65c0
fe80:1018:100:0:50:56ff:fe56:4455/128   ::       UCI   d7b61332-7441-4bee-8b4b-e29816af65c0
ff02:1018:100::1:ff00:2/128    ::                UCI   d7b61332-7441-4bee-8b4b-e29816af65c0
ff02:1018:100::1:ff56:4455/128 ::                UCI   d7b61332-7441-4bee-8b4b-e29816af65c0
```

Figure 4-6. *T1DR Blue forwarding table*

T1DR Blue forwards the packet to its next hop T0DR (100.64.16.2);
notice the subnet used: it is listed as the Tier-0–Tier-1 transit subnet.

3. T0DR receives the packet, removes the header, and inspects the destination. T0DR checks its forwarding table and identifies that the prefix exists, with a gateway or next hop of 100.64.16.5.

```
HOST TRANSPORT NODE 1> get logical-router 8a0762ce-e31a-4447-9379-8a0d36c3c65c forwarding
                    Logical Routers Forwarding Table
------------------------------------------------------------------------------------------

Flags Legend: [U: Up], [G: Gateway], [C: Connected], [I: Interface]
[H: Host], [R: Reject], [B: Blackhole], [F: Soft Flush], [E: ECMP]


          Network              Gateway        Type       Interface UUID
==================================================================================
0.0.0.0/0                    169.254.0.2      UGE    a1852c52-9305-440b-8505-54f6534f7e2c
0.0.0.0/0                    169.254.0.3      UGE    a1852c52-9305-440b-8505-54f6534f7e2c
192.168.190.0/24             100.64.64.1      UG     5c7ab3ba-a51c-4c73-a6c2-2402848f29ad
192.168.191.0/24             100.64.16.5      UG     18ab2bb9-8551-4d84-8fe2-38a9169dfbc8
```

Figure 4-7. *T0DR forwarding table*

Notice the Interface UUID in the right-hand side column in Figure 4-7. This value can be copied and pasted into the search in the NSX-T Manager user interface. This will provide the details of the interface and what it connects to.

This is not the only method of obtaining the interface information.

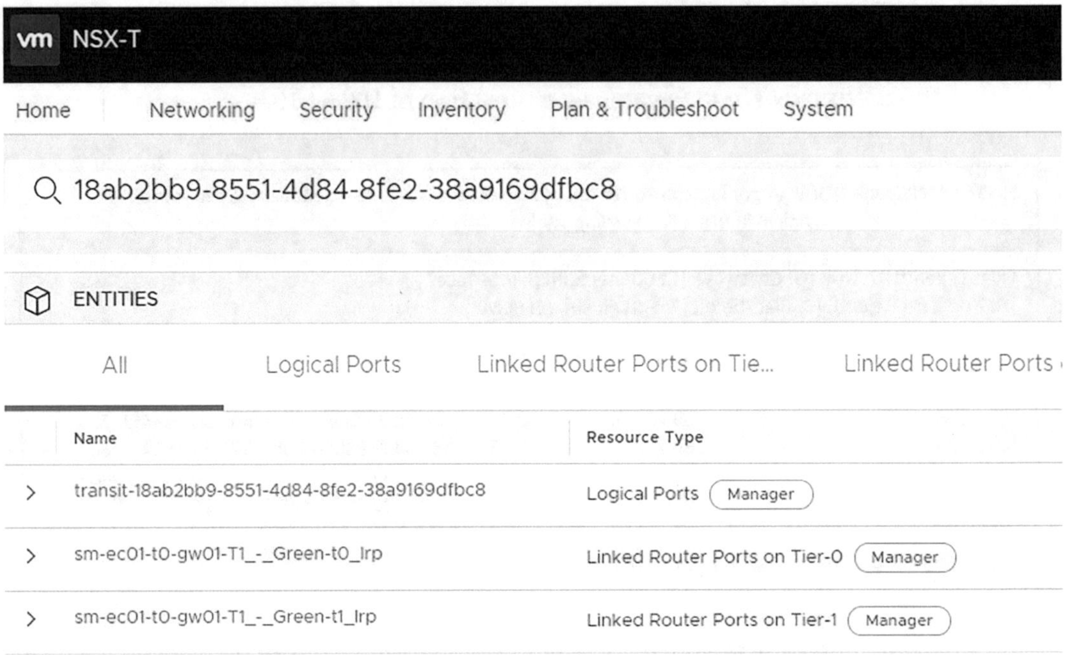

vm NSX-T

Home   Networking   Security   Inventory   Plan & Troubleshoot   System

Q 18ab2bb9-8551-4d84-8fe2-38a9169dfbc8

ENTITIES

All   Logical Ports   Linked Router Ports on Tie...   Linked Router Ports

	Name	Resource Type
>	transit-18ab2bb9-8551-4d84-8fe2-38a9169dfbc8	Logical Ports (Manager)
>	sm-ec01-t0-gw01-T1_-_Green-t0_lrp	Linked Router Ports on Tier-0 (Manager)
>	sm-ec01-t0-gw01-T1_-_Green-t1_lrp	Linked Router Ports on Tier-1 (Manager)

Figure 4-8. *Identifying an Interface UUID using NSX-T Manager UI*

Based on the output in Figure 4-8, it can be determined that the next hop address is configured on the Tier-0–Tier-1 transit subnet and is linked to the T1DR Green gateway. T0DR forwards the packet to the T1DR Green gateway.

4. T1DR Green receives the packet, inspects the IP header, and checks the destination IP against its forwarding table. It sees that the destination IP sits within a subnet connected to one of its interfaces. Figure 4-9 is TDDR Green's forwarding table.

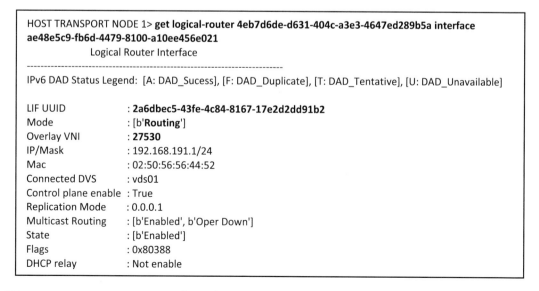

```
HOST TRANSPORT NODE 1> get logical-router 4eb7d6de-d631-404c-a3e3-4647ed289b5a forwarding
                  Logical Routers Forwarding Table
-------------------- -------------------------------------------------------------------

Flags Legend: [U: Up], [G: Gateway], [C: Connected], [I: Interface]
[H: Host], [R: Reject], [B: Blackhole], [F: Soft Flush], [E: ECMP]


        Network                  Gateway            Type      Interface UUID
==========================================================================================
0.0.0.0/0                       100.64. 16.4        UG    feb042ad-06ab-411b-9675-6547e0e42a3b
100.64.16.4/31                   0.0. 0.0           UCI   feb042ad-06ab-411b-9675-6547e0e42a3b
192.168.191.0/24                 0.0.0.0            UCI   2a6dbec5-43fe-4c84-8167-17e2d2dd91b2
::/0                       fcbf:9ce6:3dc7:7802::1   UG    feb042ad-06ab-411b-9675-6547e0e42a3b
fcbf:9ce6:3dc7:7802::/64            ::              UCI   feb042ad-06ab-411b-9675-6547e0e42a3b
fe80:1318:100:0:50:56ff:fe56:4455/128   ::          UCI   feb042ad-06ab-411b-9675-6547e0e42a3b
ff02:1318:100::1:ff00:2/128        ::              UCI   feb042ad-06ab-411b-9675-6547e0e42a3b
ff02:1318:100::1:ff56:4455/128     ::              UCI   feb042ad-06ab-411b-9675-6547e0e42a3b
```

Figure 4-9. *T1DR Green forwarding table*

Figure 4-10 shows the interface details; notice it lists an Overlay VNI ID. This is a segment ID and can be used to obtain details of where the packet should be forwarded so that VM 3 receives it.

```
HOST TRANSPORT NODE 1> get logical-router 4eb7d6de-d631-404c-a3e3-4647ed289b5a interface
ae48e5c9-fb6d-4479-8100-a10ee456e021
                Logical Router Interface
------------------------------------------------------------------------
IPv6 DAD Status Legend:  [A: DAD_Sucess], [F: DAD_Duplicate], [T: DAD_Tentative], [U: DAD_Unavailable]

LIF UUID              : 2a6dbec5-43fe-4c84-8167-17e2d2dd91b2
Mode                 : [b'Routing']
Overlay VNI          : 27530
IP/Mask              : 192.168.191.1/24
Mac                  : 02:50:56:56:44:52
Connected DVS        : vds01
Control plane enable : True
Replication Mode     : 0.0.0.1
Multicast Routing    : [b'Enabled', b'Oper Down']
State                : [b'Enabled']
Flags                : 0x80388
DHCP relay           : Not enable
```

Figure 4-10. *T1DR Green downlink port for the App Segment*

Next, the destination transport node where the packet needs to be forwarded must be determined. There are a few tables that provide relevant details to acquire this information.

Figure 4-11 shows the ARP table of segment VNI 27530, VM 3 IP address, 192.168.191.2, and MAC address 00:50:56:93:0e:1e.

```
HOST TRANSPORT NODE 1> get logical-switch 27530 arp-table
        Logical Switch ARP Table
---------------------------------------------------

        Host Kernel Entry
=================================================
    IP                        MAC              Flags

        LCP Entry
=================================================
    IP                        MAC
    192.168.191.2        00:50:56:93:0e:1e
```

Figure 4-11. *App Segment ARP table on Host Transport Node 1*

The MAC table of the segment in Figure 4-12 displays the details of VM 3 MAC address, which TEP interface MAC address it is mapped to (Outer MAC), and the IP address of that TEP interface.

```
HOST TRANSPORT NODE 1> get logical-switch 71681 mac-table
            Logical Switch MAC Table
-----------------------------------------------------------------

            Host Kernel Entry
===============================================================
  Inner MAC              Outer MAC         Outer IP         Flags

        LCP Remote Entry
===============================================================
  Inner MAC              Outer MAC         Outer IP
  00:50:56:93:0e:1e   00:50:56:6b:57:fc   192.168.65.25

            LCP Local Entry
===============================================================
  Inner MAC              Outer MAC         Outer IP
```

Figure 4-12. *App Segment MAC table on Host Transport Node 1*

From Figure 4-12, VM 3 MAC address is attached to MAC address 00:50:56:6b:57:fc, with IP address 192.168.65.25.

It is important to note that this MAC table only shows details relevant to NSX-T Overlay networks. That is, the inner MACs are VM MAC addresses, outer MACs are TEP interface MAC addresses, and the outer IPs are TEP IP addresses.

5. The packet is encapsulated in a GENEVE header and is either forwarded or routed to the Host Transport Node with MAC 00:50:56:6b:57:fc and IP 192.168.65.25. The mechanism for packet delivery is dependent on the destination TEP address; if it is in the same subnet, it is switched. If the packet is in a different subnet, it is forwarded to the gateway and then follows standard packet routing methods to reach the destination Host Transport Node.

    The packet capture in Figure 4-13 shows the packet as it leaves Host Transport Node 1 TEP interface.

```
> Frame 6: 132 bytes on wire (1056 bits), 132 bytes captured (1056 bits)
> Ethernet II, Src: VMware_6f:58:a0 (00:50:56:6f:58:a0), Dst: VMware_65:33:9a (00:50:56:65:33:9a)
> Internet Protocol Version 4, Src: 192.168.65.28, Dst: 192.168.65.25
> User Datagram Protocol, Src Port: 59169, Dst Port: 6081
> Generic Network Virtualization Encapsulation, VNI: 0x006b8a
> Ethernet II, Src: 02:50:56:56:44:52 (02:50:56:56:44:52), Dst: VMware_93:0e:1e (00:50:56:93:0e:1e)
> Internet Protocol Version 4, Src: 192.168.190.2, Dst: 192.168.191.2
> Internet Control Message Protocol
```

Figure 4-13. *Packet capture on Host Transport Node 1's TEP interface*

6. The packet arrives at the destination Host transport Node; it is processed through the IO chain and is forwarded to the destination VM. This completes the East-West packet walk. Figure 4-14 is a diagram displaying the completed packet walk with relevant interface and address details shown in Figure 4-13.

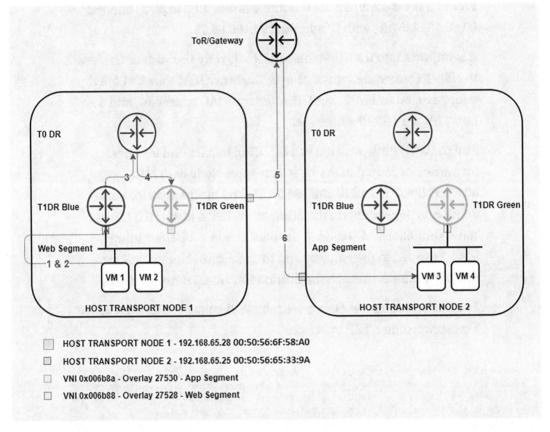

Figure 4-14. *East-West packet walk diagram with address details*

Outer Header

- **Source MAC:** 00:50:56:6F:58:A0 (Host Transport Node 1 TEP MAC address)

- **Destination MAC:** 00:50:56:65:33:9A (Host Transport Node 2 TEP MAC address)

- **Source IP:** 192.168.65.28 (Host Transport Node 1 TEP IP address)

- **Destination IP:** 192.168.65.25 (Host Transport Node 2 TEP IP address)

- **Virtual Network Identifier (VNI):** 0x006b8a (overlay 27530 – App Segment)

Inner Header

- **Source MAC:** 02:50:56:56:44:52 (virtual MAC used across various LIFs)

- **Destination MAC:** 00:50:56:93:0E:1E (VM 3 MAC address)

- **Source IP:** 192.168.190.2 (VM 1 IP address)

- **Destination IP:** 192.168.191.2 (VM 3 IP address)

East-West Logical Routing with Stateful Services

If stateful services need to be configured, common practice is to configure these services on a Tier-1 gateway. This is because stateful services cannot be distributed; an Edge cluster must be attached to the Tier-1 gateway. Once an Edge cluster is attached to the Tier-1 gateway, a T1SR is instantiated on the Edge Nodes. This Service Router is configured in Active-Standby; for example, if there are two Edge Nodes in the Edge cluster, both will have a T1SR instantiated on them. One of the Edge Nodes will host the active T1SR, while the other will have the standby SR.

Having a stateful service configured and an SR instantiated on the Edge Nodes greatly influences the data path. The diagram in Figure 4-15 exhibits the change in behavior.

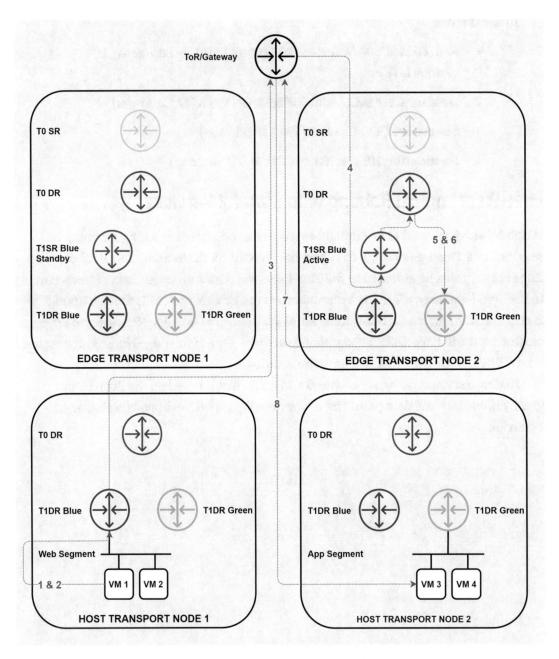

Figure 4-15. *East-West Logical Routing with a stateful service*

Traffic flowing between the two VMs must now route through the Edge Node where the SR is active. If VM 1 and VM 3 were both attached to T1DR Green, because there is no Edge cluster or stateful service attached, the process detailed in *East-West Logical Routing without stateful services*, in the previous section, would be followed.

In this example, T1-Blue references both Tier-1 logical constructs DR and SR as mentioned earlier in this chapter. VM 1 on Host Transport Node 1 needs to send data to VM 3 sitting on Host Transport Node 2. Both VMs sit on separate segments and T1 gateways. However, T1-Blue now has an Edge cluster attached, as depicted in the diagram by the existence of the T1SR Blue Active and Standby Logical Routers on both Edge Transport Nodes. This changes the forwarding table of T1DR Blue.

Figure 4-16 shows T1DR Blue forwarding table after attaching an Edge cluster.

```
HOST TRANSPORT NODE 1> get logical-router b9ba5b04-9055-42cb-897e-0242307393c2 forwarding
                    Logical Routers Forwarding Table
-------------------------------------------------------------------------------------
Flags Legend: [U: Up], [G: Gateway], [C: Connected], [I: Interface]
[H: Host], [R: Reject], [B: Blackhole], [F: Soft Flush], [E: ECMP]


           Network                      Gateway          Type      Interface UUID
=====================================================================================
0.0.0.0/0                            169.254.0.2         UG    5e898298-4970-412d-a55f-5aca31995281
169.254.0.0/28                       0.0.0.0             UCI   5e898298-4970-412d-a55f-5aca31995281
192.168.190.0/24                     0.0.0.0             UCI   5f14f9ca-84bb-4cc9-b380-1280af909de4
::/0                                 fe80::50:56ff:fe56:5300  UG  f6e3b85c-6384-4c9e-8078-5b3f132088a1
fe80::50:56ff:fe56:5300/128          ::                  UCI   f6e3b85c-6384-4c9e-8078-5b3f132088a1
fe80:1518:100:0:50:56ff:fe56:4452/128  ::                UCI   f6e3b85c-6384-4c9e-8078-5b3f132088a1
ff02:1518:100::1:ff56:4452/128       ::                  UCI   f6e3b85c-6384-4c9e-8078-5b3f132088a1
ff02:1518:100::1:ff56:5300/128       ::                  UCI   f6e3b85c-6384-4c9e-8078-5b3f132088a1
```

Figure 4-16. *T1-Blue forwarding table with an attached Edge cluster*

If you compare Figure 4-16 to Figure 4-6, which was T1DR Blue forwarding table prior to attaching an Edge cluster, notice the default route that is plumbed now has a different next hop gateway of 169.254.0.2, whereas, in Figure 4-6, it was 100.64.16.2. If you refer to the list of components in the section named *Logical Components used in NSX-T*, the address 169.254.0.0/25 belongs to the Internal Transit Subnet, which is a link between the DR and SR components.

There are several ways to identify which Edge Node has the active SR component for T1-Blue. This example will use the NSX-T Manager user interface. Figure 4-17 shows which Edge Node is active for the SR component.

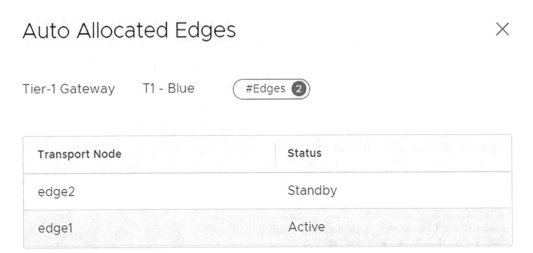

Auto Allocated Edges   ✕

Tier-1 Gateway   T1 - Blue   #Edges 2

Transport Node	Status
edge2	Standby
edge1	Active

Figure 4-17. *T1-Blue Active Edge Node*

The Edge Nodes have a new vrf instantiated on them for the SR component of the Tier-1 gateway. Figure 4-18 is the output of the command *get logical-routers* on Edge Node 2.

```
EDGE TRANSPORT NODE 2> get logical-routers
Logical Router
UUID                                    VRF  LR-ID Name            Type
736a80e3-23f6-5a2d-81d6-bbefb2786666  0    0                      TUNNEL
4eb7d6de-d631-404c-a3e3-4647ed289b5a  9    10249 DR-T1 - Blue     DISTRIBUTED_ROUTER_TIER1
d999a545-6917-488e-aaa5-f643e03642ba  10   12289 SR-T1 - Blue     SERVICE_ROUTER_TIER1
9cd30eb7-c757-41dc-b228-a8029965398b  11   10250 DR-T1 - Green    DISTRIBUTED_ROUTER_TIER1
```

Figure 4-18. *Edge Node 2 Logical Routers*

Notice there is now an SR component for T1-Blue, but there isn't one for T1-Green. Once again there are several ways to check the configuration of T1SR Blue; this example uses the command *get logical-router <UUID of T1SR – Blue> interfaces*. This will list all interfaces associated with this vrf. This command will also list the DR interface details at the same time.

Figure 4-19 is T1SR Blue backplane port. Refer to Figure 4-16; the next hop gateway is 169.254.0.2, which is the same as the backplane port on T1SR Blue.

The logical components section of this chapter states that a backplane port is a port used for communication between the DR and SR components of a Logical Router. This shows that there is a logical link between the DR and SR components of T1-Blue, where the SR is the upstream gateway for the DR component.

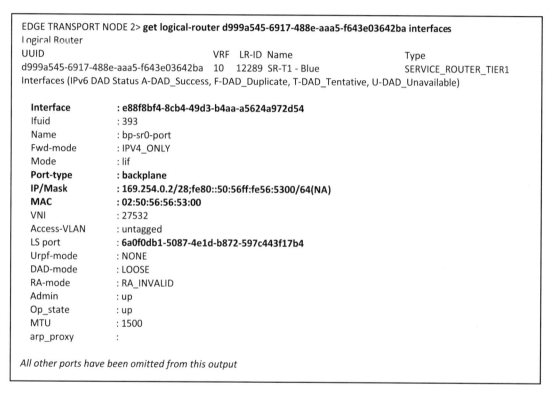

```
EDGE TRANSPORT NODE 2> get logical-router d999a545-6917-488e-aaa5-f643e03642ba interfaces
Logical Router
UUID                                     VRF  LR-ID  Name                     Type
d999a545-6917-488e-aaa5-f643e03642ba     10   12289  SR-T1 - Blue             SERVICE_ROUTER_TIER1
Interfaces (IPv6 DAD Status A-DAD_Success, F-DAD_Duplicate, T-DAD_Tentative, U-DAD_Unavailable)

    Interface         : e88f8bf4-8cb4-49d3-b4aa-a5624a972d54
    Ifuid             : 393
    Name              : bp-sr0-port
    Fwd-mode          : IPV4_ONLY
    Mode              : lif
    Port-type         : backplane
    IP/Mask           : 169.254.0.2/28;fe80::50:56ff:fe56:5300/64(NA)
    MAC               : 02:50:56:56:53:00
    VNI               : 27532
    Access-VLAN       : untagged
    LS port           : 6a0f0db1-5087-4e1d-b872-597c443f17b4
    Urpf-mode         : NONE
    DAD-mode          : LOOSE
    RA-mode           : RA_INVALID
    Admin             : up
    Op_state          : up
    MTU               : 1500
    arp_proxy         :

All other ports have been omitted from this output
```

Figure 4-19. *T1SR Blue backplane port*

 This is only relevant when there is an Edge cluster attached to a Tier-1 gateway.

Now that the configuration changes have been highlighted, the remainder of this section will walk through a step-by-step process of routing packets within this new logical topology.

Packet Flow from VM 1 to VM 3

1. VM 1 needs to send a packet to VM 3; it checks the destination IP addresses. As the destination is in a different subnet, it forwards the packet to its default gateway.

   VM 1 default gateway is a downlink interface on T1DR Blue. Figure 4-20 displays the downlink interface on T1DR Blue.

```
HOST TRANSPORT NODE 1> get logical-router b9ba5b04-9055-42cb-897e-0242307393c2 interfaces
LIF UUID              : deb8083e-a2a9-4114-8db2-889220b5f413
Mode                  : [b'Routing']
Overlay VNI           : 27528
IP/Mask               : 192.168.190.1/24
Mac                   : 02:50:56:56:44:52
Connected DVS          : vds01
Control plane enable   True
Replication Mode      : 0.0.0.1
Multicast Routing     : [b'Enabled', b'Oper Down']
State                 : [b'Enabled']
Flags                 : 0x388
DHCP relay            : Not enable
DAD-mode              : ['LOOSE']
RA-mode               : ['UNKNOWN']
```

Figure 4-20. *T1DR Blue downlink interface*

2. T1DR Blue receives the packet on its downlink interface and inspects the destination IP address. It checks the IP against its forwarding table and doesn't find a matching prefix. T1DR Blue forwarding table can be seen in Figure 4-21.

```
HOST TRANSPORT NODE 1> get logical-router b9ba5b04-9055-42cb-897e-0242307393c2 forwarding
                       Logical Routers Forwarding Table
-----------------------------------------------------------------------------------
Flags Legend: [U: Up], [G: Gateway], [C: Connected], [I: Interface]
[H: Host], [R: Reject], [B: Blackhole], [F: Soft Flush], [E: ECMP]


          Network                   Gateway          Type        Interface UUID
==================================================================================
0.0.0.0/0                          169.254. 0.2       UG    f6e3b85c-6384-4c9e-8078-5b3f132088a1
169.254.0.0/28                       0.0.0.0          UCI   f6e3b85c-6384-4c9e-8078-5b3f132088a1
192.168.190.0/24                     0.0.0.0          UCI   5f14f9ca-84bb-4cc9-b380-1280af909de4
::/0                           fe80::50:56ff:fe56:5300 UG   f6e3b85c-6384-4c9e-8078-5b3f132088a1
fe80::50:56ff:fe56:5300/128              ::           UCI   f6e3b85c-6384-4c9e-8078-5b3f132088a1
fe80:1518:100:0:50:56ff:fe56:4452/128    ::           UCI   f6e3b85c-6384-4c9e-8078-5b3f132088a1
ff02:1518:100::1:ff56:4452/128           ::           UCI   f6e3b85c-6384-4c9e-8078-5b3f132088a1
ff02:1518:100::1:ff56:5300/128           ::           UCI   f6e3b85c-6384-4c9e-8078-5b3f132088a1
```

Figure 4-21. *T1DR Blue forwarding table*

As no matching prefix was found, the packet is forwarded to the next hop (169.254.0.2) using the default route. This next hop IP address was identified as being a backplane port on T1SR Blue. As the active SR for T1DR Blue resides on Edge Node 2, the packet is sent to Host Transport Node 1 TEP interface, encapsulated with a GENEVE header, and routed to Edge Node 2 TEP interface. Figure 4-22 is a packet capture from Transport Node 1 TEP interface showing the packet being sent from Host Transport Node 1 to Edge Node 2.

```
> Frame 19: 132 bytes on wire (1056 bits), 132 bytes captured (1056 bits)
> Ethernet II, Src: VMware_6f:58:a0 (00:50:56:6f:58:a0), Dst: BrocadeC_b7:bd:14 (cc:4e:24:b7:bd:14)
> Internet Protocol Version 4, Src: 192.168.65.28, Dst: 192.168.66.63
> User Datagram Protocol, Src Port: 59169, Dst Port: 6081
> Generic Network Virtualization Encapsulation, VNI: 0x006b8c
> Ethernet II, Src: 02:50:56:56:44:52 (02:50:56:56:44:52), Dst: 02:50:56:56:53:00 (02:50:56:56:53:00)
> Internet Protocol Version 4, Src: 192.168.190.2, Dst: 192.168.191.2
> Internet Control Message Protocol
```

Figure 4-22. *Packet capture on Transport Node 1 TEP interface*

Outer Header

- **Source MAC:** 00:50:56:6f:58:a0 (Host Transport Node 1 TEP MAC address)

- **Destination MAC:** cc:4e:24:b7:bd:14 (top of rack switch/gateway MAC address)

- **Source IP:** 192.168.65.28 (Host Transport Node 1 TEP IP address)

- **Destination IP:** 192.168.66.63 (Edge Node 2 TEP IP address)

- **Virtual Network Identifier (VNI):** 0x006b8c (overlay 27532 – transit segment)

Inner Header

- **Source MAC:** 02:50:56:56:44:52 (virtual MAC used across various LIFs)

- **Destination MAC:** 02:50:56:56:53:00 (MAC address of the backplane port on Edge Node 2, for the gateway 169.254.0.2)

- **Source IP:** 192.168.190.2 (VM 1 IP address)

- **Destination IP:** 192.168.191.2 (VM 2 IP address)

3. The packet is forwarded to Edge Node 2 through the physical switch.

4. The packet arrives on the host where Edge Transport Node 2 resides, and forwards it to the Edge node. The packet is de-encapsulated once received on the Edge Nodes vNic, and it is forwarded to T1SR Blue. T1SR Blue receives the packet; it checks its forwarding table, doesn't find a match, and forwards the packet to its next hop of 100.64.16.2 as part of its default route. Figure 4-23 is the T1SR Blue forwarding table.

```
EDGE TRANSPORT NODE 2> get forwarding
Logical Router
UUID                          VRF   LR-ID  Name              Type
d999a545-6917-488e-aaa5-f643e03642ba  10   12289  SR-T1 - Blue          SERVICE_ROUTER_TIER1
IPv4 Forwarding Table
IP Prefix            Gateway IP        Type    UUID                                     Gateway MAC
0.0.0.0/0            100.64.16.2       route   2ded6094-01f2-4026-a2a7-33e2cbd97673
100.64.16.2/31                         route   2ded6094-01f2-4026-a2a7-33e2cbd97673
100.64.16.3/32                         route   7209cbaf-5b4c-5138-a80d-fed2cf104f3f
127.0.0.1/32                           route   80849cdd-8adb-46a7-82c0-9e4c298a839c
169.254.0.0/28                         route   36a52f05-fafe-4082-bf8f-2b7ef936f312
169.254.0.1/32                         route   1b5076c8-33d8-529a-b9ee-1cbfc4bc5e28
169.254.0.2/32                         route   7209cbaf-5b4c-5138-a80d-fed2cf104f3f
192.168.190.0/24                       route   5f14f9ca-84bb-4cc9-b380-1280af909de4
192.168.190.1/32                       route   1b5076c8-33d8-529a-b9ee-1cbfc4bc5e28
```

Figure 4-23. *T1SR-Blue forwarding table*

Based on the IP of the next hop, the IP address is a port on a Tier-0 gateway. This can be confirmed by issuing the command *get logical-router <UUID of Tier-0 DR> interfaces*; refer to Figure 4-24.

```
EDGE TRANSPORT NODE 2> get logical-router 8a0762ce-e31a-4447-9379-8a0d36c3c65c interfaces
    Interface           : 5c7ab3ba-a51c-4c73-a6c2-2402848f29ad
    Ifuid               : 376
    Name                : t0-gw01-T1_-_Blue-t0_lrp
    Fwd-mode            : IPV4_ONLY
    Internal name       : downlink-376
    Mode                : lif
    Port-type           : downlink
    IP/Mask             : 100.64.16.2/31;fcbf:9ce6:3dc7:7800::1/64(NA);fe80::50:56ff:fe56:4452/64(NA)
    MAC                 : 02:50:56:56:44:52
    VNI                 : 27529
    Access-VLAN         : untagged
    LS port             : f5978026-187b-4a21-b447-a5202962e114
    Urpf-mode           : PORT_CHECK
    DAD-mode            : LOOSE
    RA-mode             : SLAAC_DNS_TRHOUGH_RA(M=0, O=0)
    Admin               : up
    Op_state            : up
    MTU                 : 1500
    arp_proxy           :
```

Figure 4-24. *T0DR downlink interface*

As can be seen in Figure 4-24, the IP address 100.64.16.2 belongs to a downlink port on the Tier-0 gateway.

The command "get logical-router interface 2ded6094-01f2-4026-a2a7-33e2cbd97673" would have resulted in the same information.

5. T0DR performs a route lookup and identifies the destination prefix with a next hop of 100.64.16.5. Based on the IP addressing we know, this is within the Tier-0–Tier-1 transit subnet and can be determined that the address resides on T1-Green. Figure 4-25 is T0DR forwarding table.

```
EDGE TRANSPORT NODE 2> get logical-router 8a0762ce-e31a-4447-9379-8a0d36c3c65c forwarding
UUID                                         VRF LR-ID  Name                Type
8a0762ce-e31a-4447-9379-8a0d36c3c65c    6    8193   DR-edge-cl01-t0-gw01  DISTRIBUTED_ROUTER_TIER0
IPv4 Forwarding Table
IP Prefix              Gateway IP        Type    UUID                              Gateway MAC
192.168.191.0/24      100.64.16.5       route   18ab2bb9-85514d84-8fe2-38a9169dfbc8
```

Figure 4-25. *T0DR forwarding table*

To verify, issue the command *get logical-router <UUID of T0DR>
neighbor*. This will list any directly attached neighbors. When run
on a T0, this will list both logically connected components and the
upstream gateways if they are configured.

Figure 4-26 displays T0DR neighbors; notice the IP of the neighbor is
the same as the next hop address for prefix 192.168.191.0/24.

```
EDGE TRANSPORT NODE 2> get logical-router 8a0762ce-e31a-4447-9379-8a0d36c3c65c  neighbor
Logical Router
UUID          : 8a0762ce-e31a-4447-9379-8a0d36c3c65c
VRF           : 6
LR-ID         : 8193
Name          : DR-edge-cl01-t0-gw01
Type          : DISTRIBUTED_ROUTER_TIER0
  Interface   : 18ab2bb9-85514d84-8fe2-38a9169dfbc8
  IP          : 100.64.16.5
  MAC         : 02:50:56:56:44:55
  State       : perm
```

Figure 4-26. *T0DR neighbor*

To determine what the interface belongs to, copy the interface ID,
and paste it into the search in the NSX-T Manager user interface. You
should see an output like Figure 4-27.

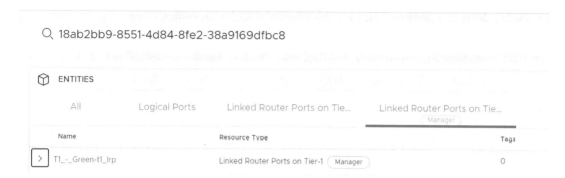

Figure 4-27. *Identifying neighbor details using NSX-T Manager*

> From this, we can infer that the interface is a logical link between T0DR and T1-Green.
>
> The packet is forwarded to the next hop, 100.64.16.5.

6. T1DR Green inspects the packet and identifies the destination IP address of 192.168.191.2 sits within a local prefix. It identifies which downlink port and segment VNI the prefix belongs to. Once the segment is identified, the destination transport node must be identified. The destination MAC address of the virtual machine must be obtained. There is an ARP and MAC cache on the Edge Nodes that is populated when ARP requests are sent and received. Figure 4-28 is the remote ARP cache on the Edge Node. If the entry doesn't exist, an ARP request is sent.

```
EDGE TRANSPORT NODE 2> get logical-switch remote  arp-cache 27530
    VM IP                    VM MAC                    VM IPv6
  192.168.191.2           00:50:56:93:0e:1e            None
```

Figure 4-28. *Edge Node App Segments remote ARP cache*

 The VNI can be found on the downlink interface of T1DR Green or issuing the command get logical-switches.

7. Next, the destination transport node must be identified. The
    Edge Node stores this information in the MAC address table for
    the logical segment. To see this information, issue command *get
    logical-switch <Segment UUID> mac-address-table*. Figure 4-29
    shows an example of the output from this command.

```
EDGE TRANSPORT NODE 2> get logical-switch 5a270e8f-1882-4ccf-a77c-f6c907a91390 mac-address-table
Logical Switch
UUID       : 5a270e8f-1882-4ccf-a77c-f6c907a91390
VNI      : 27530
Device     : fp-eth0
ENCAP      : GENEVE
Replication : mtep
routing-domain: 8a0762ce-e31a-4447-9379-8a0d36c3c65c
Enable Hub  : False
MAC-Table:
  MAC             : 00:50:56:93:0e:1e
    Tunnel        : 298f0212-a073-550a-b1fc-f29ad32742c3
    IFUID         : 366
    LOCAL         : 192.168.66.61
    REMOTE        : 192.168.65.21
    ENCAP         : GENEVE
    SOURCE        : Static
```

Figure 4-29. *App Segment's MAC address table*

From the ARP table in Figure 4-28, we see that VM 3 MAC address
is 00:50:56:93:0E:1E. Figure 4-29 shows that this MAC address is
resolved from remote TEP 192.168.65.21. The packet must now be
routed from the Edge TEP IP to the Host Transport Node TEP IP.

Figure 4-30 is a packet capture on the Edge VM TEP interface, while a
ping request is issued from VM 1 192.168.190.2 to VM 3 192.168.191.2,
displaying the source and destination TEP addresses in the packet
header.

```
> Frame 129: 132 bytes on wire (1056 bits), 132 bytes captured (1056 bits)
> Ethernet II, Src: VMware_93:6a:83 (00:50:56:93:6a:83), Dst: BrocadeC_b7:bd:14 (cc:4e:24:b7:bd:14)
∨ Internet Protocol Version 4, Src: 192.168.66.61, Dst: 192.168.65.21
      0100 .... = Version: 4
      .... 0101 = Header Length: 20 bytes (5)
    > Differentiated Services Field: 0x00 (DSCP: CS0, ECN: Not-ECT)
      Total Length: 118
      Identification: 0x0000 (0)
    > Flags: 0x40, Don't fragment
      Fragment Offset: 0
      Time to Live: 64
      Protocol: UDP (17)
      Header Checksum: 0x35d4 [validation disabled]
      [Header checksum status: Unverified]
      Source Address: 192.168.66.61
      Destination Address: 192.168.65.21
> User Datagram Protocol, Src Port: 36556, Dst Port: 6081
∨ Generic Network Virtualization Encapsulation, VNI: 0x006b8a
      Version: 0
      Length: 8 bytes
    > Flags: 0x40, Critical Options Present
      Protocol Type: Transparent Ethernet bridging (0x6558)
      Virtual Network Identifier (VNI): 0x006b8a
    > Options: (8 bytes)
> Ethernet II, Src: 02:50:56:56:44:52 (02:50:56:56:44:52), Dst: VMware_93:0e:1e (00:50:56:93:0e:1e)
∨ Internet Protocol Version 4, Src: 192.168.190.2, Dst: 192.168.191.2
      0100 .... = Version: 4
      .... 0101 = Header Length: 20 bytes (5)
    > Differentiated Services Field: 0x00 (DSCP: CS0, ECN: Not-ECT)
      Total Length: 60
      Identification: 0x10d9 (4313)
    > Flags: 0x00
      Fragment Offset: 0
      Time to Live: 125
      Protocol: ICMP (1)
      Header Checksum: 0x2e92 [validation disabled]
      [Header checksum status: Unverified]
      Source Address: 192.168.190.2
      Destination Address: 192.168.191.2
∨ Internet Control Message Protocol
      Type: 8 (Echo (ping) request)
      Code: 0
      Checksum: 0x4924 [correct]
      [Checksum Status: Good]
      Identifier (BE): 1 (0x0001)
      Identifier (LE): 256 (0x0100)
      Sequence Number (BE): 1079 (0x0437)
      Sequence Number (LE): 14084 (0x3704)
```

Figure 4-30. *Packet capture on Edge Nodes' TEP interface*

Outer Packet Header

- **Source MAC:** 00:50:56:93:6a:83 (Edge VM first TEP interface)

- **Destination MAC:** cc:4e:24:b7:bd:14 (ToR/gateway MAC address)

- **Source IP:** 192.168.66.61 (Edge TEP IP)

- **Destination IP:** 192.168.65.21 (Host Transport Node 2 TEP IP)

- **User Datagram Protocol Destination Port:** 6081 (GENEVE)

- **Virtual Network Identifier (VNI):** 0x006b8a (overlay 27530 – App Segment)

Inner Packet Header

- **Source IP:** 192.168.190.2 (VM 1 IP address)

- **Destination IP:** 192.168.191.2 (VM 3 IP address)

- **Internet Control Message Protocol:** Type 8 Echo request

8. The GENEVE packet is sent from the Edge VM TEP interface to its gateway. The packet is re-encapsulated, changing the destination MAC address to that of Host Transport Node 2 TEP interface MAC Address.

9. The gateway routes the packet to the Host Transport Node 2 TEP IP address.

10. Host Transport Node 2 receives the packet on its TEP interface; it de-encapsulates the packet as it moves through the IO chain. Once this process is complete, the packet is forwarded to VM 3.

Figure 4-31 is a completed packet walk diagram with interface details.

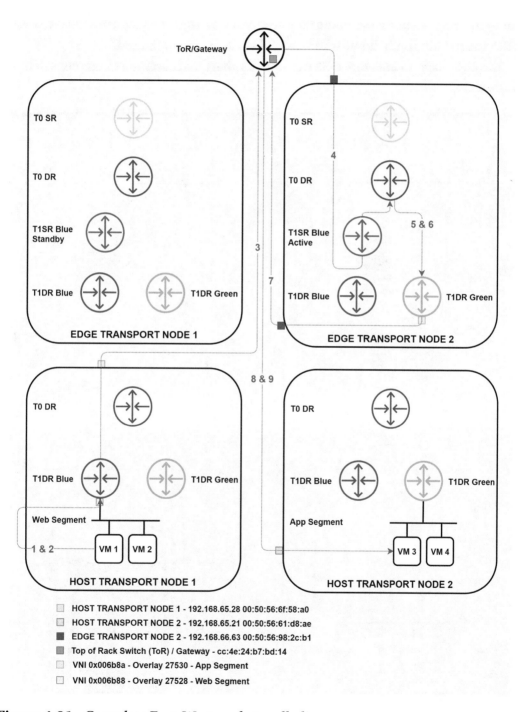

Figure 4-31. *Complete East-West packet walk diagram*

Packet Flow from VM 3 to VM 1

This section will focus on the traffic flow from VM 3 to VM 1; this information is relevant as the return traffic path differs when stateful services are configured.

The flow diagram in Figure 4-32 has step numbers that correlate to the steps in the packet walk.

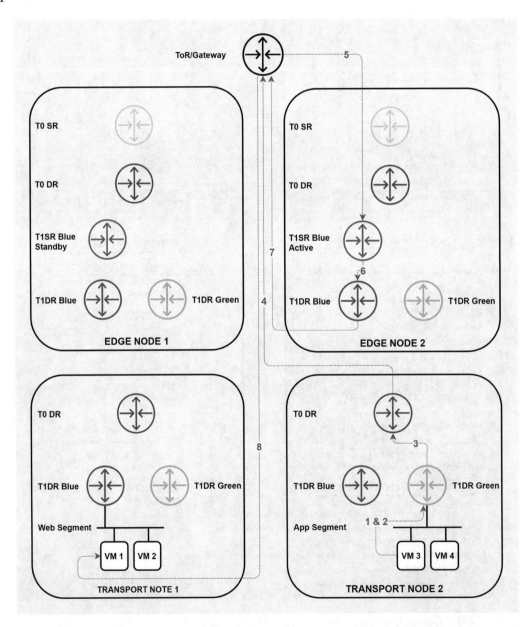

Figure 4-32. *East-West Logical Routing return traffic with stateful services*

1. VM 3 checks the destination IP address of VM 1 (192.168.190.2) against its own subnet. As the destination IP address is in a different subnet, VM 3 must send the packet to its gateway. It checks its ARP table for its gateway; if it doesn't exist, it sends an ARP request for the gateway IP.

    The MAC address resolved is a virtual MAC address that is used within NSX-T. Now that the ARP request is complete, VM 3 sends the packet to its default gateway.

    Figure 4-33 shows T1DR Green downlink interface details on Host Transport Node 2. The MAC address and IP address match the ARP response received on VM 3.

```
HOST TRANSPORT NODE 2> get logical-router 9cd30eb7-c757-41dc-b228-a8029965398b interface
Logical Router Interfaces
-----------------------------------------------------------------------
IPv6 DAD Status Legend:  [A: DAD_Success], [F: DAD_Duplicate], [T: DAD_Tentative], [U: DAD_Unavailable]

LIF UUID               : c69924cf-adf9-42cf-b997-0e93ff2da87e
Mode                   : [b'Routing']
Overlay VNI            : 27530
IP/Mask                : 192.168.191.1/24
Mac                    : 02:50:56:56:44:52
Connected DVS          : vds01
Control plane enable   : True
Replication Mode       : 0.0.0.1
Multicast Routing      : [b'Enabled', b'Oper Down']
State                  : [b'Enabled']
Flags                  : 0x388
DHCP relay             : Not enable
DAD-mode               : ['LOOSE']
RA-mode                : ['UNKNOWN']
```

Figure 4-33. *TDR Green downlink interface on Host Transport Node 2*

2. T1DR Green receives the packet, removes the header, and inspects the destination. It checks its forwarding table and does not find the prefix; the closest match is a default route pointing to 100.64.16.4, which belongs to the T0–T1 transit subnet. Figure 4-34 is the forwarding table from T1DR Green.

```
HOST TRANSPORT NODE 2> get logical-router 9cd30eb7-c757-41dc-b228-a8029965398b forwarding
                    Logical Routers Forwarding Table
---------------------------------------------------------------------------------
Flags Legend: [U: Up], [G: Gateway], [C: Connected], [I: Interface]
[H: Host], [R: Reject], [B: Blackhole], [F: Soft Flush], [E: ECMP]

        Network              Gateway        Type      Interface UUID
===================================================================================
0.0.0.0/0                   100.64.16.4     UG    247c9f76-d49e-4c69-81d5-1a3d7aa58179
100.64.16.4/31              0.0.0.0         UCI   363db8d6-e7f2-4ad3-a7ec-8820ab1ee41c
192.168.191.0/24            0.0.0.0         UCI   c69924cf-adf9-42cf-b997-0e93ff2da87e
```

Figure 4-34. *T1DR Green forwarding table*

From this output, the LIF UUID can be copied and pasted into NSX-T Manager to determine what it belongs to. Figure 4-35 shows the LIF details in the NSX-T Manager interface.

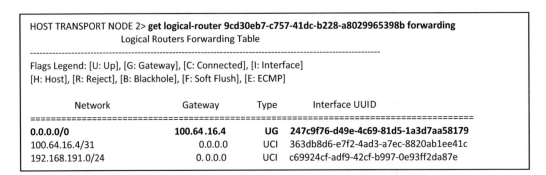

Figure 4-35. *Identifying the LIF in NSX-T Manager*

3. The interface is a link between T1DR Green and the T0DR. As T1DR Green does not have a stateful service configured, the packet does not have to leave the transport node and is forwarded to T0DR.

    T0DR receives and inspects the packet to determine the destination. It checks the destination IP against its forwarding table and verifies that the prefix exists.

```
HOST TRANSPORT NODE 2> get logical-router 8a0762ce-e31a-4447-9379-8a0d36c3c65c forwarding

                    Logical Routers Forwarding Table

--------------------------------------------------------------------------------------------
Flags Legend: [U: Up], [G: Gateway], [C: Connected], [I: Interface]
[H: Host], [R: Reject], [B: Blackhole], [F: Soft Flush], [E: ECMP]

            Network                    Gateway       Type      Interface UUID
=======================================================================================================
0.0.0.0/0                            169.254.0.2     UGE    a1852c52-9305-440b-8505-54f6534f7e2c
0.0.0.0/0                            169.254.0.3     UGE    a1852c52-9305-440b-8505-54f6534f7e2c
192.168.190.0/24                     100.64.16.3     UG     5c7ab3ba-a51c-4c73-a6c2-2402848f29ad
```

Figure 4-36. *T0DR Forwarding Table*

Based on the output in Figure 4-36, prefix 192.168.190.0/24 is known via 100.64.16.3.

Figure 4-37 shows that the interface is a logical link between the Tier-0 and T1-Blue logical gateways.

Q 28512ed5-66a1-44dd-88c4-71d05ee1a970

⬡ ENTITIES

| | All | Logical Ports | Linked Router Ports on Tie... | Linked Router Ports on Tie... |

Name	Resource Type
> sm-ec01-t0-gw01-T1_-_Blue-t0_lrp	Linked Router Ports on Tier-0 (Manager)

Figure 4-37. *Logical link between T0DR and T1 Blue SR*

4. The packet is now forwarded over a GENEVE tunnel from Host Transport Node 2, through the switch, to Edge Transport Node 2, which has the active SR for T1SR Blue.

Figure 4-38 is a packet capture output on the TEP interface on the active Edge VM.

```
>  Frame 9: 132 bytes on wire (1056 bits), 132 bytes captured (1056 bits)
>  Ethernet II, Src: BrocadeC_b7:bd:14 (cc:4e:24:b7:bd:14), Dst: VMware_93:55:d1 (00:50:56:93:55:d1)
v  Internet Protocol Version 4, Src: 192.168.65.21, Dst: 192.168.66.60
       0100 .... = Version: 4
       .... 0101 = Header Length: 20 bytes (5)
    >  Differentiated Services Field: 0x00 (DSCP: CS0, ECN: Not-ECT)
       Total Length: 118
       Identification: 0x0000 (0)
    >  Flags: 0x40, Don't fragment
       Fragment Offset: 0
       Time to Live: 63
       Protocol: UDP (17)
       Header Checksum: 0x36d5 [validation disabled]
       [Header checksum status: Unverified]
       Source Address: 192.168.65.21
       Destination Address: 192.168.66.60
>  User Datagram Protocol, Src Port: 61630, Dst Port: 6081
v  Generic Network Virtualization Encapsulation, VNI: 0x006b89
       Version: 0
       Length: 8 bytes
    >  Flags: 0x40, Critical Options Present
       Protocol Type: Transparent Ethernet bridging (0x6558)
       Virtual Network Identifier (VNI): 0x006b89
    >  Options: (8 bytes)
>  Ethernet II, Src: 02:50:56:56:44:52 (02:50:56:56:44:52), Dst: 02:50:56:56:44:55 (02:50:56:56:44:55)
v  Internet Protocol Version 4, Src: 192.168.191.2, Dst: 192.168.190.2
       0100 .... = Version: 4
       .... 0101 = Header Length: 20 bytes (5)
    >  Differentiated Services Field: 0x00 (DSCP: CS0, ECN: Not-ECT)
       Total Length: 60
       Identification: 0x04e2 (1250)
    >  Flags: 0x00
       Fragment Offset: 0
       Time to Live: 126
       Protocol: ICMP (1)
       Header Checksum: 0x3989 [validation disabled]
       [Header checksum status: Unverified]
       Source Address: 192.168.191.2
       Destination Address: 192.168.190.2
>  Internet Control Message Protocol
```

Figure 4-38. *Edge TEP interface packet capture*

The following information can be gleaned from Figure 4-38.

Outer Packet Header

- **Source MAC:** cc:4e:24:b7:bd:14 (ToR/gateway MAC address)

- **Destination MAC:** 00:50:56:93:55:d1 (Edge TEP interface MAC)

- **Source IP:** 192.168.65.21 (Host Transport Node 2 TEP IP)

- **Destination IP:** 192.168.66.60 (Edge TEP IP)

- **User Datagram Protocol Destination Port:** 6081 (GENEVE)

- **Virtual Network Identifier (VNI):** 0x006b8a (overlay 27529 – transit segment)

Inner Packet Header

- **Source IP:** 192.168.191.2 (VM 3 IP address)

- **Destination IP:** 192.168.190.2 (VM 1 IP address)

5. Edge Transport Node 2 receives the packet, de-encapsulates it, and forwards it to T1SR Blue.

   T1SR Blue checks its prefix table to see if it has a match for 192.168.190.2/24. It finds a match and determines that the prefix is local. Refer to Figure 4-39, which shows T1SR Blue forwarding table. Notice that the prefix 192.168.190.0/24 does not have a gateway IP specified. This means that there is no next hop associated with it and it is available locally.

```
EDGE TRANSPORT NODE 2> get logical-router d999a545-6917-488e-aaa5-f643e03642ba forwarding
Logical Router
UUID                                      VRF  LR-ID  Name                  Type
d999a545-6917-488e-aaa5-f643e03642ba      10   12289  SR-T1 - Blue          SERVICE_ROUTER_TIER1
IPv4 Forwarding Table
IP Prefix       Gateway IP      Type    UUID                             Gateway MAC
0.0.0.0/0       100.64.64.0     route   2ded6094-01f2-4026-a2a7-33e2cbd97673
100.64.16.2/31                  route   2ded6094-01f2-4026-a2a7-33e2cbd97673
100.64.16.3/32                  route   7209cbaf-5b4c-5138-a80d-fed2cf104f3f
169.254.0.0/28                  route   36a52f05-fafe-4082-bf8f-2b7ef936f312
169.254.0.1/32                  route   1b5076c8-33d8-529a-b9ee-1cbfc4bc5e28
169.254.0.2/32                  route   7209cbaf-5b4c-5138-a80d-fed2cf104f3f
192.168.13.0/24                 route   c83f1741-3d41-4a90-80c4-caea021672d0
192.168.13.1/32                 route   1b5076c8-33d8-529a-b9ee-1cbfc4bc5e28
192.168.190.0/24                route   5f14f9ca-84bb-4cc9-b380-1280af909de4
192.168.190.1/32                route   1b5076c8-33d8-529a-b9ee-1cbfc4bc5e28
```

Figure 4-39. *T1SR Blue forwarding table*

T1SR Blue forwards the packet to T1DR Blue using its backplane port. Remember, the SR is responsible for stateful services and will not directly perform packet routing and switching between workloads, the DR is responsible for this, and this is the reason the packet is forwarded to the DR component.

6. T1DR Blue DR checks its ARP cache for the destination IP and MAC address, so it can determine which transport node to send the packet to. Figure 4-40 is the arp cache on Edge Node 2.

```
EDGE TRANSPORT NODE 2> get logical-switch remote arp-cache 27528
    VM IP                          VM MAC                      VM IPv6
    192.168.190.2                  00:50:56:93:a7:99           None
```

Figure 4-40. *Remote ARP cache, Web Segment on Edge Transport Node 2*

Several tables are updated at the same time as the ARP cache; one of those is the MAC address table associated with the logical-switch that VM 1 is attached to. Figure 4-41 displays the contents of the MAC address table; using the output from this table, the packet can be forwarded *or* routed to the required destination endpoint.

```
EDGE TRANSPORT NODE 2> get logical-switch ef1d79ce-2555-4197-bb41-1739e3488455 mac-address-table
Logical Switch
UUID        : ef1d79ce-2555-4197-bb41-1739e3488455
VNI         : 27528
Device      : fp-eth1
ENCAP       : GENEVE
Replication : mtep
routing-domain: b9ba5b04-9055-42cb-897e-0242307393c2
Enable Hub  : False
MAC-Table:
   MAC              : 00:50:56:93:a7:99
      Tunnel        : 87c508e0-a849-53e6-a681-952e17fbe8d2
      IFUID         : 380
      LOCAL         : 192.168.66.60
      REMOTE        : 192.168.65.26
      ENCAP         : GENEVE
      SOURCE        : Static
```

Figure 4-41. *App Segments MAC address table*

VM 1 MAC address is available at remote TEP 192.168.65.26, which is Host Transport Node 1. The packet is encapsulated with a GENEVE header and routed to Host Transport Node 1, through the switch.

7. The switch receives the packet and forwards it to Host Transport Node 1.

8. Host Transport Node 1 receives the packet and de-encapsulates the packet as it moves through the IO chain. The packet is then forwarded to VM 1. Figure 4-42 displays the packet as it ingresses Host Transport Node 1 network interface.

```
> Frame 39: 132 bytes on wire (1056 bits), 132 bytes captured (1056 bits)
> Ethernet II, Src: BrocadeC_b7:bd:14 (cc:4e:24:b7:bd:14), Dst: VMware_65:b4:4d (00:50:56:65:b4:4d)
∨ Internet Protocol Version 4, Src: 192.168.66.60, Dst: 192.168.65.26
     0100 .... = Version: 4
     .... 0101 = Header Length: 20 bytes (5)
   > Differentiated Services Field: 0x00 (DSCP: CS0, ECN: Not-ECT)
     Total Length: 118
     Identification: 0x0000 (0)
   > Flags: 0x40, Don't fragment
     Fragment Offset: 0
     Time to Live: 63
     Protocol: UDP (17)
     Header Checksum: 0x36d0 [validation disabled]
     [Header checksum status: Unverified]
     Source Address: 192.168.66.60
     Destination Address: 192.168.65.26
> User Datagram Protocol, Src Port: 38614, Dst Port: 6081
∨ Generic Network Virtualization Encapsulation, VNI: 0x006b88
     Version: 0
     Length: 8 bytes
   > Flags: 0x40, Critical Options Present
     Protocol Type: Transparent Ethernet bridging (0x6558)
     Virtual Network Identifier (VNI): 0x006b88
   > Options: (8 bytes)
> Ethernet II, Src: 02:50:56:56:44:52 (02:50:56:56:44:52), Dst: VMware_93:a7:99 (00:50:56:93:a7:99)
> Internet Protocol Version 4, Src: 192.168.191.2, Dst: 192.168.190.2
> Internet Control Message Protocol
```

Figure 4-42. *Packet capture on Transport Node 1's network interface*

Outer Packet Header

- **Source MAC:** cc:4e:24:b7:bd:14 (ToR/gateway MAC address)

- **Destination MAC:** 00:50:56:65:b4:4d (Host Transport Node 1 TEP interface)

- **Source IP:** 192.168.66.60 (Edge Node 2 TEP IP)

- **Destination IP:** 192.168.65.26 (Host Transport Node 1 TEP IP)

- **User Datagram Protocol Destination Port:** 6081 (GENEVE)

- **Virtual Network Identifier (VNI):** 0x006b8a (overlay 27528 – Web Segment)

Inner Packet Header

- **Source IP:** 192.168.191.2 (VM 3 IP address)

- **Destination IP:** 192.168.190.2 (VM 1 IP address)

Figure 4-43 is a completed packet walk diagram with interface details.

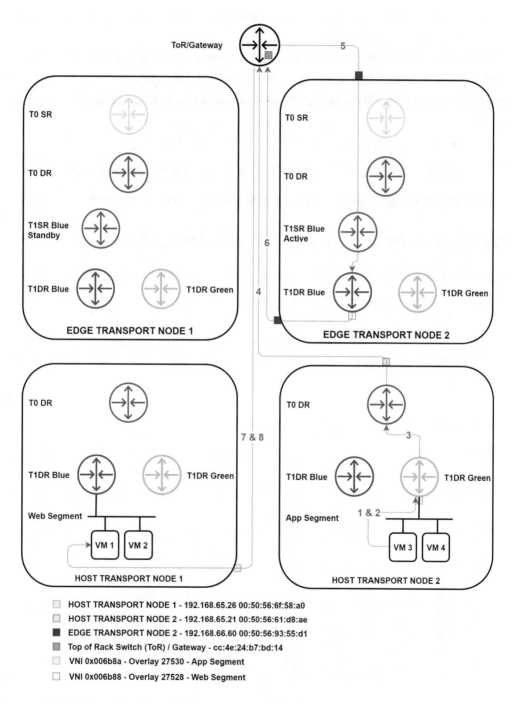

Figure 4-43. *Complete East-West return traffic diagram*

North-South Logical Routing

North-South Logical Routing, put simply, is traffic that enters and exits (ingresses and egresses) the NSX-T environment.

When using overlay segments, this encompasses all traffic that traverses the Edge Nodes. With VLAN-backed segments, data will ingress and egress the hosts as a standard portgroup normally would. This section focuses on dataflow when using overlay segments.

This section will cover two scenarios to depict traffic flow:

- North-South Logical Routing without stateful services configured

- North-South Logical Routing with stateful services configured

North-South Logical Routing Without Stateful Services

The previous section that covered East-West Logical Routing displayed the change in behavior when stateful services were configured. This change can also be seen with North-South traffic.

To be able to understand the impact of enabling stateful services, readers must first understand how North-South Logical Routing operates without stateful services configured.

The logical diagram provided in Figure 4-44 is the environment that will be discussed in this section.

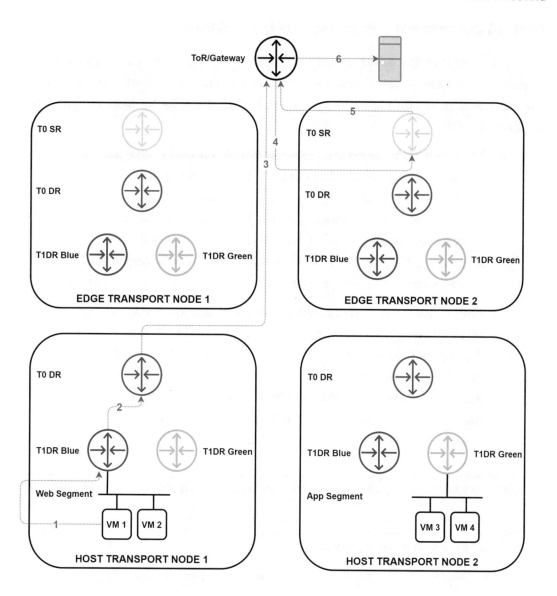

Figure 4-44. *North-South logical diagram without stateful services*

This diagram shows VM 1 communicating with the utility server through Edge Node 2. If no stateful services are configured, then ingress and egress packets will be load-balanced across both Edge Nodes. The path highlighted in this diagram is the packet that was captured.

Packet Flow from VM 1 to an External Utility Server

VM 1 sitting on Host Transport Node 1 needs to communicate with the utility server that resides on a host that is not enabled for NSX-T. This is considered North-South traffic as the packets must flow through the Edge Nodes, leaving the NSX-T domain and into the physical network.

1. VM 1 checks the destination IP address and compares it against its own IP and subnet. It determines that the destination IP is in a different subnet and therefore it must encapsulate the packet and send it to its default gateway. It checks its ARP table for the correct entry for its default gateway. If it exists, it sends the packet to the gateway, and if it does not exist, it sends an ARP request and waits for a reply before sending the packet.

   VM 1 sends the packet to its default gateway, and the packet is received on the routing or downlink interface on T1DR Blue. The packet is de-encapsulated, and the destination is checked. The destination in this case is 192.168.63.101; T1DR Blue checks its forwarding table and does not find a match for the prefix; the closest is the default route pointing to next hop gateway 100.64.16.0. Figure 4-45 is the T1DR Blue forwarding table.

```
HOST TRANSPORT NODE 1> get logical-router b9ba5b04-9055-42cb-897e-0242307393c2 forwarding
                      Logical Routers Forwarding Table
-----------------------------------------------------------------------------------------
Flags Legend: [U: Up], [G: Gateway], [C: Connected], [I: Interface]
[H: Host], [R: Reject], [B: Blackhole], [F: Soft Flush], [E: ECMP]


          Network              Gateway           Type      Interface UUID
=========================================================================================
0.0.0.0/0                   100.64.16.0          UG    2ded6094-01f2-4026-a2a7-33e2cbd97673
100.64.16.0/31              0.0.0.0              UCI   2ded6094-01f2-4026-a2a7-33e2cbd97673
169.254.0.0/28              0.0.0.0              UCI   f6e3b85c-6384-4c9e-8078-5b3f132088a1
192.168.190.0/24            0.0.0.0              UCI   5f14f9ca-84bb-4cc9-b380-1280af909de4
```

Figure 4-45. *T1DR Blue forwarding table*

Based on the IP address, it can be presumed that it belongs to an interface on the T0DR. To verify this, copy the Interface UUID and paste it into NSX-T Manager. Figure 4-46 shows the output from the NSX-T Manager user interface.

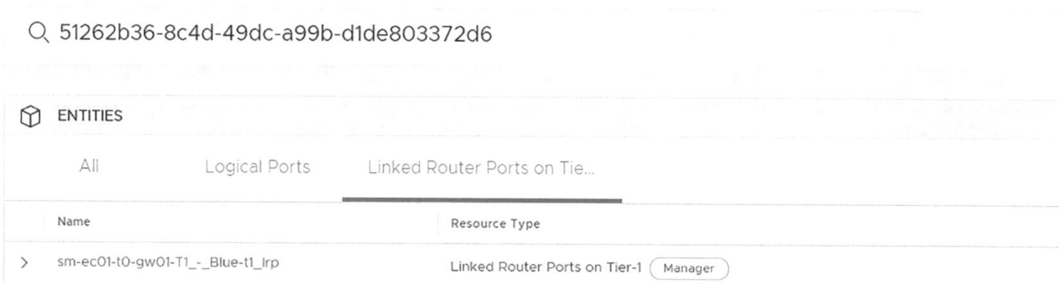

Q 51262b36-8c4d-49dc-a99b-d1de803372d6

ENTITIES		
All	Logical Ports	Linked Router Ports on Tie...

Name	Resource Type
> sm-ec01-t0-gw01-T1_-_Blue-t1_lrp	Linked Router Ports on Tier-1 (Manager)

Figure 4-46. *Identifying the interface UUID in NSX-T Manager*

The interface is a linked router port that connects T1 - Blue to the Tier-0 gateway.

2. T1DR Blue forwards the packet to T0DR; the packet is received on T0DR linked *or* routing link port. T0DR de-encapsulates the packet and inspects the destination IP. It checks its forwarding table for an entry that matches 192.168.63.101; as there is no match, the two default routes pointing to 169.254.0.2 and 169.254.0.3.

```
HOST TRANSPORT NODE 1>  get logical-router 8a0762ce-e31a-4447-9379-8a0d36c3c65c forwarding
                Logical Routers Forwarding Table
-------------------------------------------------------------------------------------------------
Flags Legend: [U: Up], [G: Gateway], [C: Connected], [I: Interface]
[H: Host], [R: Reject], [B: Blackhole], [F: Soft Flush], [E: ECMP]


        Network              Gateway          Type        Interface UUID
===============================================================================================
0.0.0.0/0                  169.254.0.2        UGE   a1852c52-9305-440b-8505-54f6534f7e2c
0.0.0.0/0                  169.254.0.3        UGE   a1852c52 -9305-440b-8505-54f6534f7e2c
```

Figure 4-47. *T0DR forwarding table on Host Transport Node 1*

These IP addresses can be identified as belonging to the SR component on the T0 gateway. Like the previous example, the SR component of the T0 resides on the Edge Nodes. The following two images confirm the location of the Logical Router components and addresses as depicted in Figure 4-47.

Figure 4-48 is Edge Node 1's backplane port.

```
EDGE TRANSPORT NODE 1> get logical-router 2ff833ab-b5ac-4840-beb6-bd873c0664a5 interface
Logical Router
UUID                        VRF  LR-ID  Name                    Type
2ff833ab-b5ac-4840-beb6-bd873c0664a5  5    9226  SR-edge-cl01-t0-gw01      SERVICE_ROUTER_TIER0
Interfaces (IPv6 DAD Status A-DAD_Success, F-DAD_Duplicate, T-DAD_Tentative, U-DAD_Unavailable)

    Interface        : 119b15ce-da2a-479b-b669-1e89259cac12
    Ifuid            : 325
    Name             : bp-sr0-port
    Fwd-mode         : IPV4_ONLY
    Internal name    : downlink-325
    Mode             : lif
    Port-type        : backplane
    IP/Mask          : 169.254.0.2/25;fe80::50:56ff:fe56:5300/64(NA)
    MAC              : 02:50:56:56:53:00
    VNI              : 67587
    Access-VLAN      : untagged
    LS port          : 73ee3328-68ce-4127-af15-82799e865308
    Urpf-mode        : NONE
    DAD-mode         : LOOSE
    RA-mode          : RA_INVALID
    Admin            : up
    Op_state         : up
    MTU              : 1500
    arp_proxy        :
```

Figure 4-48. *Edge Node 1 backplane port*

Figure 4-49 is Edge Node 2's backplane port.

```
EDGE TRANSPORT NODE 2> get logical-router 2650b6dd-c278-4873-8dbb-824ff6a4d34d interface
Logical Router
UUID                          VRF   LR-ID  Name                  Type
2ff833ab-b5ac-4840-beb6-bd873c0664a5  5    9226  SR-sm-edge-cl01-t0-gw01      SERVICE_ROUTER_TIER0
Interfaces (IPv6 DAD Status A-DAD_Success, F-DAD_Duplicate, T-DAD_Tentative, U-DAD_Unavailable)

        Interface           : 119b15ce-da2a-479b-b669-1e89259cac12
        Ifuid               : 325
        Name                : bp-sr0-port
        Fwd-mode            : IPV4_ONLY
        Internal name       : downlink-325
        Mode                : lif
        Port-type           : backplane
        IP/Mask             : 169.254.0.3/25;fe80::50:56ff:fe56:5300/64(NA)
        MAC                 : 02:50:56:56:53:01
        VNI                 : 67587
        Access-VLAN         : untagged
        LS port             : 73ee3328-68ce-4127-af15-82799e865308
        Urpf-mode           : NONE
        DAD-mode            : LOOSE
        RA-mode             : RA_INVALID
        Admin               : up
        Op_state            : up
        MTU                 : 1500
        arp_proxy           :
```

Figure 4-49. *Edge Node 2 backplane port*

3. T0DR forwards the packet over one of the backplane links, through the switch, to one of the SR. The path the packet takes is dependent on the hashing algorithm used by the hypervisor. This will be covered in the next chapter.

    It is possible to identify the paths the packet may take. To do so, obtain the VNI ID from the backplane ports. This VNI ID will be the same across the T0DR and SR counterparts. In this example the VNI ID is **67587**. The command *get logical-switch 67587 mac-table* will list the details as shown in Figure 4-50.

    Figure 4-50 shows the MAC address table for the transit segment, with VNI 67587.

```
HOST TRANSPORT NODE 1> get logical-switch 67587 mac-table
                Logical Switch MAC Table
---------------------------------------------------------------------

                Host Kernel Entry
==============================================================================
   Inner MAC        Outer MAC        Outer IP     Flags
02:50:56:56:53:01   ff:ff:ff:ff:ff:ff   192.168.66.61   0xf
02:50:56:56:53:00   ff:ff:ff:ff:ff:ff   192.168.66.63   0xf


                LCP Remote Entry
==============================================================================
   Inner MAC        Outer MAC        Outer IP

                LCP Local Entry
==============================================================================
   Inner MAC        Outer MAC        Outer IP
```

Figure 4-50. *Transit segment MAC Table*

The inner MAC addresses listed previously are the MAC addresses attached to the backplane ports on the Edge Nodes.

- 02:50:56:56:53:01 is the MAC address of 169.254.0.3 on Edge Node 1; 192.168.66.61 is Edge Node 1 first TEP interface.

- 02:50:56:56:53:00 is the MAC address of 169.254.0.2 on Edge Node 2; 192.168.66.63 is Edge Node 2 first TEP interface.

It is not possible to predetermine which path the packet will take; packets will be balanced across both SRs.

The WireShark output in Figure 4-51 is the packet as it leaves the Host Transport Node.

```
> Frame 14: 132 bytes on wire (1056 bits), 132 bytes captured (1056 bits)
> Ethernet II, Src: VMware_65:33:9a (00:50:56:65:33:9a), Dst: BrocadeC_b7:bd:14 (cc:4e:24:b7:bd:14)
∨ Internet Protocol Version 4, Src: 192.168.65.25, Dst: 192.168.66.63
      0100 .... = Version: 4
      .... 0101 = Header Length: 20 bytes (5)
    > Differentiated Services Field: 0x00 (DSCP: CS0, ECN: Not-ECT)
      Total Length: 118
      Identification: 0x0000 (0)
    > Flags: 0x40, Don't fragment
      Fragment Offset: 0
      Time to Live: 64
      Protocol: UDP (17)
      Header Checksum: 0x35ce [validation disabled]
      [Header checksum status: Unverified]
      Source Address: 192.168.65.25
      Destination Address: 192.168.66.63
> User Datagram Protocol, Src Port: 61882, Dst Port: 6081
∨ Generic Network Virtualization Encapsulation, VNI: 0x010803
      Version: 0
      Length: 8 bytes
    > Flags: 0x40, Critical Options Present
      Protocol Type: Transparent Ethernet bridging (0x6558)
      Virtual Network Identifier (VNI): 0x010803
    > Options: (8 bytes)
> Ethernet II, Src: 02:50:56:56:44:52 (02:50:56:56:44:52), Dst: 02:50:56:56:53:00 (02:50:56:56:53:00)
> Internet Protocol Version 4, Src: 192.168.190.2, Dst: 192.168.63.101
> Internet Control Message Protocol
```

Figure 4-51. *Transport Node 1 egress packet capture*

Outer Packet Header

- **Source MAC:** 00:50:56:65:33:9a (Host Transport Node 1 TEP interface)

- **Destination MAC:** cc:4e:24:b7:bd:14 (ToR/gateway MAC address)

- **Source IP:** 192.168.65.25 (Host Transport Node 1 TEP IP)

- **Destination IP:** 192.168.66.63 (Edge Node 2 TEP IP)

- **User Datagram Protocol Destination Port:** 6081 (GENEVE)

- **Virtual Network Identifier (VNI):** 0x010803 (overlay 67587 – transit segment)

Inner Packet Header

- **Source MAC:** 02:50:56:56:44:52 (virtual MAC used across various LIFs)

- **Destination MAC:** 02:50:56:56:53:00 (Edge Node 2 backplane port MAC address)

- **Source IP:** 192.168.190.2 (VM 1 IP address)

- **Destination IP:** 192.168.63.101 (utility server IP address)

4. Figure 4-52 is the capture output on Edge Node 2 TEP interface.

```
> Frame 22: 132 bytes on wire (1056 bits), 132 bytes captured (1056 bits)
> Ethernet II, Src: BrocadeC_b7:bd:14 (cc:4e:24:b7:bd:14), Dst: VMware_93:cf:ee (00:50:56:93:cf:ee)
∨ Internet Protocol Version 4, Src: 192.168.65.25, Dst: 192.168.66.63
     0100 .... = Version: 4
     .... 0101 = Header Length: 20 bytes (5)
   > Differentiated Services Field: 0x00 (DSCP: CS0, ECN: Not-ECT)
     Total Length: 118
     Identification: 0x0000 (0)
   > Flags: 0x40, Don't fragment
     Fragment Offset: 0
     Time to Live: 63
     Protocol: UDP (17)
     Header Checksum: 0x36ce [validation disabled]
     [Header checksum status: Unverified]
     Source Address: 192.168.65.25
     Destination Address: 192.168.66.63
> User Datagram Protocol, Src Port: 61882, Dst Port: 6081
∨ Generic Network Virtualization Encapsulation, VNI: 0x010803
     Version: 0
     Length: 8 bytes
   > Flags: 0x40, Critical Options Present
     Protocol Type: Transparent Ethernet bridging (0x6558)
     Virtual Network Identifier (VNI): 0x010803
   > Options: (8 bytes)
> Ethernet II, Src: 02:50:56:56:44:52 (02:50:56:56:44:52), Dst: 02:50:56:56:53:00 (02:50:56:56:53:00)
> Internet Protocol Version 4, Src: 192.168.190.2, Dst: 192.168.63.101
> Internet Control Message Protocol
```

Figure 4-52. *Edge Node 2 ingress packet capture*

Outer Packet Header

- **Source MAC:** cc:4e:24:b7:bd:14 (ToR/gateway MAC address)

- **Destination MAC:** 00:50:56:93:cf:ee (Edge Node 2 TEP MAC address)

- **Source IP:** 192.168.65.25 (Host Transport Node 1 TEP IP)

- **Destination IP:** 192.168.66.63 (Edge Node 2 TEP IP)

- **User Datagram Protocol Destination Port:** 6081 (GENEVE)

- **Virtual Network Identifier (VNI):** 0x010803 (overlay 67587 – transit segment)

Inner Packet Header

- **Source MAC:** 02:50:56:56:44:52 (virtual MAC used across various LIFs)

- **Destination MAC:** 02:50:56:56:53:00 (Edge Node 2 backplane port MAC address)

- **Source IP:** 192.168.190.2 (VM 1 IP address)

- **Destination IP:** 192.168.63.101 (utility server IP address)

Figure 4-51 shows that the packet has left the Host Transport Node and is being routed to Edge Node 2 TEP interface. The inner packet header in Figure 4-52 shows the communication between VM 1 within NSX-T and the utility server that sits outside of the NSX-T domain.

Edge Node 2 receives the packet and removes the outer packet header. The inner packet header is inspected, and the packet is sent to the backplane port with MAC 02:50:56:56:53:00.

The capture output in Figure 4-53 is from the backplane interface on Edge Node 2.

```
> Frame 1: 74 bytes on wire (592 bits), 74 bytes captured (592 bits)
> Ethernet II, Src: 02:50:56:56:44:52 (02:50:56:56:44:52), Dst: 02:50:56:56:53:00 (02:50:56:56:53:00)
∨ Internet Protocol Version 4, Src: 192.168.190.2, Dst: 192.168.63.101
     0100 .... = Version: 4
     .... 0101 = Header Length: 20 bytes (5)
   > Differentiated Services Field: 0x00 (DSCP: CS0, ECN: Not-ECT)
     Total Length: 60
     Identification: 0x0367 (871)
   > Flags: 0x00
     Fragment Offset: 0
     Time to Live: 126
     Protocol: ICMP (1)
     Header Checksum: 0xbaa1 [validation disabled]
     [Header checksum status: Unverified]
     Source Address: 192.168.190.2
     Destination Address: 192.168.63.101
> Internet Control Message Protocol
```

Figure 4-53. *Packet capture on Edge Node 2 backplane port*

Notice that the outer packet header has been removed; there is no longer a GENEVE header or any VNI details. These details are only relevant when the packet moves through the GENEVE tunnels – in other words, between Host and Edge Transport Nodes. Once the packet is received on the TEP interface, the outer packet header is removed, and the packet is forwarded to the required port internally.

Edge Node 2 performs a lookup to see if it has a match for 192.168.63.101.

- **Prefix found:** If it finds a match that has multiple paths, it uses a hashing algorithm to pick an egress interface. If there is only a single path, that path is used to forward the packet.

- **Default route:** If it does not find a match and has a default route, the default route is used. If there are multiple paths for the default route, a hashing algorithm is used to pick an egress interface or else the packet is forwarded over the path available.

- **No match:** If no match is found and there is no default route, the packet is dropped.

```
EDGE TRANSPORT NODE 2(tier0_sr)> get forwarding
Sat Aug 14 2021 UTC 05:08:42.969
Logical Router
UUID                                      VRF  LR-ID  Name                  Type
2650b6dd-c278-4873-8dbb-824ff6a4d34d  4    9227   SR-edge-cl01-t0-gw01  SERVICE_ROUTER_TIER0

IP Prefix          Gateway IP          Type   UUID                                        Gateway MAC
192.168.63.0/24    10.50.0.1           route  d2a5e701-2448-40db-8b23-3f3002b99d21  00:50:56:86:b0:9d
                   10.51.0.1                                                        00:50:56:86:38:91
```

Figure 4-54. *T0SR forwarding table*

The output in Figure 4-54 shows the prefix is known. As can be seen in Figure 4-54, the prefix 192.168.63.0/24 exists; 192.168.63.101 sits within this subnet. The packet is forwarded through one of the paths available.

Figure 4-55 shows a packet capture on the uplink interface of Edge Node 2.

```
> Frame 3: 74 bytes on wire (592 bits), 74 bytes captured (592 bits)
> Ethernet II, Src: VMware_93:cf:ee (00:50:56:93:cf:ee), Dst: VMware_86:b0:9d (00:50:56:86:b0:9d)
∨ Internet Protocol Version 4, Src: 192.168.190.2, Dst: 192.168.63.101
     0100 .... = Version: 4
     .... 0101 = Header Length: 20 bytes (5)
   > Differentiated Services Field: 0x00 (DSCP: CS0, ECN: Not-ECT)
     Total Length: 60
     Identification: 0x0a9c (2716)
   > Flags: 0x00
     Fragment Offset: 0
     Time to Live: 126
     Protocol: ICMP (1)
     Header Checksum: 0xb36c [validation disabled]
     [Header checksum status: Unverified]
     Source Address: 192.168.190.2
     Destination Address: 192.168.63.101
> Internet Control Message Protocol
```

Figure 4-55. *Edge Node 2 packet egress to the physical network*

The capture in Figure 4-55 shows the packet as it leaves the Edge uplink interface and therefore leaves the NSX-T domain. Once again, there are no GENEVE headers added to this packet as it is not being sent to another transport node.

5. The gateway receives the packet, checks its routing table, and then forwards it to the utility server.

6. The utility server receives the packet and processes it accordingly.

Figure 4-56 is a completed packet walk diagram with interface details.

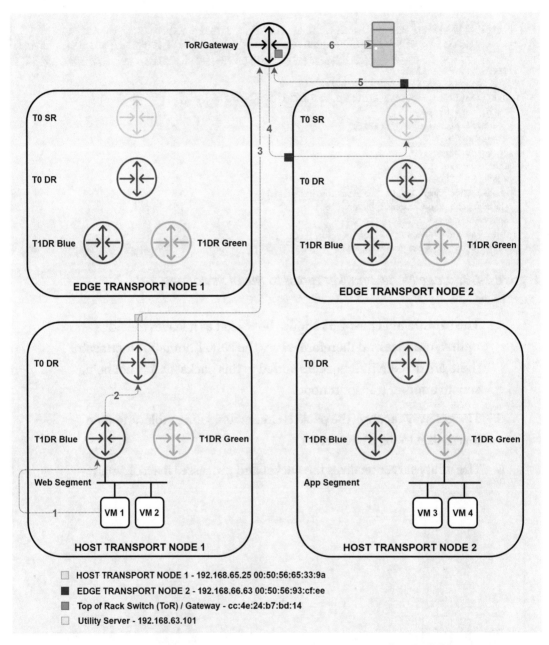

Figure 4-56. *Complete South-North packet walk diagram with interface details*

Packet Flow from the Physical Network to VM 1

This section will demonstrate packet flow from an external network into NSX-T. The logical diagram in Figure 4-57 has been provided so that readers have a better understanding of the topology.

This section will display communication from the utility server at IP address 192.168.63.101 to VM 1 at IP address 192.168.190.2.

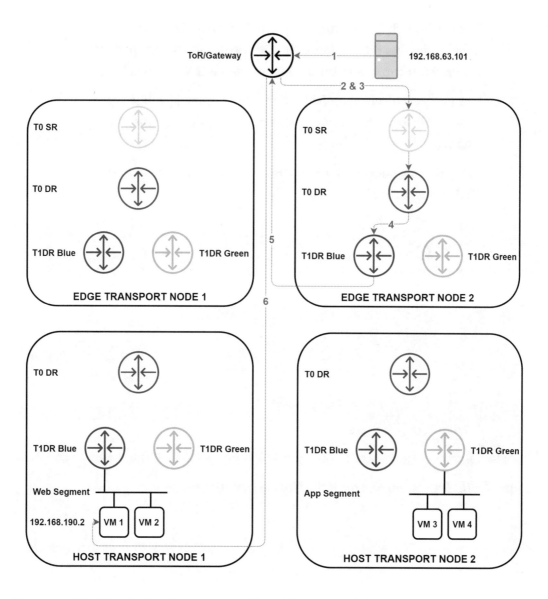

Figure 4-57. *North-South return traffic with no stateful services*

1. The utility server must send the packet to its default gateway, as VM 1 IP address sits within a different subnet. The utility server checks its ARP table for an entry of its default gateway. If it does not exist, it sends an ARP request and, once it receives a reply, encapsulates the packet and sends it to its default gateway.

   Refer to the logical diagram; the utility server default gateway sits on the core switch.

2. The core switch has learned the prefix 192.168.190.0/24 from the Edge Nodes that it is peered with. The core switch picks a path to the prefix, encapsulates the packet, and sends it to the next hop.

3. The packet is received on Edge Node 2 and de-encapsulated, the header is inspected, and the destination is checked against the routing table.

   The following packet is received on the uplink interface of Edge Node 2 shown in Figure 4-58.

```
> Frame 3: 74 bytes on wire (592 bits), 74 bytes captured (592 bits)
> Ethernet II, Src: Cisco_86:c0:7d (6c:20:56:86:c0:7d), Dst: VMware_93:cf:ee (00:50:56:93:cf:ee)
∨ Internet Protocol Version 4, Src: 192.168.63.101, Dst: 192.168.190.2
     0100 .... = Version: 4
     .... 0101 = Header Length: 20 bytes (5)
   > Differentiated Services Field: 0x00 (DSCP: CS0, ECN: Not-ECT)
     Total Length: 60
     Identification: 0x3757 (14167)
   > Flags: 0x00
     Fragment Offset: 0
     Time to Live: 126
     Protocol: ICMP (1)
     Header Checksum: 0x86b1 [validation disabled]
     [Header checksum status: Unverified]
     Source Address: 192.168.63.101
     Destination Address: 192.168.190.2
> Internet Control Message Protocol
```

Figure 4-58. *Ingress packet on Edge Node 2 uplink interface*

Packet Data

- **Source MAC:** 6c:20:56:86:c0:7d (top of rack switch)

- **Destination MAC:** 00:50:56:98:69:82 (Edge Node 2 uplink interface)

- **Source IP:** 192.168.63.101 (utility server IP address)

- **Destination IP:** 192.168.190.2 (VM 1 IP address)

Notice that the packet has not been encapsulated in a GENEVE header. This is because it has just ingressed from the physical network and there are no GENEVE tunnels upstream of the edge appliances.

The SR component of the T0 Logical Router is where the uplink interfaces reside. Figure 4-59 shows the uplink interfaces of the T0SR on Edge Node 2.

```
EDGE TRANSPORT NODE 2> get logical-router 2650b6dd-c278-4873-8dbb-824ff6a4d34d interface
Logical Router
UUID                                    VRF  LR-ID  Name              Type
2650b6dd-c278-4873-8dbb-824ff6a4d34d     4    9227   SR-edge-cl01-t0-gw01      SERVICE_ROUTER_TIER0
Interfaces (IPv6 DAD Status A-DAD_Success, F-DAD_Duplicate, T-DAD_Tentative, U-DAD_Unavailable)

        Interface      : d2a5e701-2448-40db-8b23-3f3002b99d21
        Ifuid          : 284
        Name           : uplink3
        Fwd-mode       : IPV4_ONLY
        Internal name  : uplink-284
        Mode           : lif
        Port-type      : uplink
        IP/Mask        : 10.50.0.3/24
        MAC            : 00:50:56:98:69:82
        VLAN           : 50
        Access-VLAN    : untagged
        LS port        : 77c5ee50-7d1a-4846-acd7-d52219fc64fe
        Urpf-mode      : STRICT_MODE
        DAD-mode       : LOOSE
        RA-mode        : SLAAC_DNS_TRHOUGH_RA(M=0, O=0)
        Admin          : up
        Op_state       : up
        MTU            : 1500
        arp_proxy      :

        Interface      : 9e325adb-689d-4529-af21-9845198c8209
        Ifuid          : 300
        Name           : uplink4
        Fwd-mode       : IPV4_ONLY
        Internal name  : uplink-300
        Mode           : lif
        Port-type      : uplink
        IP/Mask        : 10.51.0.3/24
        MAC            : 00:50:56:98:ee:c7
        VLAN           : 51
        Access-VLAN    : untagged
        LS port        : 8efdbdbe-7670-488c-8201-6d38c26e33fe
        Urpf-mode      : STRICT_MODE
        DAD-mode       : LOOSE
        RA-mode        : SLAAC_DNS_TRHOUGH_RA(M=0, O=0)
        Admin          : up
        Op_state       : up
        MTU            : 1500
        arp_proxy      :
```

Figure 4-59. *T0SR interfaces on Edge Node 2*

The forwarding table is checked to see if there is a match; prefix
192.168.190.0/24 is found with a gateway IP of 100.64.16.1.

The forwarding table on Edge Node 2 is displayed in Figure 4-60.

```
EDGE TRANSPORT NODE 2> get logical-router 2650b6dd-c278-4873-8dbb-824ff6a4d34d forwarding
Logical Router
UUID                                    VRF  LR-ID  Name              Type
2650b6dd-c278-4873-8dbb-824ff6a4d34d    4    9227   SR-edge-cl01-t0-gw01   SERVICE_ROUTER_TIER0
IPv4 Forwarding Table
IP Prefix          Gateway IP           Type    UUID                                 Gateway MAC
192.168.190.0/24   100.64.16.1          route   5c7ab3ba-a51c-4c73-a6c2-2402848f29ad
```

Figure 4-60. *T0SR forwarding table*

T0DR forwards the packet to T1DR Blue, which is also instantiated on the Edge Node. Figure 4-61 is a packet capture on the linked port on T0DR, which is the port that links T0DR and T1DR Blue.

```
> Frame 1: 74 bytes on wire (592 bits), 74 bytes captured (592 bits)
> Ethernet II, Src: 02:50:56:56:44:52 (02:50:56:56:44:52), Dst: 02:50:56:56:44:55 (02:50:56:56:44:55)
∨ Internet Protocol Version 4, Src: 192.168.63.101, Dst: 192.168.190.2
      0100 .... = Version: 4
      .... 0101 = Header Length: 20 bytes (5)
    > Differentiated Services Field: 0x00 (DSCP: CS0, ECN: Not-ECT)
      Total Length: 60
      Identification: 0x725e (29278)
    > Flags: 0x00
      Fragment Offset: 0
      Time to Live: 125
      Protocol: ICMP (1)
      Header Checksum: 0x4caa [validation disabled]
      [Header checksum status: Unverified]
      Source Address: 192.168.63.101
      Destination Address: 192.168.190.2
> Internet Control Message Protocol
```

Figure 4-61. *Egress packet capture on T0DR*

Packet Data

- **Source MAC:** 02:50:56:56:44:52 (linked port on T0DR MAC address)

- **Destination MAC:** 02:50:56:56:44:55 (linked port on T1DR Blue MAC address)

4. T1DR Blue receives the packet and inspects the header. T1DR Blue checks its forwarding table for an entry that matches the destination IP 192.168.190.2. It finds a match and sees that it has a downlink port attached that matches the prefix; this is shown in Figure 4-62.

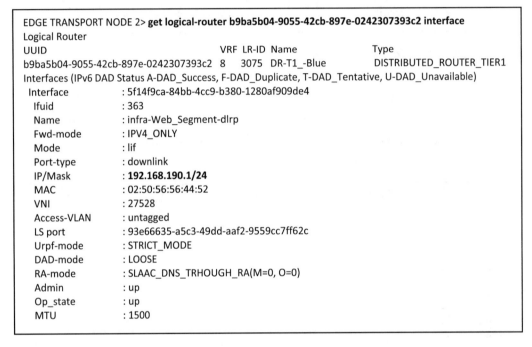

Figure 4-62. *T1DR Blue downlink port*

T1DR Blue must now find which transport node the destination IP resides in. To do so, it uses the VNI found attached to the downlink port, as shown in Figure 4-62. It checks the ARP cache and finds the destination IP and MAC address, as can be seen in Figure 4-63.

```
EDGE TRANSPORT NODE 2> get logical-switch remote arp-cache 27528

  VM IP                          VM MAC                      VM IPv6
  192.168.190.2                  00:50:56:93:a7:99           None
```

Figure 4-63. *VNI 27528 ARP cache on Edge Node 2*

Now that VM 1 MAC address is known, the tunnel endpoint address where VM 1 resides must be determined. To accomplish this, the MAC address table associated with the logical-switch is checked.

```
EDGE TRANSPORT NODE 2> get logical-switch ef1d79ce-2555-4197-bb41-1739e3488455 mac-address-table
Logical Switch
UUID                    : ef1d79ce-2555-4197-bb41-1739e3488455
VNI                     : 27528
Device                  : fp-eth1
ENCAP                   : GENEVE
Replication             : mtep
routing-domain          : 8a0762ce-e31a-4447-9379-8a0d36c3c65c
Enable Hub              : False
MAC-Table:
   MAC                  : 02:50:56:56:44:52
      Port              : 93e66635-a5c3-49dd-aaf2-9559cc7ff62c
      IFUID             : 362
      SOURCE            : Static
   MAC                  : 00:50:56:93:a7:99
      Tunnel            : 2877f3e0-9a35-5bd9-b39b-892b800416b7
      IFUID             : 368
      LOCAL             : 192.168.66.62
      REMOTE            : 192.168.65.26
      ENCAP             : GENEVE
      SOURCE            : Static
```

Figure 4-64. *Web Segment MAC address table on Edge Node 2*

Figure 4-64 shows VM 1 MAC address 00:50:56:93:a7:99 exists on Remote Tunnel Endpoint 192.168.65.26, which is Host Transport Node 1. T1DR Blue forwards the packet to the tunnel endpoint interface on Edge Node 2 (192.168.66.62). As the packet is being transmitted from T1DR Blue logical port to the TEP interface, it has not been encapsulated in a GENEVE header.

Once the packet is received on the TEP interface, it is encapsulated in a GENEVE header and sent to Host Transport Node 1 TEP interface.

The WireShark output in Figure 4-65 is a packet capture on Edge Node 2 TEP interface, which the same packet from Figure 4-61, however, has now been encapsulated with a GENEVE header.

```
> Frame 7: 132 bytes on wire (1056 bits), 132 bytes captured (1056 bits)
> Ethernet II, Src: VMware_93:14:ad (00:50:56:93:14:ad), Dst: BrocadeC_b7:bd:14 (cc:4e:24:b7:bd:14)
> Internet Protocol Version 4, Src: 192.168.66.62, Dst: 192.168.65.26
> User Datagram Protocol, Src Port: 38614, Dst Port: 6081
> Generic Network Virtualization Encapsulation, VNI: 0x006b88
> Ethernet II, Src: 02:50:56:56:44:52 (02:50:56:56:44:52), Dst: VMware_93:a7:99 (00:50:56:93:a7:99)
> Internet Protocol Version 4, Src: 192.168.63.101, Dst: 192.168.190.2
> Internet Control Message Protocol
```

Figure 4-65. *Packet after being encapsulated with a GENEVE header on Edge Node 2*

Outer Header

- **Source MAC:** 00:50:56:93:14:ad (Edge Node 2 TEP interface)

- **Destination MAC:** cc:4e:24:b7:bd:14 (gateway MAC address)

- **Source IP:** 192.168.66.62 (Edge Node 2 TEP IP)

- **Destination IP:** 192.168.65.26 (Host Transport Node 1 TEP IP)

- **Virtual Network Identifier (VNI):** 0x006b88 (overlay 27528 – Web Segment)

Inner Header

- **Source MAC:** 02:50:56:56:44:52 (LIF virtual MAC address)

- **Destination MAC:** 00:50:56:93:a7:99 (VM 1 MAC address)

- **Source IP:** 192.168.63.101 (utility server VM IP address)

- **Destination IP:** 192.168.190.2 (VM 1 IP address)

5. The packet is routed over the physical network fabric and sent to Host Transport Node 1 TEP interface.

6. The packet is de-encapsulated as it passes through the IO chain on Host Transport Node 1. Once complete, the packet is forwarded to VM 1.

Figure 4-66 is a completed packet walk diagram with interface details.

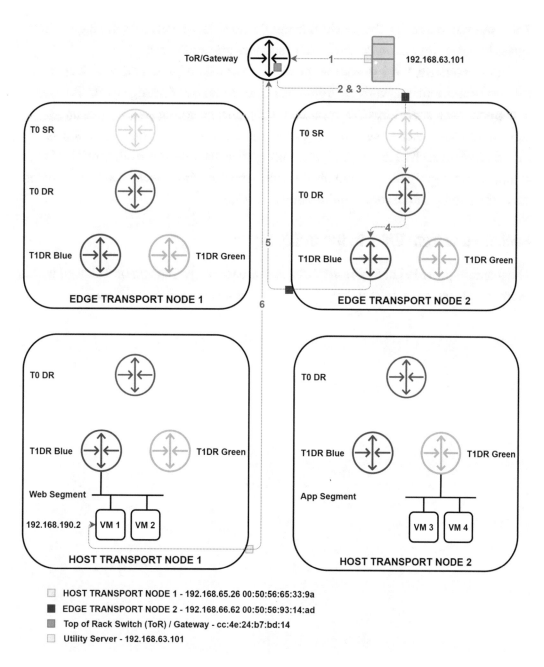

Figure 4-66. *Complete North-South packet walk with interface details*

North-South Logical Routing with Stateful Services

This example will be like the previous example; however, it will show the ingress and egress behavior for packets when stateful services are configured.

In this scenario, VM 1 IP address needs to be translated to IP address 172.25.0.10 prior to communicating with the utility server as it egresses the Edge Node. For this to happen, Network Address Translation (NAT) must be configured. Source and Destination NAT will be used and are both a stateful service. As such T1SR Blue is instantiated on each of the Edge Nodes. One will be active and the other will be in standby. The steps in this section display this behavior with a packet walk and do not cover the configuration steps for the stateful service.

Packet Flow from VM 1 to the Utility Server

The diagram provided in Figure 4-67 displays the topology that will be followed in this example. The steps in this section correlate to the step numbers in the diagram.

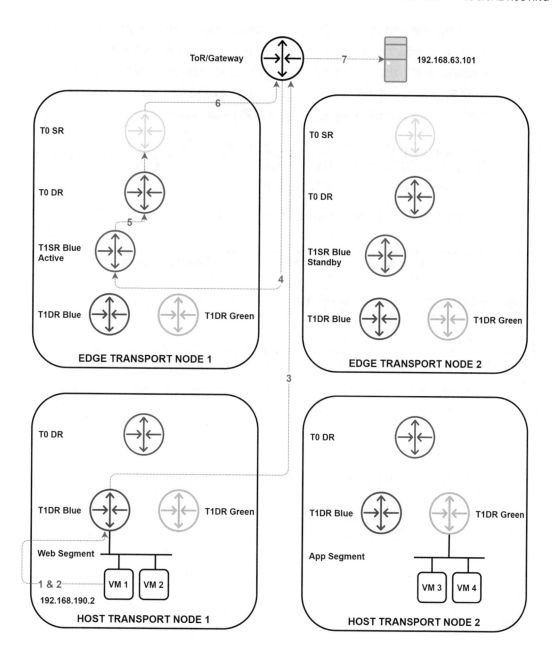

Figure 4-67. *North-South traffic with stateful services*

1. VM 1 begins with checking the destination IP and determines if it sits in a different subnet. VM 1 must send the packet to its default gateway; it checks its ARP table to ensure it has an entry for its default gateway; if it doesn't, it sends an ARP request, waits for a response, and sends the packet to its default gateway.

2. T1DR Blue checks its forwarding table for the destination address, 192.168.63.101. It does not have a match for the prefix, so it uses its default route pointing to 169.254.0.2.

   Figure 4-68 is the forwarding table on T1DR Blue.

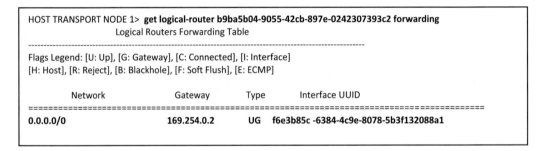

Figure 4-68. *T1DR Blue forwarding table*

The backplane port on Host Transport Node 1 that links to gateway 169.254.0.2 is associated with VNI 67599, which can be seen in Figure 4-69.

```
HOST TRANSPORT NODE 1> get logical-router b9ba5b04-9055-42cb-897e-0242307393c2 interface
                Logical Router Interfaces
---------------------------------------------------------------------------
IPv6 DAD Status Legend:  [A: DAD_Sucess], [F: DAD_Duplicate], [T: DAD_Tentative], [U: DAD_Unavailable]

LIF UUID              : f6e3b85c-6384-4c9e-8078-5b3f132088a1
Mode                  : [b'Routing-Backplane']
Overlay VNI           : 67599
IP/Mask               : 169.254.0.1/28;  fe80::50:56ff:fe56:4452/128(U)
Mac                   : 02:50:56:56:44:52
Connected DVS         : vds01
Control plane enable  : True
Replication Mode      : 0.0.0.1
Multicast Routing     : [b'Enabled', b'Oper Down']
State                 : [b'Enabled']
Flags                 : 0x90308
DHCP relay            : Not enable
DAD-mode              : ['LOOSE']
RA-mode               : ['SLAAC_DNS_THROUGH_RA(M=0, O=0)']
```

Figure 4-69. *T1DR Blue backplane port details*

To forward the packet, T1DR Blue sends the packet to its neighbor, T1SR Blue, which resides on Edge Node 1. The neighbor details of T1DR Blue can be checked on Host Transport Node 1 by issuing the command *get logical-router <T1DR Blue UUID> neighbors*.

Figure 4-70 is the neighbor table for T1DR Blue.

```
HOST TRANSPORT NODE 1> get logical-router b9ba5b04-9055-42cb-897e-0242307393c2 neighbor
                Logical Routers Neighbors
-----------------------------------------------------------------------------------------------------------
Flags Legend: [S: Static], [V: Valid], [P: Proxy], [I: Interface]
[N: Nascent], [L: Local], [D: Deleted], [K: linKlif]

      Network           Mac           Flags   State  SrcPort     Refcnt      Lif UUID
============================================================================================================
169.254.0.2        02:50:56:56:53:00   V     598    2214592677   2    f6e3b85c-6384-4c9e-8078-5b3f132088a1
169.254.0.1        02:50:56:56:44:52   VI    permanent  0        1    f6e3b85c-6384-4c9e-8078-5b3f132088a1
192.168.190.2      00:50:56:98:77:b8   VL    598    67109057     2    5f14f9ca-84bb-4cc9-b380-1280af909de4
192.168.190.1      02:50:56:56:44:52   VI    permanent  0        1    5f14f9ca-84bb-4cc9-b380-1280af909de4
```

Figure 4-70. *T1DR Blue neighbors*

The transport node where the neighbor IP and MAC address are instantiated must now be determined. These details can be checked by issuing the command *get logical-switch <VNI> mac-table*; in this case the VNI would be 67599.

141

Pay close attention to the inner MAC and outer IP fields in Figure 4-71.

```
HOST TRANSPORT NODE 1> get logical-switch 67599 mac-table
              Logical Switch MAC Table
----------------------------------------------------------------------

                    Host Kernel Entry
===================================================================
    Inner MAC        Outer MAC        Outer IP     Flags
  02:50:56:56:53:00  ff:ff:ff:ff:ff:ff   192.168.66.11   0x1

                    LCP Remote Entry
===================================================================
    Inner MAC        Outer MAC        Outer IP

                    LCP Local Entry
===================================================================
    Inner MAC        Outer MAC        Outer IP
```

Figure 4-71. *VNI 67599 MAC table*

The inner MAC is the MAC address of the next hop gateway 169.254.0.2. The outer IP is the TEP IP address of an Edge Node.

- 02:50:56:56:53:00 is 169.254.0.2 MAC address.

- 192.168.66.11 is Edge Node 1 second TEP interface

The packet must now be encapsulated with a GENEVE header and forwarded out of one of Host Transport Node 1 TEP interfaces through the switch to 192.168.66.11.

3.   The switch receives the packet and forwards it to Edge Node 1.

4.   The packet capture displayed in Figure 4-72 is received on Edge Node 1 TEP interface 192.168.66.11.

```
> Frame 6: 132 bytes on wire (1056 bits), 132 bytes captured (1056 bits)
> Ethernet II, Src: BrocadeC_b7:bd:14 (cc:4e:24:b7:bd:14), Dst: VMware_86:93:2b (00:50:56:86:93:2b)
> Internet Protocol Version 4, Src: 192.168.65.2, Dst: 192.168.66.11
> User Datagram Protocol, Src Port: 61882, Dst Port: 6081
> Generic Network Virtualization Encapsulation, VNI: 0x01080f
> Ethernet II, Src: 02:50:56:56:44:52 (02:50:56:56:44:52), Dst: 02:50:56:56:53:00 (02:50:56:56:53:00)
> Internet Protocol Version 4, Src: 192.168.190.2, Dst: 192.168.63.101
> Internet Control Message Protocol
```

Figure 4-72. *Edge Node 1 TEP ingress packet capture*

Outer Packet Header

- **Source MAC:** cc:4e:24:b7:bd:14 (ToR/gateway MAC address)

- **Destination MAC:** 02:50:56:86:93:2b (Edge Node 1 TEP interface)

- **Source IP:** 192.168.65.2 (Host Transport Node 1 TEP IP address)

- **Destination IP:** 192.168.66.11 (Edge Node 1 TEP IP address)

- **Virtual Network Identifier (VNI):** 0x01080f (overlay 67599 – transit segment)

Inner Packet Header

- **Source MAC:** 02:50:56:56:44:52 (T1DR Blue virtual MAC address)

- **Destination MAC:** 02:50:56:56:53:00 (Edge Node 1 backplane port MAC address)

- **Source IP:** 192.168.190.2 (VM 1 IP address)

- **Destination IP:** 192.168.63.101 (utility server IP address)

T1SR Blue checks the destination IP address against its forwarding table; it does not have a matching prefix and must use its default route. Figure 4-73 is the forwarding table on T1SR Blue.

```
EDGE TRANSPORT NODE 1> get logical-router d999a545-6917-488e-aaa5-f643e03642ba forwarding
Logical Router
UUID                                    VRF   LR-ID  Name              Type
d999a545-6917-488e-aaa5-f643e03642ba    12    12290  SR-T1 - Blue      SERVICE_ROUTER_TIER1
IPv4 Forwarding Table
IP Prefix              Gateway IP          Type    UUID                                    Gateway MAC
0.0.0.0/0             100.64.128.0         route   2ded6094-01f2-4026-a2a7-33e2cbd97673    02:50:56:56:44:52
169.254.0.0/28                            route   21a4c389-c9f1-4e0a-9b73-068845e76621
169.254.0.1/32                            route   1b5076c8-33d8-529a-b9ee-1cbfc4bc5e28
192.168.190.0/24                         route   5f14f9ca-84bb-4cc9-b380-1280af909de4
192.168.190.1/32                         route   1b5076c8-33d8-529a-b9ee-1cbfc4bc5e28
```

Figure 4-73. *T1SR Blue forwarding table*

The gateway IP associated with the default route belongs to the T0DR gateway. This can be checked by issuing the command *get logical-router interface <uuid>*. The UUID in Figure 4-73 is T1SR Blue interface UUID which links to T0DR's downlink interface. This can be seen from the interface name.

Figure 4-74 displays the interface details.

```
EDGE TRANSPORT NODE 1> get logical-router interface 2ded6094-01f2-4026-a2a7-33e2cbd97673
interface          : 2ded6094-01f2-4026-a2a7-33e2cbd97673
ifuid              : 407
VRF                : d999a545-6917-488e-aaa5-f643e03642ba
name               : sm-edge-cl01-t0-gw01-T1_-_Blue_lrp
mode               : lif
IP/Mask            : 100.64.128.1/31;fe80::50:56ff:fe56:4455/64(NA);fcbf:9ce6:3dc7:7800::2/64(NA)
Fwd-mode           : IPV4_ONLY
MAC                : 02:50:56:56:44:55
VNI                : 67598
LS port            : 9ac8f2c7-0ff9-4201-a382-12bc2496bc82
urpf-mode          : NONE
admin              : up
op_state           : up
MTU                : 1500
arp_proxy          :
```

Figure 4-74. *Checking gateway interface UUID*

To confirm this, issue the command *get logical-router <T0DR UUID> interfaces*.

Figure 4-75 shows the downlink port details on T0DR.

```
EDGE TRANSPORT NODE 1> get logical-router 8a0762ce-e31a-4447-9379-8a0d36c3c65c interfaces
Logical Router
UUID                                      VRF  LR-ID  Name                    Type
8a0762ce-e31a-4447-9379-8a0d36c3c65c       4    8193  DR-sm-edge-cl01-t0-gw01   DISTRIBUTED_ROUTER_TIER0
Interfaces (IPv6 DAD Status A-DAD_Success, F-DAD_Duplicate, T-DAD_Tentative, U-DAD_Unavailable)

Interface      : 5c7ab3ba-a51c-4c73-a6c2-2402848f29ad
  Ifuid        : 376
  Name         : edge-cl01-t0-gw01-T1_-_Blue_lrp
  Fwd-mode     : IPV4_ONLY
  Internal name : downlink-376
  Mode         : lif
  Port-type    : downlink
  IP/Mask      : 100.64.128.0/31;fcbf:9ce6:3dc7:7800::1/64(NA);fe80::50:56ff:fe56:4452/64(NA)
  MAC          : 02:50:56:56:44:52
  VNI          : 67598
  Access-VLAN  : untagged
  LS port      : 7ee11313-b429-4ea2-a687-8e0f6dcfd0fb
  Urpf-mode    : PORT_CHECK
  DAD-mode     : LOOSE
  RA-mode      : SLAAC_DNS_TRHOUGH_RA(M=0, O=0)
  Admin        : up
  Op_state     : up
  MTU          : 1500
  arp_proxy    :
```

Figure 4-75. *T0DR downlink interface*

The packet is now forwarded to the downlink interface on T0DR.

5. T0DR receives the packet and attempts to match the destination IP to a prefix in its forwarding table. It finds a matching entry in the forwarding table with two interfaces associated. Upon checking the interfaces, they are assigned to T0SR's uplink interfaces. The packet is forwarded to T0SR, which then forwards the frame out of one of its uplink interfaces to the gateway.

6. The gateway receives the packet and then forwards it to the utility server.

7. The utility server receives the frame and processes it accordingly.

Figure 4-76 is a completed packet walk diagram with interface details.

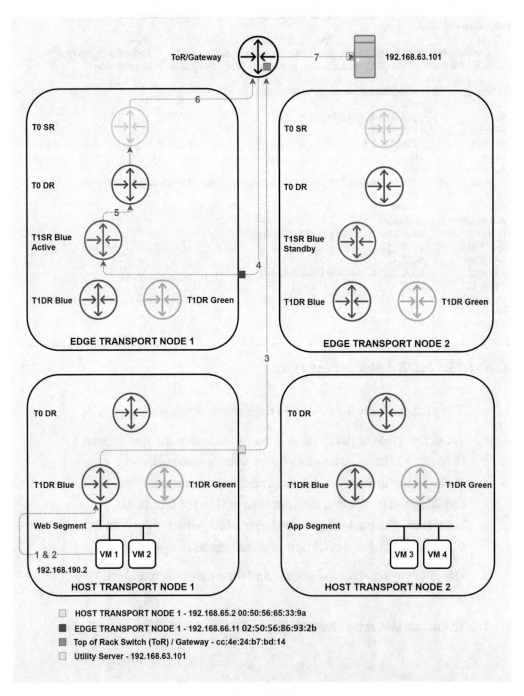

Figure 4-76. *Complete packet walk South-North with interface details*

NAT operation was not covered in this packet walk.

Packet Flow from the Utility Server to VM 1

This example will highlight packet flow behavior as it is sent back to VM 1. It will not show the return flow when the packets ingress via the Edge Node with the active SR. This is because similar behavior has already been covered in the previous sections.

This section will focus on what happens to packets if they arrive on the Edge Node that has the Standby SR. The reason for this is, while only one Edge has the active SR for T1SR Blue, both Edge Nodes are still peering with the top of rack switches and propagating the prefix. Therefore, the physical network sees multiple paths through both Edge Nodes to get to the prefix.

As an example, the image in Figure 4-77 shows the second top of rack switch routing table.

```
SSH@Leaf-2#show ip route 172.25.0.10
Type Codes - B:BGP D:Connected O:OSPF R:RIP S:Static; Cost - Dist/Metric
BGP  Codes - i:iBGP e:eBGP
OSPF Codes - i:Inter Area 1:External Type 1 2:External Type 2
     Destination            Gateway     Port    Cost    Type Uptime
1    172.25.0.10/32         10.51.0.2   ve 51   20/0    Be  1m41s
     172.25.0.10/32         10.51.0.3   ve 51   20/0    Be  1m41s
```

Figure 4-77. *Top of rack switch 2's BGP routing table*

Notice that the IP that is being translated is known via 10.51.0.2 and 10.51.0.3.

- **10.51.0.2** is attached to Edge Node 1.

- **10.51.0.3** is attached to Edge Node 2.

The diagram provided in Figure 4-78 highlights both the steps that will be followed in this section and the topology that will be utilized.

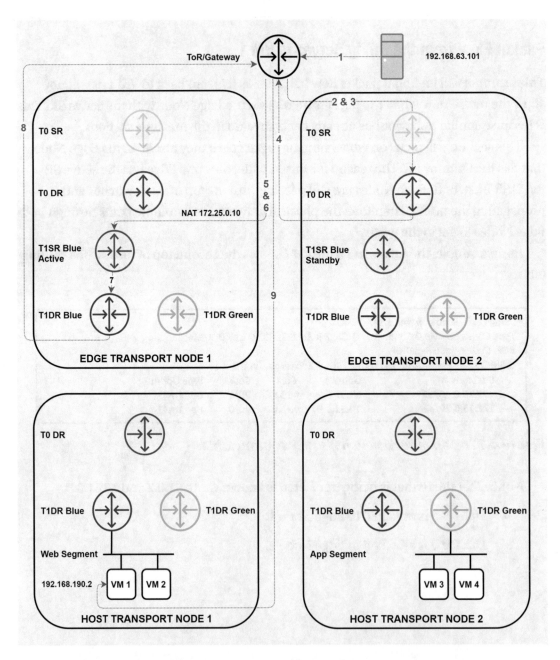

Figure 4-78. *North-South return traffic with stateful services*

1. The utility server needs to send a packet to VM 1. As it is in a different subnet, it encapsulates the packet and forwards it through its default gateway.

2. The core switch inspects the packet and checks the destination IP address against its routing table. It has two entries, both learned via eBGP with equal cost. These are both Edge Nodes. The switch encapsulates and sends the packet to Edge Node 2.

3. The packet capture in Figure 4-79 shows the packet arriving on Edge Node 2 uplink interface.

```
> Frame 1: 74 bytes on wire (592 bits), 74 bytes captured (592 bits)
> Ethernet II, Src: Cisco_33:f0:6d (6c:20:56:33:f0:6d), Dst: VMware_86:ca:18 (00:50:56:86:ca:18)
v Internet Protocol Version 4, Src: 192.168.63.101, Dst: 172.25.0.10
     0100 .... = Version: 4
     .... 0101 = Header Length: 20 bytes (5)
  > Differentiated Services Field: 0x00 (DSCP: CS0, ECN: Not-ECT)
     Total Length: 60
     Identification: 0x7195 (29077)
  > Flags: 0x00
     Fragment Offset: 0
     Time to Live: 126
     Protocol: ICMP (1)
     Header Checksum: 0x1efb [validation disabled]
     [Header checksum status: Unverified]
     Source Address: 192.168.63.101
     Destination Address: 172.25.0.10
> Internet Control Message Protocol
```

Figure 4-79. *Packet captured on Edge 2 uplink interface*

Packet Header

- **Source MAC:** 6c:20:56:33:f0:6d (ToR-2 MAC address)

- **Destination MAC:** 00:50:56:86:ca:18 (Edge Node 2 uplink interface MAC address)

- **Source IP:** 192.168.63.101 (utility server IP address)

- **Destination IP:** 172.25.0.10 (192.168.190.2 DNAT IP address)

Ordinarily, the forwarding table is checked for a match and the packet is forwarded to the T0DR across the backplane port, and then it is forwarded onto the T1 gateway. However, this is where having the stateful service changes this behavior.

The T0SR on Edge Node 2 checks its forwarding table and finds a
match with a gateway IP of 100.64.128.1. Figure 4-80 is the T0SR
forwarding table on Edge Node 2.

```
EDGE TRANSPORT NODE 2> get logical-router 2ff833ab-b5ac-4840-beb6-bd873c0664a5 forwarding 172.25.0.10/32
Logical Router
UUID                                      VRF  LR-ID  Name                          Type
2ff833ab-b5ac-4840-beb6-bd873c0664a5      5    9226   SR-sm-edge-cl01-t0-gw01       SERVICE_ROUTER_TIER0
IPv4 Forwarding Table
IP Prefix          Gateway IP              Type    UUID                                    Gateway MAC
172.25.0.10/32     100.64.128.1            route   5c7ab3ba-a51c-4c73-a6c2-2402848f29ad
```

Figure 4-80. *T0SR forwarding table on Edge 2*

The T0SR would normally forward the packet out through T0DR and
across its intra-tier downlink port to T1SR Blue on the same Edge
Node. At this point, if a packet capture is taken on the T1SR Blue
uplink port 100.64.128.1, there *shouldn't* be any packets captured.

Figure 4-81 is a packet capture on the T1SR Blue uplink interface on
Edge Node 2.

```
EDGE TRANSPORT NODE 2> start capture interface 2ded6094-01f2-4026-a2a7-33e2cbd97673 direction dual

0 packets captured
0 packets received by filter
0 packets dropped by kernel
```

Figure 4-81. *Packet capture on Edge Node 2 on T1SR Blue uplink interface*

As can be seen, no packets have been forwarded to the uplink
interface on T1SR Blue on Edge Node 2 from T0DR. Figure 4-82
shows the reason for this.

```
EDGE TRANSPORT NODE 2>  get logical-router d999a545-6917-488e-aaa5-f643e03642ba interfaces
    Interface          : 2ded6094-01f2-4026-a2a7-33e2cbd97673
    Ifuid              : 407
    Name               : edge-cl01-t0-gw01-T1_-_Blue_lrp
    Fwd-mode           : IPV4_ONLY
    Mode               : lif
    Port-type          : uplink
    IP/Mask            : 100.64.128.1/31;fe80::50:56ff:fe56:4455/64(NA);fcbf:9ce6:3dc7:7800::2/64(NA)
    MAC                : 02:50:56:56:44:55
    VNI                : 71696
    Access-VLAN        : untagged
    LS port            : 9ac8f2c7-0ff9-4201-a382-12bc2496bc82
    Urpf-mode          : NONE
    DAD-mode           : LOOSE
    RA-mode            : SLAAC_DNS_TRHOUGH_RA(M=0, O=0)
    Admin              : up
    Op_state           : down
    MTU                : 1500
```

Figure 4-82. *T1SR Blue uplink interface on Edge Node 2*

 The uplink interface on Edge Node 2 has an Op_state of down. This is intended behavior when the SR is the standby router.

Figure 4-83 shows packet capture output on the T1SR Blue uplink interface on Edge Node 1, which is the active SR.

```
EDGE TRANSPORT NODE 1>  start capture interface 2ded6094-01f2-4026-a2a7-33e2cbd97673 direction dual

07:43:03.605186 02:50:56:56:44:52 > 02:50:56:56:44:55, ethertype IPv4 (0x0800), length 74: 192.168.63.101 >
192.168.190.2: ICMP echo request, id 1, seq 258, length 40
<base64>AIBWVkRVAIBWVkRSCABFAAA8ChQAAHwBqz4KuQALwKi+AggATFkAAQECYWJjZGVmZ2hpamtsbW5vc
HFyc3R1dndhYmNkZWWZnaGk=</base64>

07:43:03.613614 02:50:56:56:44:55 > 02:50:56:56:44:52, ethertype IPv4 (0x0800), length 74: 192.168.190.2 >
192.168.63.101: ICMP echo reply, id 1, seq 258, length 40
<base64>AIBWVkRSAIBWVkRVCABFAAA8xe0AAD8BLGXAqL4CCrkACwAAVFkAAQECYWJjZGVmZ2hpamtsbW5vc
HFyc3R1dndhYmNkZWWZnaGk=</base64>
```

Figure 4-83. *Packet capture on Edge Node 1 T1SR Blue uplink interface*

4. The packet has been forwarded from T0DR on Edge Node 2 to the ToR/core switch.

5. The ToR/core switch then forwards the packet to Edge Node 1.

6. Edge Node 1 receives the packet, removes the outer header, and forwards the packet to T1SR Blue.

    To quickly summarize this step, the packet ingresses on Edge Node 2 uplink interface. The T0SR checks its forwarding table, finds a matching prefix, and forwards it to the T0DR on Edge Node 2. The T0DR then forwards the packet to the active T1SR Blue uplink of 100.64.128.1, which is active on Edge Node 1, through the ToR/core switch. The packet hasn't yet been encapsulated in a GENEVE header.

7. Once the packet has passed through the service routers, the address is translated back to VM 1 original IP address of 192.168.190.2. T1SR Blue checks its forwarding table and confirms it has an entry for 192.168.190.0/24. Figure 4-84 is the forwarding table on T1SR Blue.

```
EDGE TRANSPORT NODE 1> get logical-router d999a545-6917-488e-aaa5-f643e03642ba forwarding
Logical Router
UUID                    VRF  LR-ID Name              Type
d999a545-6917-488e-aaa5-f643e03642ba  12   12290 SR-T1 - Blue            SERVICE_ROUTER_TIER1
IPv4 Forwarding Table
IP Prefix      Gateway IP            Type   UUID                            Gateway MAC
0.0.0.0/0      100.64.128.0          route  2ded6094-01f2-4026-a2a7-33e2cbd97673
100.64.64.0/31                       route  2ded6094-01f2-4026-a2a7-33e2cbd97673
100.64.64.1/32                       route  7209cbaf-5b4c-5138-a80d-fed2cf104f3f
127.0.0.1/32                         route  fc56978f-12ac-4089-a356-a04bec869e82
169.254.0.0/28                       route  21a4c389-c9f1-4e0a-9b73-068845e76621
169.254.0.1/32                       route  1b5076c8-33d8-529a-b9ee-1cbfc4bc5e28
169.254.0.2/32                       route  7209cbaf-5b4c-5138-a80d-fed2cf104f3f
172.25.0.10/32                       route  fc56978f-12ac-4089-a356-a04bec869e82
192.168.190.0/24                     route  5f14f9ca-84bb-4cc9-b380-1280af909de4
192.168.190.1/32                     route  1b5076c8-33d8-529a-b9ee-1cbfc4bc5e28
```

Figure 4-84. *T1SR Blue forwarding table on Edge Node 1*

T1SR Blue checks the UUID attached to the prefix and sees that the prefix is attached to a downlink logical port on T1DR Blue. Figure 4-85 lists the interface details for T1DR Blue.

```
EDGE TRANSPORT NODE 1> get logical-router d999a545-6917-488e-aaa5-f643e03642ba interfaces
interface            : 5f14f9ca-84bb-4cc9-b380-1280af909de4
ifuid                : 363
VRF                  : b9ba5b04-9055-42cb-897e-0242307393c2
name                 : infra-Web_Segment-dlrp
mode                 : lif
 Port-type           : downlink
IP/Mask              : 192.168.190.1/24
Fwd-mode             : IPV4_ONLY
MAC                  : 02:50:56:56:44:52
VNI                  : 67589
LS port              : 93e66635-a5c3-49dd-aaf2-9559cc7ff62c
urpf-mode            : STRICT_MODE
admin                : up
op_state             : up
MTU                  : 1500
```

Figure 4-85. *T1DR Blue interface*

T1SR Blue forwards the packet to T1DR Blue using the backplane port.

8. T1DR Blue checks its ARP and MAC tables to identify which transport node 192.168.190.2 resides on. Figure 4-86 shows Edge Node 1's arp cache for the segment.

```
EDGE TRANSPORT NODE 1> get logical-switch remote arp-cache 67589
    VM IP                    VM MAC                   VM IPv6
  192.168.190.2           00:50:56:98:77:b8           None
```

Figure 4-86. *Web Segment – VNI 67589 ARP cache*

Now that the MAC address is known, the MAC address table can be referenced. In doing so, the Tunnel Endpoint where VM 1 resides will be known. Figure 4-87 displays the MAC address table, which shows the Tunnel Endpoint where VM 1 MAC address is located.

```
EDGE TRANSPORT NODE 1> get logical-switch ef1d79ce-2555-4197-bb41-1739e3488455 mac-address-table
Sat Aug 14 2021 UTC 08:22:43.517
Logical Switch
UUID     : ef1d79ce-2555-4197-bb41-1739e3488455
VNI      : 67589
Device   : fp-eth0
ENCAP    : GENEVE
Replication : mtep
routing-domain: b9ba5b04-9055-42cb-897e-0242307393c2
Enable Hub  : False
MAC-Table:
   MAC            : 02:50:56:56:44:52
      Port        : 93e66635-a5c3-49dd-aaf2-9559cc7ff62c
      IFUID       : 362
      SOURCE      : Static
   MAC            : 00:50:56:98:77:b8
      Tunnel      : 2877f3e0-9a35-5bd9-b39b-892b800416b7
      IFUID       : 368
      LOCAL       : 192.168.66.10
      REMOTE      : 192.168.65.2
      ENCAP       : GENEVE
      SOURCE      : Static
```

Figure 4-87. *Web Segment MAC address table on Edge Node 1*

The packet is forwarded out of TEP interface 192.168.66.10 on Edge
Node 1; as this occurs it is encapsulated with a GENEVE header and
sent to its default gateway. It is then routed to Host Transport Node 1
TEP of 192.168.65.2.

Shown in Figure 4-88 is a packet capture on interface 192.168.66.10.

```
> Frame 20: 132 bytes on wire (1056 bits), 132 bytes captured (1056 bits)
> Ethernet II, Src: VMware_86:94:0f (00:50:56:86:94:0f), Dst: BrocadeC_b7:bd:14 (cc:4e:24:b7:bd:14)
> Internet Protocol Version 4, Src: 192.168.66.10, Dst: 192.168.65.2
> User Datagram Protocol, Src Port: 53229, Dst Port: 6081
> Generic Network Virtualization Encapsulation, VNI: 0x010805
> Ethernet II, Src: 02:50:56:56:44:52 (02:50:56:56:44:52), Dst: VMware_86:c4:34 (00:50:56:86:c4:34)
> Internet Protocol Version 4, Src: 192.168.63.101, Dst: 192.168.190.2
> Internet Control Message Protocol
```

Figure 4-88. *Packet capture on Edge Node 1 TEP interface*

Outer Header

- **Source MAC:** 00:50:56:86:94:0f (Edge Node 1 TEP interface MAC address)

- **Destination MAC:** cc:4e:24:b7:bd:14 (ToR/core switch MAC address)

- **Source IP:** 192.168.66.10 (Edge Node 1 TEP IP address)

- **Destination IP:** 192.168.65.2 (Host Transport Node 1 TEP IP address)

- **Virtual Network Identifier (VNI):** 0x010805 (overlay 67589 – Web Segment)

Inner Header

- **Source MAC:** 02:50:56:56:44:52 (virtual MAC used across various LIFs)

- **Destination MAC:** 00:05:56:86:c4:34 (VM 1 MAC address)

- **Source IP:** 192.168.63.101 (utility server IP address)

- **Destination IP:** 192.168.190.2 (VM 1 IP address)

9. Host Transport Node 1 receives the packet; it is de-encapsulated as it moves through the IO chain. Once this process is complete, the packet is forwarded to VM 1.

Figure 4-89 is a completed packet walk diagram with interface details.

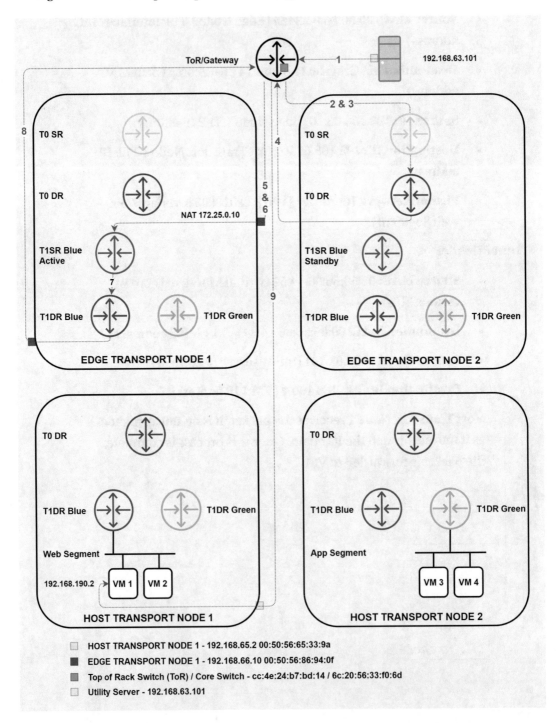

Figure 4-89. *Complete North-South packet walk diagram with interface details*

Logical Routing Between Sites

This section provides an overview of packet flow between federated NSX-T sites across two stretched segments. For further details on NSX-T Federation, refer to the book *Multi-Site Network and Security Services with NSX-T* by Iwan Hoogendoorn.

Figure 4-90 is the topology that will be discussed in this example.

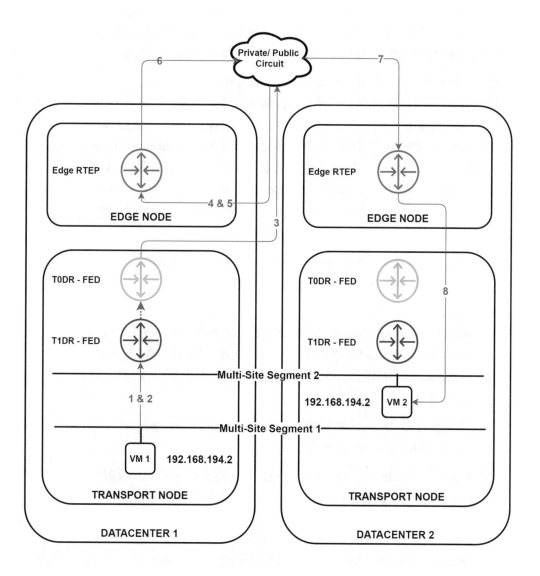

Figure 4-90. *NSX-T Federation packet flow*

1. VM 1 needs to send a packet to VM 2 in datacenter 2. It checks the destination IP and determines that it is in a different subnet. It checks its ARP table for its default gateway if no entry exists it ARPs for the default gateway and waits for a response. Once the entry exists, it forwards the packet to the gateway.

2. T1DR-FED receives the packet on its downlink port and inspects the destination. It does not have an entry in its forwarding table for 192.168.195.3. T1DR-FED has a default route with the next hop gateway of T0DR-FED. T1DR-FED forwards to the next hop.

3. T0DR-FED receives the packet, inspects the destination, and matches the IP with a prefix in its forwarding table. The next hop gateway has been learned via the upstream gateway. The packet must be sent to T0SR-FED. With federated deployments a single Edge node is active for a segment, to determine which Edge is active the VTEP-GROUP is checked. Once the active member is determined, the packet is sent to the TEP interface on the host transport node, encapsulated, and sent to the active Edge.

4. The switch receives the packet, inspects the destination, and forwards it accordingly.

5. The Edge Node in datacenter 1 receives the packet, de-encapsulates it, inspects the destination, and knows the IP and MAC addresses of VM 2 exist in datacenter 2. The packet is sent to the RTEP interface, encapsulated, and sent to the edge in datacenter 2.

6. The switch receives the packet, checks the destination, and forwards the packet accordingly.

7. The Edge Node in datacenter 2 receives the packet on its RTEP interface. The packet is de-encapsulated, the destination is checked. The Edge knows that VM 2 sits on the local transport node, and the packet is forwarded through the edge's TEP interface, encapsulated, and sent to the transport node.

8. The transport node receives the packet; the packet is de-encapsulated as it moves through the IO chain and then sent to VM 2.

Summary

In this chapter you have learned the benefits of Logical Routing, the various components used in NSX-T for Logical Routing, and Logical Routing architecture and have seen how packets flow in different situations.

Chapter 5 will discuss data plane availability and how NSX-T ensures a component outage does not render the environment offline.

CHAPTER 5

Data Plane Availability

Readers should now be familiar with NSX-T Logical Routing operations.

 This chapter explores the data plane in further detail and will cover the mechanisms built into the NSX-T platform to provide data plane availability. By the end of this chapter, readers should have an in-depth understanding of:

- NSX-T Edge deployment considerations

- Inter-SR routing

- Bidirectional forwarding detection (BFD) within the NSX-T platform

- Use of equal cost multipathing (ECMP) in NSX-T

This chapter will start by providing readers an understanding of Edge Nodes, including the logical constructs within an Edge Node, logical wiring, deployment considerations, data plane availability within an Edge cluster, and why Edge Nodes are important for NSX-T data plane availability.

It will then proceed to uncover other mechanisms used within NSX-T to provide data plane availability, such as BFD and ECMP, not only within the Edge Nodes but also to and from the Host Transport Nodes.

Edge Cluster Deployment Considerations

A common obstacle faced when deploying NSX-T is the Edge cluster. Often the most important considerations are overlooked, such as Edge Node placement, cluster configuration, data paths, resiliency, and service placement.

© Shashank Mohan 2022
S. Mohan, *NSX-T Logical Routing*, https://doi.org/10.1007/978-1-4842-7458-3_5

As was discussed in the previous chapter, the Edge Nodes are responsible for North-South traffic into and out of the NSX-T environment and providing stateful services. As the Edge Nodes play such a vital role, their configuration and deployment must be given an appropriate amount of attention.

This section will discuss Edge Nodes in more detail and deployment options for multiple scenarios. This section will not cover NSX-T Federation spanning multiple regions or NSX-T Multisite.

Defining Edge Nodes

The preceding chapters of this book introduced the concept of Edge Nodes and the critical role they play in NSX-T. Before administrators or engineers design or deploy Edge clusters, they should first understand the intricacies that surround Edge Nodes.

An Edge cluster can be thought of as a pool of resources, in which various Logical Routing and switching components are instantiated.

Edge Node Logical Routing Components

- **Tier-0 gateways:** When a Tier-0 gateway is configured and has an Edge cluster associated with it, it has two components instantiated on the Edge Nodes: the Tier-0 DR and the Tier-0 SR components. The functionality of these components was discussed in Chapter 4 and will not be reiterated here.

- **Tier-1 gateways:** Tier-1 gateways behave differently to Tier-0 gateways. When a user creates a Tier-1 gateway without an Edge cluster or stateful service attached to it, the DR component is instantiated on all Edge cluster members. With this configuration, the Tier-1 gateway is in an Active-Active availability mode. This means all Edge Nodes in the Edge cluster can perform packet routing and forwarding operations.

If an Edge cluster is attached to the gateway, the Tier-1 gateway moves from Active-Active to Active-Standby. After performing this action, the SR counterpart to the Tier-1 gateway is instantiated on the Edge Nodes. However, as this configuration is meant for stateful services, packet routing and forwarding operations for this Tier-1 can no longer be distributed among all Edge Nodes. One of the Edge Nodes will have the active SR component, while the rest of the cluster members will have the standby SR component. In the event of a primary Edge Node failure, the active SR component will move to one of the other Edge cluster members.

NSX-T automatically elects which Edge Node hosts the active SR component without any user interaction. The node that is elected is not deterministic; however, active SR placement can be made to be deterministic with the use of failure domains.

Unlike Tier-0 gateways, an Edge Node or cluster can host many Tier-1 gateways. For specific details around the maximum configurable components for NSX-T, please visit `https://configmax.vmware.com`.

Edge Node Wiring

A critical aspect of data plane availability revolves around the Edge Nodes. As these appliances govern traffic that ingresses and egresses the NSX-T domain, they must be properly configured when being deployed.

Each Edge node has a nested N-VDS instantiated on it. This fact is often overlooked, as it is not easily seen via the user interface. This N-VDS has virtual uplink interfaces which must be plumbed into the vNIC of the Edge virtual machine so it can communicate with the physical network.

If users choose to use a Bare Metal Edge, the additional layer of VDS network complexity is removed, as the Bare Metal Edge node has direct access to its physical network interfaces and can be configured as such. This comes at the sacrifice of flexibility and mobility of the Edge Nodes. As they are not virtual appliances, they cannot move as easily.

The following sections will explore both deployment options.

Edge Virtual Appliance Wiring

Understanding how to properly wire an Edge virtual appliance makes deploying the appliances much easier. The first step in being able to understand this is to first visualize the internal networking of an Edge Node.

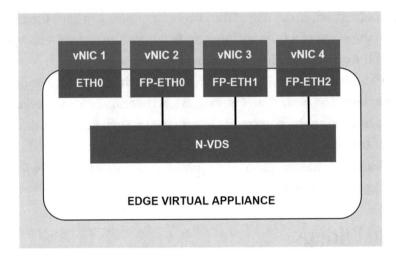

Figure 5-1. *NSX-T Edge virtual appliance internal wiring*

Figure 5-1 is a visual representation of an Edge virtual appliance. Think of the surrounding gray box as the virtual machine object in vSphere and the internal white box as the logical construct of the Edge virtual appliance.

Logical Interfaces

The logical interfaces that exist within the Edge virtual appliance act as uplinks to the nested N-VDS (which will be described in the following section). Appropriate configuration of these interfaces results in predictable and reliable dataflow across the Edge Nodes.

The following is a description of the logical interfaces and their functions:

- **ETH0:** This interface is reserved for management traffic. The IP address used to access and deploy the Edge Node is associated with this interface.

- **FP-ETH0:** This interface plays a critical role in both data forwarding and ensuring GENEVE tunnel availability to other transport nodes. When configured, this interface is assigned a TEP IP address and is used as an endpoint for other transport nodes within the same Overlay Transport Zone. The TEP address can be assigned using either an IP pool or be statically configured and is done during Edge deployment. These values can be changed post-deployment as well.

- **FP-ETH1:** Like FP-ETH0, this interface is also assigned a TEP address and is used for data forwarding. Use of this interface is dependent on the load balancing method used in the uplink profile. If a single uplink is configured in the uplink profile, this interface will not be used. However, if multi-TEP is configured (two or more uplink interfaces configured in the uplink profile), then this interface is used in a similar fashion to FP-ETH0. These configuration options will be displayed later in this chapter.

- **FP-ETH2:** Upon deployment of an Edge Node, this interface remains disconnected. By default, it is not used for any data forwarding. A common use case for this interface is Edge bridging.

 Edge bridging is not covered in this book; therefore, FP-ETH2 will not be referred to any further.

Nested N-VDS

Each Edge Node is deployed with a nested N-VDS. This N-VDS is used to perform routing and switching operations at the Edge of the NSX-T domain. For egress traffic, data packets are de-encapsulated, that is, the GENEVE header is stripped, and the packet is forwarded to the physical network. With ingress traffic, the packet is encapsulated with a GENEVE header and forwarded to the defined transport node.

When configured, the internal N-VDS can be associated with VLAN and Overlay Transport Zones. Generally, the Edge Node must belong to the same Overlay Transport Zone as the Host Transport Nodes and segments to be able to forward traffic for them. An Edge Node can only route traffic for objects that sit within the same Transport Zone.

Mapping the Interfaces

The interfaces mentioned previously are configured using uplink profiles. Unlike Host Transport Nodes, Edge Nodes must be configured individually; in other words, transport node profiles cannot be used.

Uplink Profiles

Uplink profile configuration was mentioned in Chapter 2, and this section will elaborate on the configuration and what impact it has on the Edge virtual appliance.

There are two ways to configure uplink profiles; the configuration applied will determine if the Edge is configured with a single TEP interface or multiple TEP interfaces or multi-TEP.

Single TEP Interface Configuration

Figure 5-2 is a logical representation of an Edge Node being deployed with a single TEP interface. The following configuration demonstrates how to configure an Edge Node with a single TEP interface.

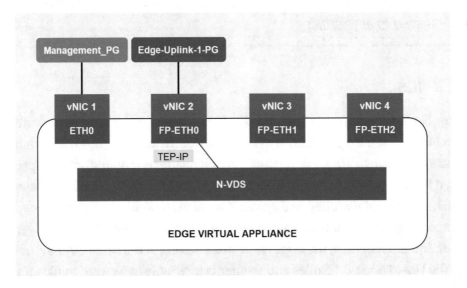

Figure 5-2. *Edge single TEP logical topology*

Creating and applying an uplink profile with a single active uplink interface configures a single active TEP interface on the Edge Node. This results in a single interface being used for data forwarding.

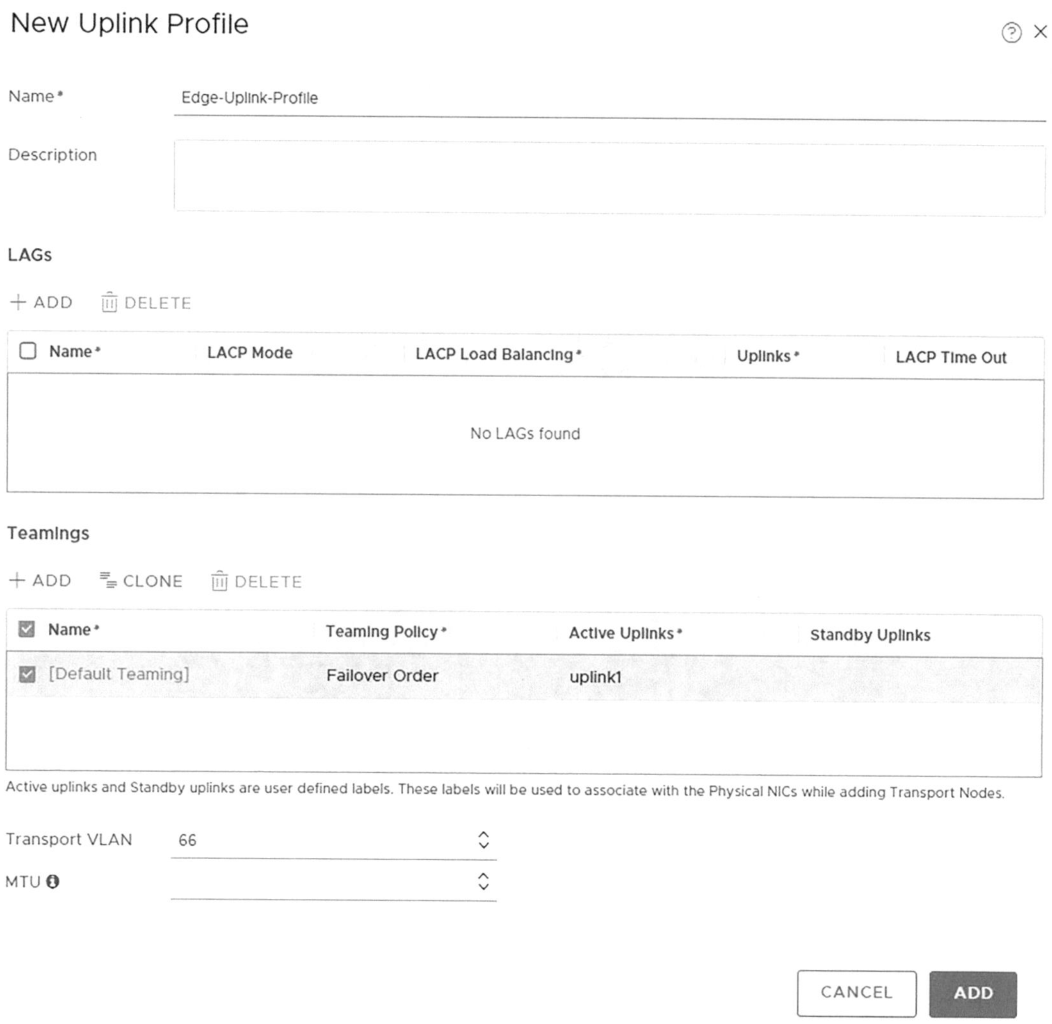

New Uplink Profile   (?) ✕

Name *	Edge-Uplink-Profile

Description

LAGs

+ ADD   🗑 DELETE

☐ Name *	LACP Mode	LACP Load Balancing *	Uplinks *	LACP Time Out
		No LAGs found		

Teamings

+ ADD   ⇶ CLONE   🗑 DELETE

☑ Name *	Teaming Policy *	Active Uplinks *	Standby Uplinks
☑ [Default Teaming]	Failover Order	uplink1	

Active uplinks and Standby uplinks are user defined labels. These labels will be used to associate with the Physical NICs while adding Transport Nodes.

Transport VLAN	66	⌄
MTU ❶		⌄

CANCEL   **ADD**

Figure 5-3. Edge single TEP configuration

Figure 5-3 displays the configuration required deploy an Edge virtual appliance with a single TEP interface. Notice under **Teamings**, the teaming policy is set to Failover Order, and under Active Uplinks, a single uplink 1 interface has been entered. The transport VLAN must also be correct; if it is not the correct VLAN, then GENEVE tunnels between the Host Transport Node and the Edge virtual appliance will not be initiated.

Multi-TEP Interface Configuration

Figure 5-4 is a logical representation of an Edge Node being deployed with multiple TEP interfaces. The following configuration demonstrates how to configure an Edge Node with a multiple TEP interfaces.

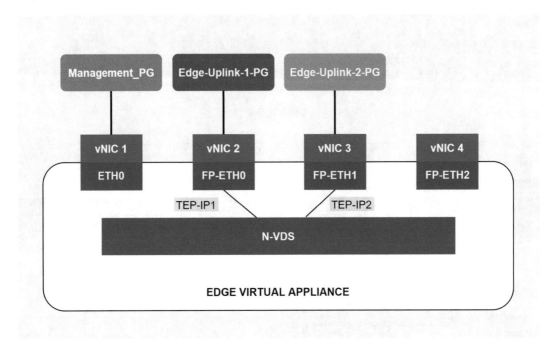

Figure 5-4. *Edge multi-TEP logical topology*

The process to configure an Edge Node with multiple TEP interfaces is the same as configuring a single TEP interface. The only difference is the configuration of the uplink interfaces in the **Teamings** section within the uplink profile.

Figure 5-5 displays the difference in configuration. Notice in the **Teamings** section, the Teaming Policy is configured as Load Balance Source and has two active uplinks.

New Uplink Profile   ⑦ ×

Name*	Edge-Uplink-MultiTEP
Description	

LAGs

+ ADD   🗑 DELETE

☐ Name*	LACP Mode	LACP Load Balancing*	Uplinks*	LACP Time Out
		No LAGs found		

Teamings

+ ADD   🗐 CLONE   🗑 DELETE

☑ Name*	Teaming Policy*	Active Uplinks*	Standby Uplinks
☑ [Default Teaming]	Load Balance Source	uplink1,uplink2	

Active uplinks and Standby uplinks are user defined labels. These labels will be used to associate with the Physical NICs while adding Transport Nodes.

Transport VLAN	66	⌄
MTU ❶		⌄

CANCEL   ADD

Figure 5-5. *Edge multi-TEP configuration*

Applying Uplink Profiles

Once the uplink profile is created, it must be applied to an Edge virtual appliance to take effect.

Single TEP Deployment

Figure 5-6 shows the deployment of an Edge Node using the single TEP uplink profile that was created in the previous section. Based on the configuration shown, the appliance will be deployed and configured with a single uplink interface, which will be plumbed into DPDK Fastpath Interface Edge-Uplink-PG. This interface is a VDS portgroup created in vCenter.

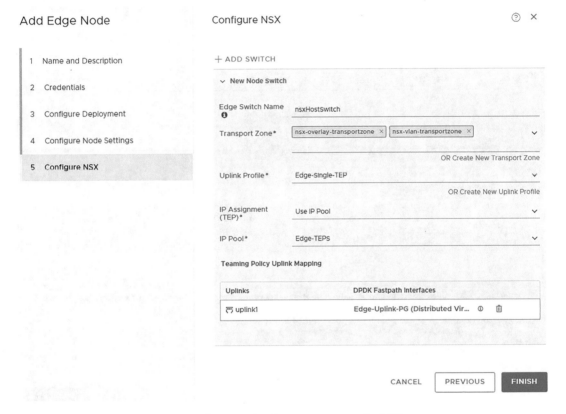

Figure 5-6. *Edge virtual appliance deployment – single TEP*

Once the appliance is deployed, you will notice that only two interfaces are actively being used and connected. Those interfaces are ETH 0 which maps to vNIC 1 and is linked to the management VDS portgroup. As mentioned earlier, this interface is responsible for management access to the Edge Node. The second is FP-ETH0, which is mapped to vNIC 2, and is linked to the Edge-Uplink-PG.

The management portgroup should be tagged with the appropriate VLAN for management, and best practice for the Edge-Uplink-PG is to configure it as a trunking portgroup. Configuring this portgroup in trunking mode allows it to pass multiple VLANs, which allows the TEP VLAN and the VLAN configured for BGP peering to pass.

Figure 5-7 is a visual representation of the configuration that was completed previously.

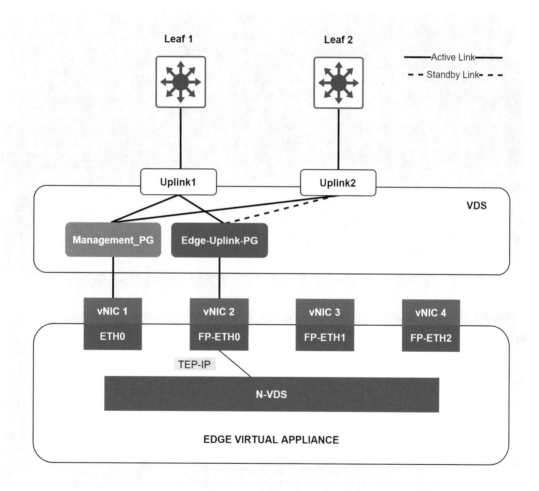

Figure 5-7. *Edge virtual appliance single interface wiring*

 The availability of the standby uplink to Leaf 2 for Edge-Uplink-PG is dependent on uplink portgroup configuration and will be covered in the following section.

Figure 5-8 displays the Edge virtual machine configuration in vCenter, showing network adapter 1 connected to management portgroup and network adapter 3 configured and attached to Edge-Uplink-2-PG.

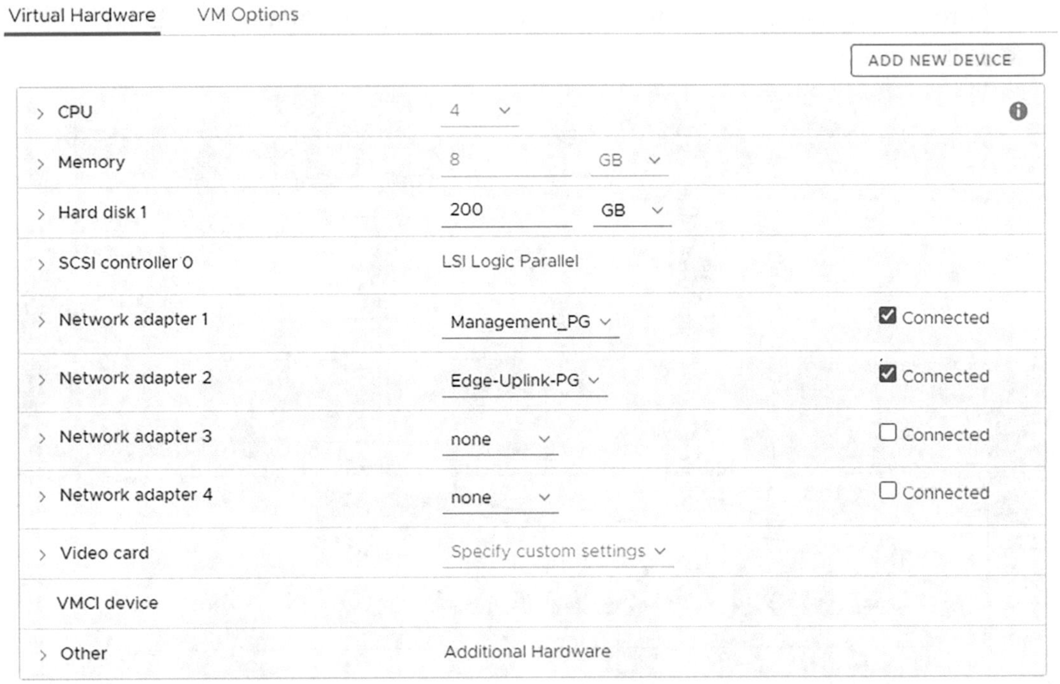

Virtual Hardware	VM Options		
			ADD NEW DEVICE
> CPU	4 ⌄		ⓘ
> Memory	8	GB ⌄	
> Hard disk 1	200	GB ⌄	
> SCSI controller 0	LSI Logic Parallel		
> Network adapter 1	Management_PG ⌄		☑ Connected
> Network adapter 2	Edge-Uplink-PG ⌄		☑ Connected
> Network adapter 3	none ⌄		☐ Connected
> Network adapter 4	none ⌄		☐ Connected
> Video card	Specify custom settings ⌄		
VMCI device			
> Other	Additional Hardware		

Figure 5-8. *Single uplink interface Edge virtual machine configuration in vCenter*

Multi-TEP Deployment

Figure 5-9 shows the deployment of an Edge virtual appliance using the multi-TEP uplink profile that was created in the uplink profiles section of this chapter.

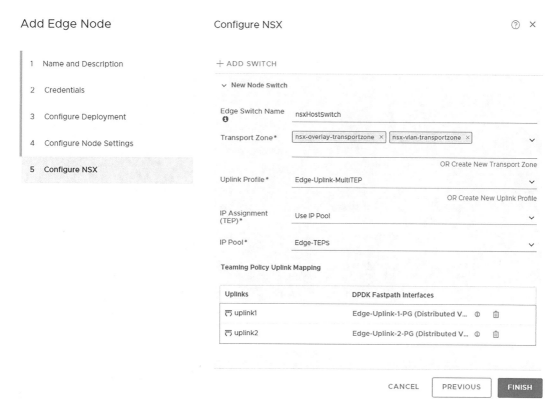

Figure 5-9. *Edge virtual appliance deployment – multi-TEP*

When comparing Figure 5-9 with Figure 5-6, there is now an additional interface available. The additional uplink interface is a result of the teaming policy that was set as part of the uplink profile in Figure 5-5. The appliance is being deployed with two uplink interfaces.

The Edge Node being deployed will have the following port mappings:

- **ETH 0:** Mapped to vNIC 1, which is attached to a management VDS portgroup

- **FP-ETH0:** Mapped to vNIC 2, which is attached to Edge-Uplink-1-PG, and is a DPDK Fastpath interface

- **FP-ETH1:** Mapped to vNIC 3, which is attached to Edge-Uplink-2-PG, which is also a DPDK Fastpath interface

Figure 5-10 is a visual representation of a multi-TEP Edge deployment.

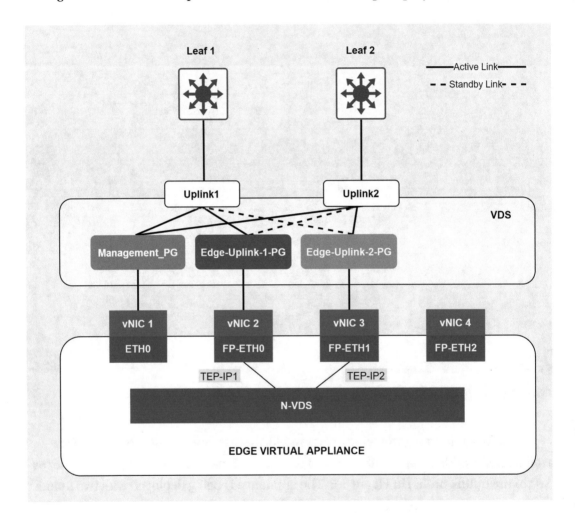

Figure 5-10. *Edge virtual appliance multiple interface wiring*

 This represents the desired end state; however, the various uplink portgroup configuration possibilities are detailed in the next section.

Figure 5-11 displays the Edge virtual machine configuration in vCenter. Note that in addition to the portgroups configured as per Figure 5-8, multi-TEP configuration has network adapter 3 configured and attached to Edge-Uplink-2-PG.

Virtual Hardware	VM Options		

				ADD NEW DEVICE
> CPU	4			ⓘ
> Memory	8	GB		
> Hard disk 1	200	GB		
SCSI controller 0	LSI Logic Parallel			
> Network adapter 1	Management_PG			☑ Connected
> Network adapter 2	Edge-Uplink-1-PG			☑ Connected
> Network adapter 3	Edge-Uplink-2-PG			☑ Connected
> Network adapter 4	none			☐ Connected
> Video card	Specify custom settings			
VMCI device				
> Other	Additional Hardware			

Figure 5-11. *Multiple uplink interface Edge virtual machine configuration in vCenter*

VDS Portgroup Uplink Configuration

Ensuring data plane connectivity to the Edge Nodes does not stop with the configuration of the Edge interfaces. It is also important to ensure that the teaming and failover settings for the uplink portgroups are configured correctly.

If these properties are not defined correctly and an uplink fails, traffic may be blackholed due to lack of connectivity to the physical network.

Blackholed traffic occurs when traffic is sent to one of the TEP interfaces of an Edge but the physical link for that TEP interface is down. The link could be down for multiple reasons but is generally to do with connectivity to the upstream switch or gateway failing.

If this situation occurs, the Edge is not aware of the link failure and GENEVE traffic is forwarded to all available interfaces, as it normally would be. Once the packets arrive on the Edge TEP interface that is plumbed into an uplink that is down, the data that is sent to this interface will be blackholed or dropped. This can be detrimental to applications and workloads, as packets are actively being dropped.

The good news is this can be avoided with proper portgroup uplink configuration. Figure 5-10 displays correct uplink portgroup configuration, using Active-Standby. This configuration can be utilized for both single TEP and multi-TEP deployments.

While this configuration is important for GENEVE traffic, remember that BGP is also peering over these uplinks. If uplink 1 were to fail, *all* traffic would flow through uplink 2, BGP included.

This may not be desired behavior for your environment. The reason for this is, if Leaf 1 hasn't failed and it was just a link failure, the Edge may still attempt to peer with Leaf 1, through Leaf 2. As a result, this means BGP peering is not deterministic and not optimal. This can be overcome by configuring named teaming, which will be covered in the next chapter.

Uplink Failure Behavior

This section will guide readers in proper configuration of the VDS portgroups and will demonstrate the impact of suboptimal configuration in contrast to having correct configuration.

The details in the following section will focus on the multi-TEP deployment option; however, the principles remain the same regardless of the deployment option.

Active/Unused Uplink Configuration

In this example, the VDS portgroup teaming is configured with a single active uplink interface. Figure 5-12 is an example of the configuration that will be discussed.

Edge-Uplink-1-PG - Edit Settings

General		
Advanced	Load balancing	Route based on physical NIC load ⌄
VLAN	Network failure detection	Link status only ⌄
Security	Notify switches	Yes ⌄
Teaming and failover	Failback	Yes ⌄
Traffic shaping		
Monitoring	Failover order ⓘ	
Miscellaneous	⇧ ⇩	

Active uplinks
   🔧 uplink1
Standby uplinks
Unused uplinks
   🔧 uplink2

Figure 5-12. *Edge uplink portgroup with a single active uplink*

With this configuration, Edge vNIC 2 (FP-ETH0) is attached to Edge-Uplink-1-PG, which has a single active uplink with no standby uplinks. If the physical link or switch fails, connectivity is not failed over to the second uplink interface.

Figure 5-13 displays the current NIC mappings for the Edge Node.

```
 PORT-ID USED-BY                    TEAM-PNIC DNAME
 67108878 Management                n/a DvsPortset-0
 67108883 vmk0                      vmnic5 DvsPortset-0
 67108884 vmk1                      vmnic4 DvsPortset-0
 67108885 vmk2                      vmnic4 DvsPortset-0
 67108886 vmk10                     vmnic4 DvsPortset-0
 67108887 vmk50                     void DvsPortset-0
 67108888 vmk11                     vmnic5 DvsPortset-0
 67109097 29306873:edge1.eth1       vmnic4 DvsPortset-0
 67109098 29306873:edge1.eth0       vmnic5 DvsPortset-0
 67109099 29306873:edge1.eth2       vmnic5 DvsPortset-0
```

Figure 5-13. *Edge Node to host vmnic mapping*

Interface statistics have been omitted from this output.

There are three interfaces listed for Edge1:

- **Edge1.eth0:** The management interface (ETH0/vNIC 1)

- **Edge1.eth1:** The first uplink interface (FP-ETH0/vNIC 2)

- **Edge1.eth2:** The second uplink interface (FP-ETH1/vNIC 3)

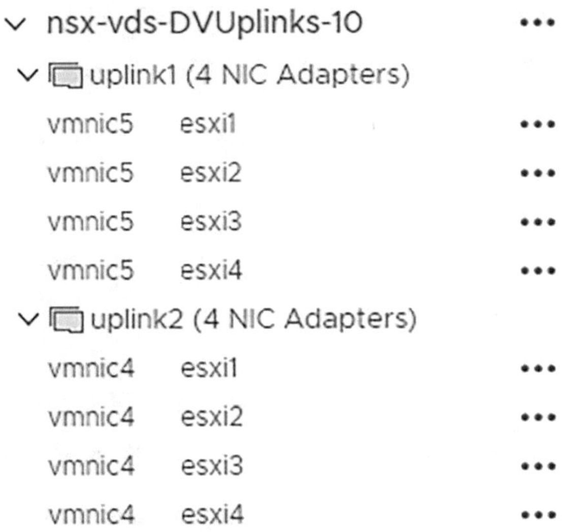

∨ nsx-vds-DVUplinks-10   •••
   ∨ 🖳 uplink1 (4 NIC Adapters)
      vmnic5   esxi1   •••
      vmnic5   esxi2   •••
      vmnic5   esxi3   •••
      vmnic5   esxi4   •••
   ∨ 🖳 uplink2 (4 NIC Adapters)
      vmnic4   esxi1   •••
      vmnic4   esxi2   •••
      vmnic4   esxi3   •••
      vmnic4   esxi4   •••

Figure 5-14. *VDS DV uplink configuration*

Figure 5-14 displays the DV uplink configuration in vCenter. Referencing Figure 5-12, Figure 5-13, and Figure 5-14, it can be determined that FP-ETH0/vNIC 2 of Edge1 will communicate with Leaf 1, and Edge-Uplink-1-PG will not failover to the second uplink in case of link or switch failure.

Figure 5-15 is a logical representation of an Edge Node that has uplink portgroups that do not have a standby uplink assigned.

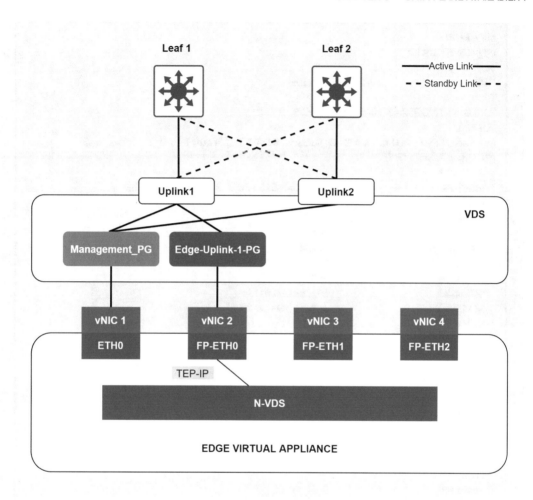

Figure 5-15. *Edge uplink portgroups with no standby uplinks*

 This configuration is not ideal for most NSX-T deployments. The next section will explain why.

Demonstrating an Uplink Failure

In this scenario, Edge Node 1 has two TEP addresses: they are 192.168.66.60 and 192.168.66.61. These interfaces can be seen in Figure 5-16.

```
edge1> vrf 0
edge1(vrf)> get int
Logical Router
UUID                    VRF   LR-ID  Name
Type
736a80e3-23f6-5a2d-81d6-bbefb2786666  0    0
TUNNEL
Interfaces (IPv6 DAD Status A-DAD_Success, F-DAD_Duplicate, T-DAD_Tentative, U-D
AD_Unavailable)

    Interface            : 915356a6-529e-5d26-8b38-4c76ef8c96b3
    Ifuid                : 258
    Name                 :
    Fwd-mode             : IPV4_ONLY
    Internal name        : uplink-258
    Mode                 : lif
    Port-type            : uplink
    IP/Mask              : 192.168.66.61/24
    MAC                  : 00:50:56:93:6a:83
    VLAN                 : 66
    Access-VLAN          : untagged
    LS port              : 226befb0-50ca-5032-aa37-679184fbe4b2
    Urpf-mode            : PORT_CHECK
    Admin                : up
    Op_state             : up
    MTU                  : 9000

    Interface            : b55b26d4-a82d-5e5f-a1d0-c4f64c356c62
    Ifuid                : 355
    Name                 :
    Fwd-mode             : IPV4_ONLY
    Internal name        : uplink-355
    Mode                 : lif
    Port-type            : uplink
    IP/Mask              : 192.168.66.60/24
    MAC                  : 00:50:56:93:55:d1
    VLAN                 : 66
    Access-VLAN          : untagged
    LS port              : 1d4aecac-2f91-59c0-8486-bb7edc00010a
    Urpf-mode            : PORT_CHECK
    Admin                : up
    Op_state             : up
    MTU                  : 9000
```

Figure 5-16. *Edge1's TEP interfaces*

In this example, the connectivity to uplink 1 which is where 192.168.66.61 sits behind will be removed. This is so readers can see the impact of not having the Edge-Uplink-1-PG failover to uplink 2.

To begin with, Figure 5-17 displays working communication from a Host Transport Node to the Edge TEP IP. This test demonstrates working communication from the Host Transport Nodes VXLAN netstack to Edge Node 1 TEP IP.

```
[root@HOST TRANSPORT NODE 1:~] vmkping ++netstack=vxlan 192.168.66.61
PING 192.168.66.31 (192.168.66.31): 56 data bytes
64 bytes from 192.168.66.61: icmp_seq=0 ttl=63 time=0.334 ms
64 bytes from 192.168.66.61: icmp_seq=1 ttl=63 time=0.362 ms
64 bytes from 192.168.66.61: icmp_seq=2 ttl=63 time=0.422 ms

--- 192.168.66.61 ping statistics ---
3 packets transmitted, 3 packets received, 0% packet loss
round-trip min/avg/max = 0.334/0.373/0.422 ms
```

Figure 5-17. *Host Transport Node vmkping before link failure*

Now the connectivity from vmnic5 which is a member of uplink 1 is disconnected on the host where Edge Node 1 resides. Figure 5-18 is a visual representation of the uplink failure.

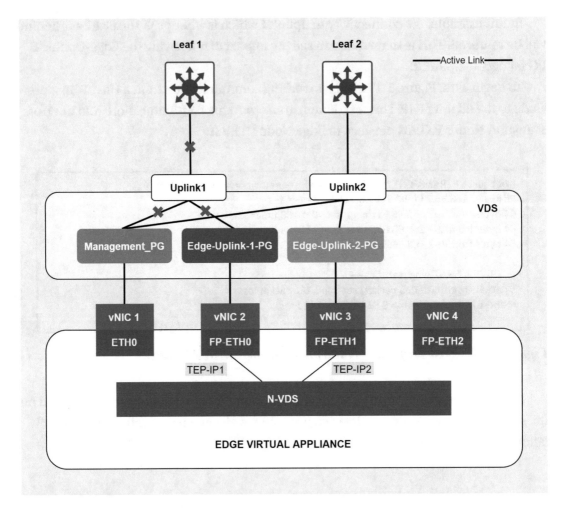

Figure 5-18. *Edge and Host uplink failure with no standby uplink*

Notice in Figure 5-19 the status of the pNIC attached to edge1.eth1 is now *fallback*.

```
PORT-ID USED-BY                          TEAM-PNIC
67108878 Management                      n/a DvsPortset-0
67108883 vmk0                            vmnic4 DvsPortset-0
67108884 vmk1                            vmnic4 DvsPortset-0
67108885 vmk2                            vmnic4 DvsPortset-0
67108886 vmk10                           vmnic4 DvsPortset-0
67108887 vmk50                           void DvsPortset-0
67108888 vmk11                           vmnic4 DvsPortset-0
67109097 29306873:en01.eth1             fallback DvsPortset-0
67109098 29306873:en01.eth0             vmnic4 DvsPortset-0
67109099 29306873:en01.eth2             vmnic4 DvsPortset-0
```

Figure 5-19. *vmnic status after a link failure*

Running the same connectivity test from the Host Transport Node, as was done in Figure 5-17, results in the output shown in Figure 5-20.

```
[root@HOST TRANSPORT NODE 1:~] vmkping ++netstack=vxlan 192.168.66.61
PING 192.168.66.61 (192.168.66.32): 56 data bytes

--- 192.168.66.61 ping statistics ---
3 packets transmitted, 0 packets received, 100% packet loss
```

Figure 5-20. *Host Transport Node vmkping after link failure*

There is now 100% packet loss; this should highlight the criticality of proper uplink configuration. As a result of the vmnic in uplink 1 failing, and there was no standby uplink configured, there was no data plane connectivity from vSphere. Edge Node 1 doesn't keep track of the host pNIC status and won't ever fail the TEP interface over. The next section will cover the ideal way to configure the uplinks to provide the most resiliency for the data plane.

Active-Standby Uplink Configuration

In this example the VDS portgroup is configured with uplink 1 as Active and uplink 2 as Standby. Figure 5-21 displays the configuration that will be tested.

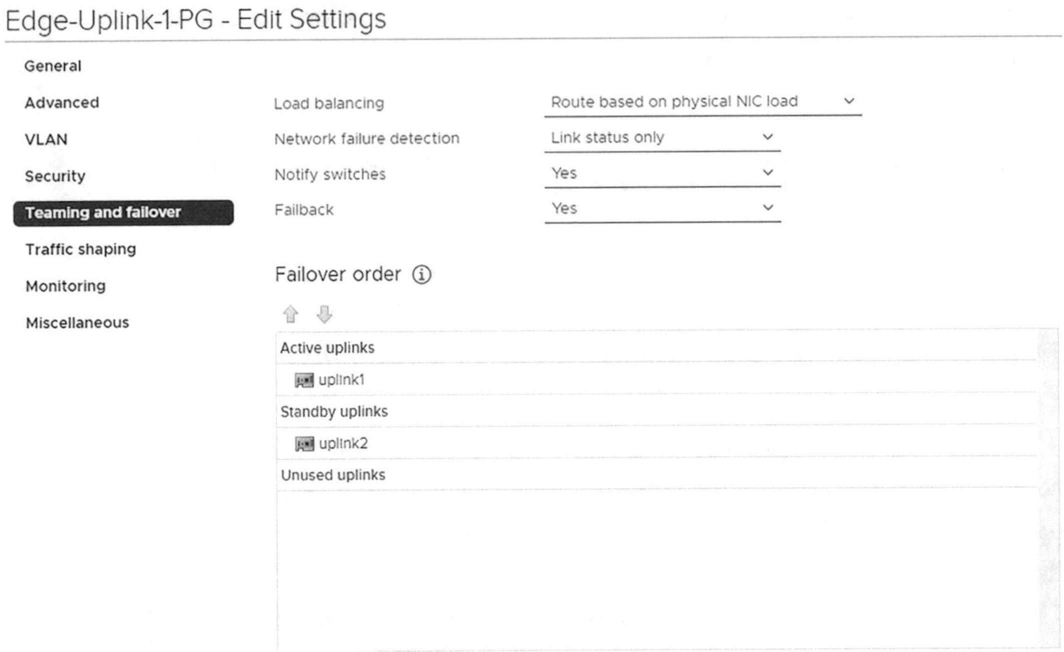

Edge-Uplink-1-PG - Edit Settings

General		
Advanced	Load balancing	Route based on physical NIC load ⌄
VLAN	Network failure detection	Link status only ⌄
Security	Notify switches	Yes ⌄
Teaming and failover	Failback	Yes ⌄
Traffic shaping		
Monitoring		
Miscellaneous		

Failover order ⓘ

⇧ ⇩

Active uplinks
📷 uplink1
Standby uplinks
📷 uplink2
Unused uplinks

Figure 5-21. *Edge uplink portgroup with Active and Standby uplinks*

As configured in the previous example, Edge vNIC 2 (FP-ETH0) is attached to
Edge-Uplink-1-PG, which now has an Active uplink and a Standby uplink configured. If
the physical link or switch fails on the active uplink interface, connectivity is failed over
to the standby uplink interface.

Figure 5-22 displays the current NIC mappings for the Edge Node.

```
PORT-ID USED-BY                          TEAM-PNIC
67108878 Management                      n/a DvsPortset-0
67108883 vmk0                            vmnic4 DvsPortset-0
67108884 vmk1                            vmnic4 DvsPortset-0
67108885 vmk2                            vmnic4 DvsPortset-0
67108886 vmk10                           vmnic4 DvsPortset-0
67108887 vmk50                           void DvsPortset-0
67108888 vmk11                           vmnic5 DvsPortset-0
67109097 29306873:edge1.eth1            vmnic5 DvsPortset-0
67109098 29306873:edge1.eth0            vmnic4 DvsPortset-0
67109099 29306873:edge1.eth2            vmnic4 DvsPortset-0
```

Figure 5-22. *Edge Node to Host vmnic mapping*

 Refer to Figure 5-10 for a logical diagram displaying Active-Standby portgroup connectivity for Edge Nodes.

Demonstrating Uplink Failure

Edge Node 1 will be tested in this section; as all its interface details are identical to the last failure scenario, they will not be repeated here. See Figure 5-16.

To start, Figure 5-23 demonstrates that there is connectivity between the Host Transport Node VXLAN stack and Edge Node 1 TEP address.

```
[root@HOST TRANSPORT NODE 1:~] vmkping ++netstack=vxlan 192.168.66.61
PING 192.168.66.31 (192.168.66.31): 56 data bytes
64 bytes from 192.168.66.61: icmp_seq=0 ttl=63 time=0.334 ms
64 bytes from 192.168.66.61: icmp_seq=1 ttl=63 time=0.362 ms
64 bytes from 192.168.66.61: icmp_seq=2 ttl=63 time=0.422 ms

--- 192.168.66.61 ping statistics ---
3 packets transmitted, 3 packets received, 0% packet loss
round-trip min/avg/max = 0.334/0.373/0.422 ms
```

Figure 5-23. *Host Transport Node to Edge TEP interface connectivity status*

Connectivity to uplink 1 (vmnic5) on the host where Edge Node 1 resides is now terminated. Figure 5-24 displays the uplink failure to Leaf 1, which leads to vSphere subsequently utilizing the standby link.

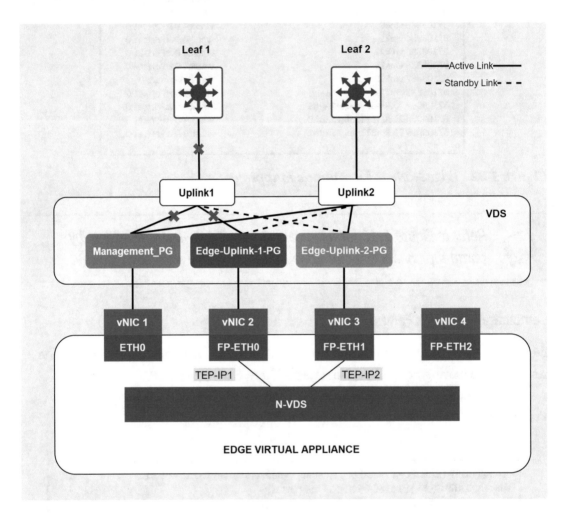

Figure 5-24. *Edge and Host uplink failure with standby uplinks*

Figure 5-25 shows edge1.eth1 now resides on vmnic4 which is part of uplink 2. The interface has failed over to the second uplink.

```
PORT-ID USED-BY                          TEAM-PNIC

67108883 vmk0                            vmnic4 DvsPortset-0
67108884 vmk1                            vmnic4 DvsPortset-0
67108885 vmk2                            vmnic4 DvsPortset-0
67108886 vmk10                           vmnic4 DvsPortset-0
67108887 vmk50                           void DvsPortset-0
67108888 vmk11                           vmnic4 DvsPortset-0
67109097 29306873:edge1.eth1            vmnic4 DvsPortset-0
67109098 29306873:edge1.eth0            vmnic4 DvsPortset-0
```

Figure 5-25. *vmnic status after link failure*

Running the vmkping command from the Host Transport Node now shows that there is still connectivity to Edge Node 1's TEP Interface.

```
[root@HOST TRANSPORT NODE 1:~] vmkping ++netstack=vxlan 192.168.66.61
PING 192.168.66.31 (192.168.66.31): 56 data bytes
64 bytes from 192.168.66.61: icmp_seq=0 ttl=63 time=0.334 ms
64 bytes from 192.168.66.61: icmp_seq=1 ttl=63 time=0.362 ms
64 bytes from 192.168.66.61: icmp_seq=2 ttl=63 time=0.422 ms

--- 192.168.66.61 ping statistics ---
3 packets transmitted, 3 packets received, 0% packet loss
round-trip min/avg/max = 0.334/0.373/0.422 ms
```

Figure 5-26. *Host Transport Node vmkping after link failure*

In this scenario, even after an uplink failure, there is connectivity between the transport nodes. This example highlights why it is crucial to ensure the teaming and failover order of the edge uplink portgroups are configured correctly.

Active-Active Uplink Configuration

It is possible to configure the teaming and failover settings with both uplinks as being active. The failover scenario will be similar to what was demonstrated in the Active-Standby section.

However, this is not the recommended approach, as traffic will be balanced across both uplinks and makes it more difficult to determine the data path, which in turn can make it more difficult to troubleshoot from an operational standpoint. Figure 5-27 displays Active-Active uplink portgroup connectivity.

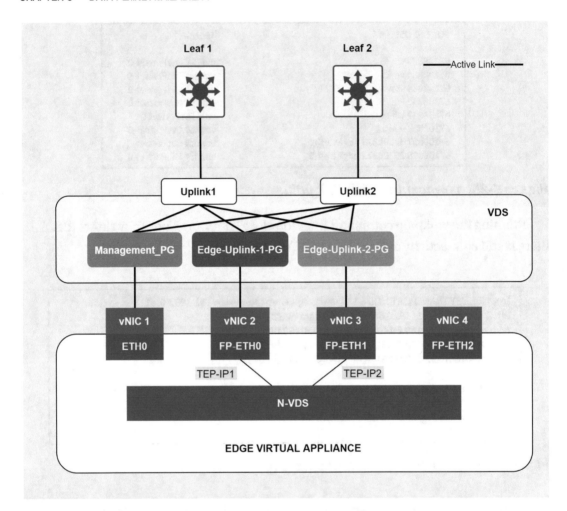

Figure 5-27. *Edge Node Active-Active portgroup wiring*

Edge Virtual Appliance Placement

Placement of the Edge virtual appliances is another critical aspect that is sometimes overlooked. As the appliances are virtual machines residing on a hypervisor cluster, they must be deployed with rules to govern their placement. This aspect is crucial to data plane availability, as it has been explored in this and previous chapters. The Edge Nodes play a large role in NSX-T.

Edge Node placement also comes down to your hypervisor cluster design. For example, if you have a dedicated cluster just for the Edge Nodes, their placement is more predictable. In this scenario, you would still require rules to ensure two Edge Nodes in the same Edge cluster do not reside on the same hypervisor. The reason for this is, if the hypervisor were to fail, multiple Edge Nodes from the same Edge cluster do not fail at the same time.

If you follow the VMware best practices, it does not call for a dedicated hypervisor cluster for the Edge Nodes; however, this does not preclude your design from including one. This decision needs to be investigated on a case-by-case basis as dedicated hardware for Edge virtual appliances can be quite costly and may not be required.

Edge virtual appliances can be deployed onto workload or management hosts, alongside workload or management virtual machines, and will generally operate just fine. If you as the administrator are aware of particularly noisy workloads on specific hosts, it may be worthwhile separating them so they are not competing for bandwidth and resources.

To maintain the data plane, there are several actions that can be taken to ensure uptime and availability:

- Deploy at least two Edge virtual appliances.

- Use DRS VM-VM anti-affinity rules; this ensures two Edge Nodes are not running on the same host.

- Use vSphere HA, with the restart policy to set high on the Edge virtual machine configuration.

- If your clusters span multiple racks, configure DRS VM-Host rules. This is so that the Edge virtual appliances are not moving across all hosts and racks and the data path becomes more predictable.

Bare Metal Edge Node Wiring

As mentioned earlier, when deploying Bare Metal Edge Nodes, the additional layer of complexity of vCenter VDS configuration is removed. This is due to the fact they are not virtual appliances and therefore not managed by vCenter.

Bare Metal Edge Nodes support up to 16 DPDK Fastpath Interfaces; however, for simplicity and the purpose of this book, the example in this chapter will cover three interfaces. Those interfaces are one for management and two for Fastpath.

For availability of the management interface, Bare Metal Edge Nodes can be configured with out-of-band interfaces. They have an additional ETH interface, configured in a bond. The interface is used as a standby link should the other fail. The other option is In-band management, which utilizes the same uplink interfaces the TEPs are configured on.

The diagram in Figure 5-28 is a visual representation of the Bare Metal Edge Node uplink configuration in this example.

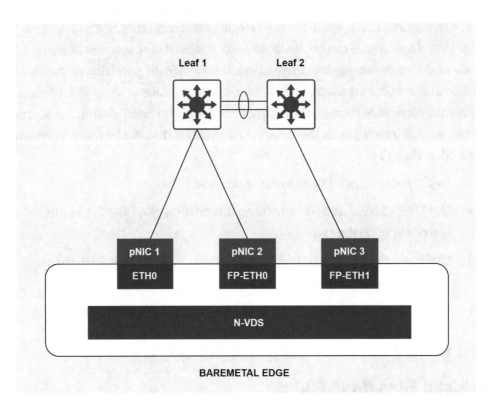

Figure 5-28. *Bare Metal Edge wiring*

After a Bare Metal Edge Node has been deployed, it must be configured. This process is like configuring the Edge virtual appliance. Each node that is deployed must have a profile applied to it, and like the virtual appliance, these profiles dictate TEP pools, uplink configuration, etc.

This section will cover multi-TEP configuration with two uplink interfaces. As there are no VDS portgroups and standby uplinks, there is no need to demonstrate VDS uplink failover conditions.

Figure 5-29 should be familiar; it displays the multi-TEP profile being applied to the Bare Metal Edge Node. Notice, all the configuration is like deploying the virtual appliance.

Edit Edge Transport Node - nsx-edge   ✕

Name*   nsx-edge

Description

+ ADD SWITCH

∨ **New Node Switch**

Edge Switch Name*   nsxHostSwitch
ⓘ

Transport Zone* | nsx-overlay-transportzone ✕ | | nsx-vlan-transportzone ✕ | ∨

                                                    OR Create New Transport Zone

Uplink Profile*   Edge-Uplink-MultiTEP   ∨

                                                    OR Create New Uplink Profile

LLDP Profile   ✕ ∨

IP Assignment   Use IP Pool   ∨
(TEP)*

IP Pool*   Edge-TEPS   ∨

Teaming Policy Uplink Mapping

Uplinks	Physical NICs
🖥 uplink1	fp-eth0
🖥 uplink2	fp-eth1

Figure 5-29. *Applying the multi-TEP profile to the Bare Metal Edge*

The Bare Metal Edge Node will have the following port mappings:

- **ETH0:** Mapped to pNIC 1; this interface will be reserved for management.

- **FP-ETH0:** Mapped to pNIC 2, which has an uplink to Leaf 1 and is a DPDK Fastpath Interface.

- **FP-ETH1:** Mapped to pNIC 3, which has an uplink to Leaf 2 and is a DPDK Fastpath Interface.

Figure 5-30 is a visual representation of a Bare Metal Edge Node with TEP interfaces assigned.

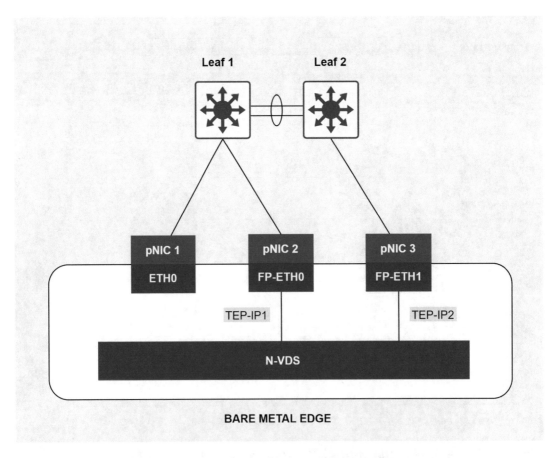

Figure 5-30. *Example Bare Metal wiring with TEP interfaces*

Physical NIC Failure

To begin, Figure 5-31 displays the TEP IP addresses of the Bare Metal Edge Node.

```
nsx-edge> get logical-router 736a80e3-23f6-5a2d-81d6-bbefb2786666 interfaces
UUID                                     VRF  LR-ID  Name              Type
736a80e3-23f6-5a2d-81d6-bbefb2786666   0    0                        TUNNEL
    Interface        : 26d2d35c-b087-5dd8-abaa-714d4372cdf4
    Ifuid            : 260
    Name             :
    Fwd-mode         : IPV4_ONLY
    Internal name    : uplink-260
    Mode             : lif
    Port-type        : uplink
    IP/Mask          : 192.168.66.21/24
    MAC              : 02:50:56:00:18:00
    VLAN             : 66
    Access-VLAN      : untagged
    Admin            : up
    Op_state         : up
    MTU              : 1600

    Interface        : 3e0596ff-1886-54cd-8226-edc8c059ed7c
    Ifuid            : 262
    Name             :
    Fwd-mode         : IPV4_ONLY
    Internal name    : uplink-262
    Mode             : lif
    Port-type        : uplink
    IP/Mask          : 192.168.66.22/24
    MAC              : 02:50:56:00:18:01
    VLAN             : 66
    Access-VLAN      : untagged
    Admin            : up
    Op_state         : up
    MTU              : 1600

Other attributes have been omitted from output
```

Figure 5-31. *Bare Metal Edge TEP addresses*

With the IP addresses now identified, initial connectivity tests from the Host Transport Node to the Bare Metal Edge Node can be conducted.

Figure 5-32 confirms connectivity between the Host Transport Node and the Bare Metal Edge Node. It is important to remember that these interfaces are connected through two different physical switches.

```
[root@HOST TRANSPORT NODE 1~] vmkping ++netstack=vxlan 192.168.66.21
PING 192.168.66.21 (192.168.66.21): 56 data bytes
64 bytes from 192.168.66.21: icmp_seq=0 ttl=63 time=1.944 ms
64 bytes from 192.168.66.21: icmp_seq=1 ttl=63 time=0.668 ms
64 bytes from 192.168.66.21: icmp_seq=2 ttl=63 time=0.536 ms

--- 192.168.66.21 ping statistics ---
3 packets transmitted, 3 packets received, 0% packet loss
round-trip min/avg/max = 0.536/1.049/1.944 ms

[root@HOST TRANSPORT NODE 1~] vmkping ++netstack=vxlan 192.168.66.22
PING 192.168.66.22 (192.168.66.22): 56 data bytes
64 bytes from 192.168.66.22: icmp_seq=0 ttl=63 time=0.738 ms
64 bytes from 192.168.66.22: icmp_seq=1 ttl=63 time=0.612 ms
64 bytes from 192.168.66.22: icmp_seq=2 ttl=63 time=1.220 ms

--- 192.168.66.22 ping statistics ---
3 packets transmitted, 3 packets received, 0% packet loss
round-trip min/avg/max = 0.612/0.857/1.220 ms
```

Figure 5-32. *Host Transport Node to Bare Metal Edge connectivity test*

To ensure that the TEP interfaces are communicating through both top of rack switches, Figure 5-33 shows the ARP entries for both TEP IP addresses.

```
SSH@Leaf-1#show arp 192.168.66.21
No.  IP Address      MAC Address      Type      Age      Port          Status
1    192.168.66.21   0250.5600.1800   Dynamic   2        1/1/1-1/1/2   Valid
SSH@Leaf-1#show arp 192.168.66.22
No.  IP Address      MAC Address      Type      Age      Port          Status
1    192.168.66.22   0250.5600.1801   Dynamic   3        1/3/4         Valid
```

Figure 5-33. *Leaf Switch ARP entry*

Correlating the details shown in Figure 5-33 with the Bare Metal Edge Node wiring diagram in Figure 5-28, it shows that the TEP interface 192.168.66.21 is being learned via the port-channel to Leaf 2, and 192.168.66.22 has been learned locally via interface 1/3/4.

Considering the Bare Metal Edge Node is not running on a hypervisor such as ESXi, it is not possible to utilize commands such as *esxtop* to determine uplink paths; however, there are multiple ways to achieve this. This book will continue to utilize the ARP entries on the switch to show where the addresses are being learned from.

The uplink from the Bare Metal Edge Node to Leaf 1 has been shut down. This simulates a switch outage or a failure. The TEP interface that was plumbed through this interface was 192.168.66.22.

Figure 5-34 shows that fp-eth1 is now down or offline.

```
Interface: fp-eth1
  ID                  : 1
  Link status:        down
  MAC address         : 00:50:56:98:9c:bb
  MTU                 : 1600
  PCI: 0000           :13:00:00
  Offload Capabilities : TX_VLAN_INSERT TX_UDP_CKSUM TX_TCP_CKSUM TX_TCP_TSO
                        RX_VLAN_STRIP RX_IPV4_CKSUM RX_UDP_CKSUM RX_TCP_CKSUM RX_TCP_LRO
  Polling Status      : inactive
  Driver              : net_vmxnet3
  Rx queue            : 4
  Tx queue            : 4
  Socket              : 0
  RX packets          : 6176456
  RX bytes            : 4507602577
  RX errors           : 0
  RX badcrc           : unknown
  RX badlen           : unknown
  RX misses           : 0
  RX nombufs          : 0
  RX pause xoff       : unknown
  RX pause xon        : unknown
  TX packets          : 25
  TX bytes            : 1572
  TX errors           : 0
  TX pause xoff       : unknown
  TX pause xon        : unknown
```

Figure 5-34. *Bare Metal Edge FP-ETH1 down*

Figure 5-35 shows an updated image of the ARP table on Leaf 1; notice the TEP interface 192.168.66.22 is now being learned from the port-channel connected to Leaf 2.

```
SSH@Leaf-1#show arp 192.168.66.22
No.  IP Address       MAC Address         Type     Age      Port          Status
1    192.168.66.22    0250.5600.1801      Dynamic  2        1/1/1-1/1/2   Valid
```

Figure 5-35. *Leaf 1 ARP entry after link failure*

Figure 5-36 displays the same test run in Figure 5-32.

```
[root@HOST TRANSPORT NODE 1:~] vmkping ++netstack=vxlan 192.168.66.22
PING 192.168.66.22 (192.168.66.22): 56 data bytes
64 bytes from 192.168.66.22: icmp_seq=0 ttl=63 time=0.869 ms
64 bytes from 192.168.66.22: icmp_seq=1 ttl=63 time=0.545 ms
64 bytes from 192.168.66.22: icmp_seq=2 ttl=63 time=0.501 ms

--- 192.168.66.22 ping statistics ---
3 packets transmitted, 3 packets received, 0% packet loss
round-trip min/avg/max = 0.501/0.638/0.869 ms
```

Figure 5-36. *Bare Metal Edge uplink 1 failure testing*

In the event of a physical uplink failure, the TEP interfaces failover to the remaining uplink; this is to prevent blackholing of traffic and packet loss. Figure 5-37 provides a visual representation.

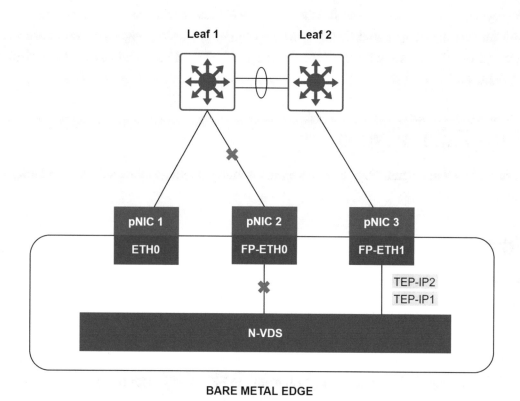

Figure 5-37. *Bare Metal Edge Node TEP failover*

Bare Metal Edge Node Placement

Bare Metal Edge Nodes can be considered simply as a standalone device. As they do not share resources with other virtual machines, they can be placed either in the same rack as the other hosts or in a dedicated rack.

Availability considerations differ to the virtual appliances; this is since Bare Metal Edge Nodes cannot move. During the planning and design of the solution, this must be considered. As an example, if there is ever a rack failure and all Bare Metal Edge Nodes are in a single rack, all North-South traffic would cease until the Bare Metal Edge Nodes are brought back online.

Bare Metal Edge Nodes are not as common as virtual appliances; they are generally deployed for specific use cases. Bare Metal Edge Nodes provide faster failover times, quicker convergence, higher throughput, and can be easier to design. This book will not cover in-depth reasoning for the deployment of Bare Metal Edge Nodes over Edge virtual appliances.

Edge Failure Types

This section will discuss Edge failure scenarios including Edge Node statuses and uplink failures.

Edge Node Status

An Edge Node can have one of three statuses:

1. **Up:** Completely operational.

2. **Up – Routing Down:** Edge node is considered up; however, routing with the upstream is considered down. If a BFD peer is configured, then a connection from the BFD peer must not be present.

3. **Down:** Nonoperational Edge Node.

For an Edge cluster to be deemed active, at least one Edge Node in the cluster must have a status of up. There are several conditions that must be met for the Edge to be considered up, which are:

- A TEP interface is up and operational.

- At least one tunnel is up and operational to another Host Transport Node or Edge.

- Not in maintenance mode.

The preceding conditions play an important role when discussing active SR placement. If an Edge Node has a status of "Up – Routing Down" or "Down" and had an active SR instantiated on it, the SR would move into a down state and a remaining Edge Node in the cluster would assume the active SR state.

Each Edge Node in an Edge cluster attached to Tier-0 gateway in an Active-Active HA mode will have an active SR. Should one of the Edge Node status move into "Up – Routing Down" or "Down," the active SR moves into a down state. The backplane port, for example, 169.254.0.2, which was running on the Edge Node that is now down, would be moved to one of the Edge Nodes that are up in the cluster. This behavior will be covered in further detail in the next section.

A Tier-0 gateway in Active-Standby would exhibit similar behavior: when the Edge Node moves into an "Up – Routing Down" or "Down" state, the SR would move into a down state. One of the remaining Edge Nodes would assume the active SR status and the backplane port would be available from the now-active Edge Node.

For an Active-Standby gateway, the backplane port does not move; it is already instantiated on the standby SR; it is just in a down state.

Service Router Uplink Failures

There are two possible scenarios when discussing service router uplink failures:

- **Partial uplink failure:** When there is more than one uplink from an SR but one or more has failed and there is still at least one uplink

- **Complete uplink failure:** When all uplinks from the SR have failed

Partial Uplink Failure

This section will discuss a typical Edge Node deployment that has two uplinks to the physical network for data transport.

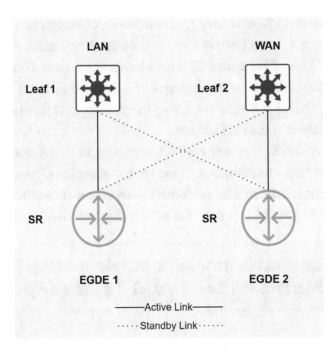

Figure 5-38. *Standard Edge uplink configuration*

Figure 5-37 displays a redundant uplink configuration on a two-node Edge cluster. The SRs are the components of the Logical Router that have uplinks to the physical network. Each SR has two uplinks, one to each top of the rack switch. Pay close attention to the zones that are available through each peer. Leaf 1 is the peer for all LAN prefixes, and Leaf 2 is for WAN.

It would be considered a partial uplink failure in this scenario if Edge 1 uplink to Leaf 1 failed.

Figure 5-38 shows a failed uplink between Edge 1 and Leaf 1.

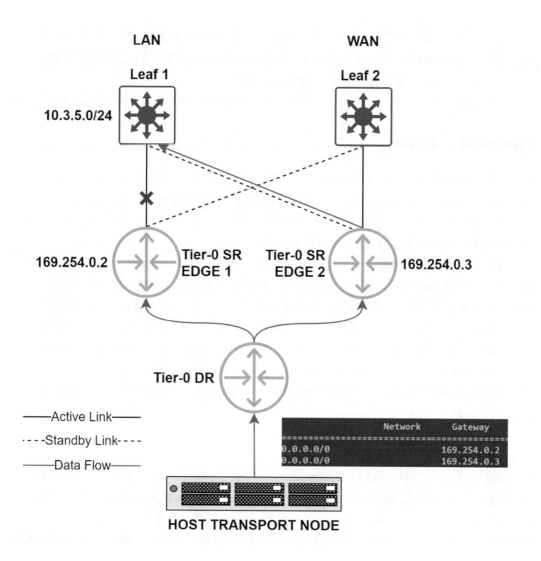

Figure 5-39. *SR with uplink failure*

If this situation occurs and workload sitting on the transport node attempts to send data to the LAN prefix, there is potential for traffic to be blackholed. This is because all transport nodes still have a default route to each SR. When traffic is forwarded to Edge 1 SR, the traffic is discarded, as it does not have the prefix in its routing table any longer. However, the traffic sent to Edge 2 SR will pass as it still has connectivity to Leaf 1.

This example demonstrates an uplink failure; however, the functionality discussed in this section is also relevant if the peering between Edge 1 and Leaf 1 was no longer established.

Inter-SR iBGP Routing

Inter-SR BGP routing is a mechanism that is used to provide resiliency against eBGP and static neighbor adjacency or uplink issues. Inter-SR iBGP routing only operates If BGP and Inter-SR iBGP are enabled on the Tier-0 gateway. BGP does not have to be the routing protocol used with the physical network.

When a Tier-0 gateway is deployed in Active-Active, all Edge Nodes in the cluster have an active SR. This provides multiple paths for packets to ingress and egress the NSX-T environment. This is beneficial from both an availability and throughput standpoint.

However, the transport nodes that are sending data to the respective active SR are not aware of the SR routing tables and where they have learned prefixes from. Host Transport Nodes have a default route pointing to each SR and use an algorithm to balance traffic sent to both active SR; this will be covered in more detail later in this chapter.

This is important because if the Edge Nodes are in an operational state (they are online, healthy to the management plane, and have at least one active uplink), then the Host Transport Nodes will continue to send packets to them, even if an SR's eBGP peering to the physical network has failed and no longer knows about the prefix the packet was being sent to. In other words, there is no mechanism for an SR to signal downstream that an upstream failure has occurred. This is not even propagated down to the DR.

If this were to occur, the SR that received the packets would silently drop them, as it would have no route to the destination. This would result in significant packet loss, as Host Transport Nodes will balance traffic across both active SRs.

To overcome this problem, Inter-SR iBGP routing can be enabled when a Tier-0 gateway is configured in the Active-Active HA mode. This is not required in Active-Standby, as there is only one active SR, and all traffic is forwarded through it.

With Inter-SR routing enabled, a GENEVE tunnel is instantiated between the SR using an internal-routing port, which is a logical interface that is specifically instantiated for Inter-SR routing. Once the tunnel is up, an iBGP peering is created between the SR.

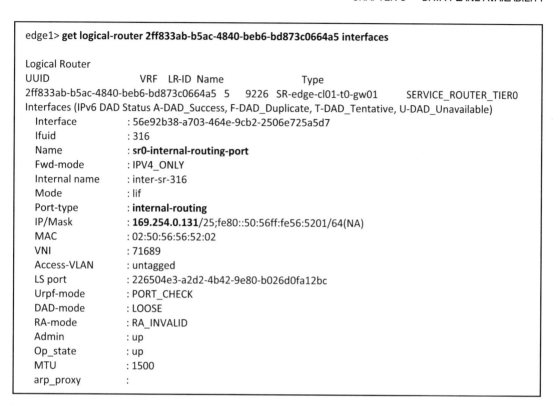

```
edge1> get logical-router 2ff833ab-b5ac-4840-beb6-bd873c0664a5 interfaces

Logical Router
UUID                        VRF   LR-ID  Name                    Type
2ff833ab-b5ac-4840-beb6-bd873c0664a5  5     9226  SR-edge-cl01-t0-gw01      SERVICE_ROUTER_TIER0
Interfaces (IPv6 DAD Status A-DAD_Success, F-DAD_Duplicate, T-DAD_Tentative, U-DAD_Unavailable)
    Interface       : 56e92b38-a703-464e-9cb2-2506e725a5d7
    Ifuid           : 316
    Name            : sr0-internal-routing-port
    Fwd-mode        : IPV4_ONLY
    Internal name   : inter-sr-316
    Mode            : lif
    Port-type       : internal-routing
    IP/Mask         : 169.254.0.131/25;fe80::50:56ff:fe56:5201/64(NA)
    MAC             : 02:50:56:56:52:02
    VNI             : 71689
    Access-VLAN     : untagged
    LS port         : 226504e3-a2d2-4b42-9e80-b026d0fa12bc
    Urpf-mode       : PORT_CHECK
    DAD-mode        : LOOSE
    RA-mode         : RA_INVALID
    Admin           : up
    Op_state        : up
    MTU             : 1500
    arp_proxy       :
```

Figure 5-40. *Service Router internal-routing port*

The port displayed in Figure 5-39 is not instantiated if Inter-SR routing is not enabled. This port is assigned with an address in the 169.254.0.128/25 range, not to be mistaken with the backplane port range of 169.254.0.0/25.

Figure 5-40 displays the iBGP configuration on Edge Node 1. This configuration is automatically populated once Inter-SR iBGP is enabled. The configuration file can be found in /etc/frr/frr.conf on the Edge Nodes.

```
root@edge1:~# cat /etc/frr/frr.conf
router bgp 65002 vrf inter_sr_vrf
 bgp router-id 10.50.0.3
 bgp log-neighbor-changes
 coalesce-time 1000
 neighbor 169.254.0.130 remote-as 65002
 neighbor 169.254.0.130 update-source 169.254.0.131
 neighbor 169.254.0.130 timers 1 3
 neighbor 169.254.0.130 graceful-restart-disable
 address-family ipv4 unicast
 redistribute static
 neighbor 169.254.0.130 next-hop-self
 neighbor 169.254.0.130 allowas-in 4
 maximum-paths ibgp 8
 import vrf route-map inter_sr_import_rmap
 import vrf default
 exit-address-family
```

Figure 5-41. *iBGP configuration on Edge Node 1*

Figure 5-41 shows the configuration for the iBGP peers that is used for Inter-SR routing. The default vrf is being imported, which has the global routing table. This configuration adds an additional path to the northbound prefixes via the iBGP peer.

Source	Destination	Protocol	Length	Info
169.254.0.131	169.254.0.130	BGP	89	KEEPALIVE Message
169.254.0.130	169.254.0.131	BGP	85	KEEPALIVE Message

Figure 5-42. *Packet capture on the internal-routing port*

Figure 5-42 is a packet capture output from the internal-routing port on Edge Node 1. It shows BGP keepalive messages sent and received from both active SRs, which means there is an active BGP session between the two SRs using the internal-routing port.

With this configuration, and the uplink failure scenario in Figure 5-38, Edge Node 1 will still be able to route to the LAN prefix through Edge Node 2. It is not a straightforward process to verify this on the Edge Nodes, as it requires diving deeper into FRRouting, which is out of scope for this book. Figure 5-43 shows that the LAN prefix 10.3.5.0/24 is reachable via 169.254.0.130 (Edge Node 2 internal-routing port).

```
Edge1> show ip bgp vrf inter_sr_vrf 10.3.5.0
BGP routing table entry for 10.3.5.0/24
Paths: (2 available, best #2, table inter_sr_vrf)
 Advertised to non peer-group peers:
 169.254.0.131
 65002
   169.254.0.130 from 169.254.0.130 (10.50.0.3)
   Origin IGP, metric 0, localpref 100, valid, internal
   Last update: Tue Aug 17 00:01:27 2021
```

Figure 5-43. *Edge Node 1 Inter-SR routes*

Notice in the global BGP routing table output in Figure 5-44, the LAN prefix cannot be seen on Edge Node 1. It is important to remember that the prefixes shown in the following are those in the default vrf; the Inter-SR routing vrf prefixes are not shown here.

```
edge1(tier0_sr)> get bgp ipv4
BGP IPv4 table version is 231
Local router ID is 10.50.0.2
Status flags: > - best, I - internal
Origin flags: i - IGP, e - EGP, ? - incomplete
```

Network	Next Hop	Metric	LocPrf	Weight	Path
> 10.32.0.0/24	100.64.64.1	0	100	32768	?
> 10.50.0.0/24	0.0.0.0	0	100	32768	?
10.51.0.0/24	10.51.0.1	0	100	0	65002 i
> 10.51.0.0/24	0.0.0.0	0	100	32768	?
> 172.25.0.10/32	100.64.64.1	0	100	32768	?
> 192.168.11.0/24	100.64.64.3	0	100	32768	?
> 192.168.13.0/24	100.64.64.1	0	100	32768	?
> 192.168.14.0/24	100.64.64.3	0	100	32768	?
> 192.168.31.0/24	100.64.64.3	0	100	32768	?
> 192.168.190.0/24	100.64.64.1	0	100	32768	?
> 192.168.191.0/24	100.64.64.7	0	100	32768	?

Figure 5-44. *Edge Node 1 routing table with a failed uplink*

Once a link failure is detected or the peering to Leaf 1 from Edge 1 is no longer established, the forwarding table on the Edge Node will be updated. Figure 5-45 displays the Edge Node 1 forwarding table after it has been updated.

```
edge1(tier0_sr)> get forwarding 10.3.5.0/24
Logical Router
UUID                          VRF   LR-ID  Name                        Type
2ff833ab-b5ac-4840-beb6-bd873c0664a5  5    9226  SR-edge-cl01-t0-gw01        SERVICE_ROUTER_TIER0
IPv4 Forwarding Table
IP Prefix             Gateway IP          Type   UUID                                      Gateway MAC
10.3.5.0/24           169.254.0.130       route  56e92b38-a703-464e-9cb2-2506e725a5d7  02:50:56:56:52:01
```

Figure 5-45. *Edge Node 1 forwarding table after suffering an uplink failure*

Figure 5-46 displays what the data path looks like after an uplink or peering failure has occurred and Inter-SR routing is enabled.

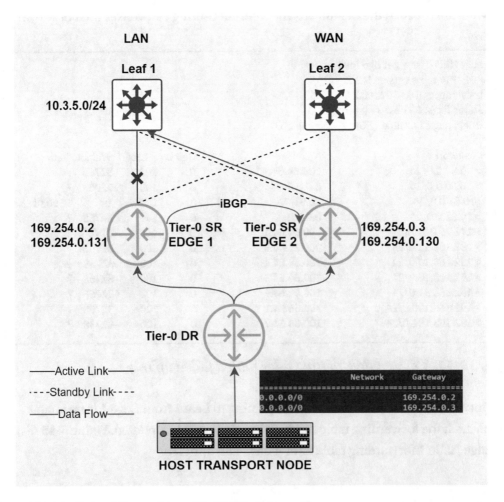

Figure 5-46. *Inter-SR routing with iBGP data path*

Any packets sent to the LAN prefix through Edge Node 1 are now sent to Edge Node 2's internal-routing port (169.254.0.130), which then performs its routing functions and forwards the packet to Leaf 1.

Complete Uplink Failure

A complete uplink failure for an SR (individual Edge Node) occurs when all uplinks have failed; this could be physical failure or the peering to the physical switches could be down.

In this situation, Inter-SR routing cannot be used, as there is no valid uplink to create the iBGP peering over. This is because the Inter-SR iBGP peering runs over the Edge Node uplinks even though it has its own dedicated interface. It is a logical interface that does not have direct upstream access and, therefore, must utilize the existing Edge uplinks.

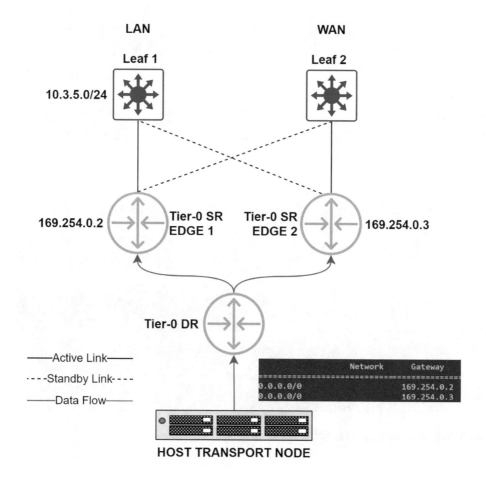

Figure 5-47. *Service Routers with no failed uplinks*

This event is much simpler to understand; refer to Figure 5-47. All uplinks are active and in a working state; the Tier-0 DR has two default routes, one to each SR. These addresses correlate to a backplane port on each Edge Node.

When an Edge Node suffers from complete uplink failure, it can no longer form any peerings and therefore cannot route traffic to the destination prefixes. Figure 5-48 is a visual representation of an SR suffering from complete uplink failure.

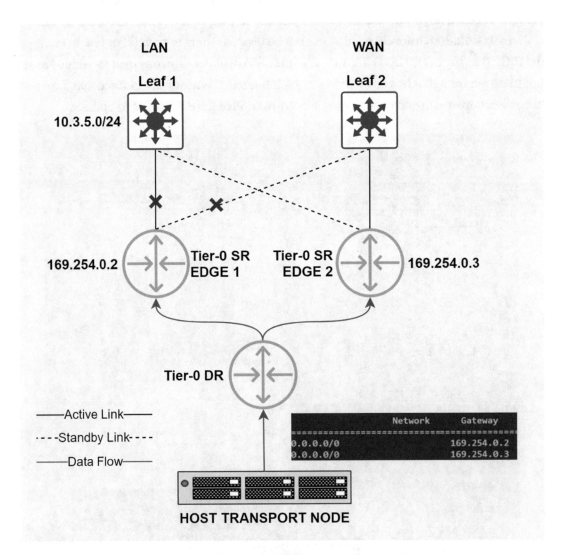

Figure 5-48. *Service Router with complete uplink failure*

Notice the Host Transport Node still has two default routes, pointing to each backplane port. The question should now arise: If there is still a default route pointing to Edge Node 1 backplane port, wouldn't that mean traffic would be forwarded to Edge Node 1, only to be discarded? The answer is no, and this is because the backplane port 169.254.0.2 no longer resides on Edge Node 1 after a complete uplink failure. Figure 5-49 shows that this is in fact the case.

```
edge1(tier0_sr)> get int | find 169.254.0.2

edge1(tier0_sr)
```

Figure 5-49. *Tier-0 SR backplane port on Edge Node 1*

Repeating the same command on Edge Node 2 will now show both backplane ports are now available on Edge Node 2.

As can be seen in Figure 5-50, both backplane ports now reside on Edge Node 2 SR. Rather than updating the routing table on each Host Transport Node, it is more efficient to move the backplane port to the remaining active SR, as this is the least disruptive approach to dataflow and requires the least resources. Once the uplinks are reinstated, the backplane port will move back to Edge Node 1 SR.

```
Edge2(tier0_sr)> get int | find 169.254.0.2
IP/Mask            :169.254.0.2/25,169.254.0.3/25;fe80::50:56ff:fe56:5300/64(NA);
                   Fe80:50:56ff:fe56:5301
```

Figure 5-50. *Tier-0 SR backplane port on Edge Node 2*

Bidirectional Forwarding Detection (BFD)

BFD is frequently discussed and used in conjunction with routing protocols. BFD provides fast peer failure detection, which results in quicker data plane recovery and higher availability.

When deploying NSX-T, BFD can be configured with external peers:

- Using BGP as the routing protocol

- Using OSPF as the routing protocol

- Using static routing

BFD is also automatically configured throughout the rest of the NSX-T fabric. The next section covers BFD within the NSX-T fabric.

BFD Usage Within the NSX-T Fabric

A BFD session is instantiated from a Host Transport Node only when it has active overlay workload on it. That is, a virtual machine must be configured and attached to a portgroup that is an NSX-T overlay segment and powered on.

Edge Nodes initiate BFD sessions once they are deployed and configured with IP addresses across their management and TEP interfaces.

The BFD sessions instantiated across the TEP interfaces of all transport nodes play a significant role in data plane availability. As covered earlier in this book, GENEVE tunnels and TEP interfaces are extremely important for overlay traffic. If a tunnel or tunnels are down, GENEVE traffic (overlay traffic) will not be able to pass between those transport nodes.

It is for this reason that BFD sessions are created between tunnel endpoints. If a peer becomes unavailable or goes down for any reason, BFD will quickly detect this, and the endpoint is declared down. Overlay traffic will not be sent to the interface that is offline but will continue to be forwarded to the remaining endpoints. This process is seamless to the end user, and there should be no visible downtime or packet loss.

The BFD timers used within the NSX-T fabric are:

- **Minimum RX Interval (Min RX):** 1000µs

- **Minimum TX Interval (Min TX):** 1000µs

- **Minimum RX TTL (Min RX TTL):** 255

- **Multiplier:** 3

The next two sections describe BFD usage within the Edge Nodes and Host Transport Nodes.

Edge Node BFD Sessions

The BFD sessions instantiated on the Edge Nodes are:

- The management interface of each Edge Node

- Each Edge TEP interface

- Edge TEP interfaces and Host Transport Node TEP interfaces

BFD sessions can be verified by using either the NSX-T Manager user interface or command line on the Edge Nodes. If using the user interface, the active GENEVE tunnels are displayed, along with their BFD diagnostic code. This directly correlates to the current BFD sessions. It is important to note that the active BFD sessions between the management interfaces are not listed in this section. Figure 5-51 displays the BFD sessions and GENEVE tunnels using the user interface.

Tunnel Endpoint

Show Status: ALL   24 UP   0 DOWN   Filter by BFD Status: ALL   ⌄

Source IP	Remote IP	Status	BFD Diagnostic Code	Remote Transport Node	Encap Interface	Encap	Tunnel Name
192.168.66.11	192.168.65.50	● Up	0 - No Diagnostic	vcfesxi3	fp-eth1	GENEVE	geneve3232252210
192.168.66.10	192.168.65.50	● Up	0 - No Diagnostic	vcfesxi3	fp-eth0	GENEVE	geneve3232252210
192.168.66.10	192.168.65.51	● Up	0 - No Diagnostic	vcfesxi3	fp-eth0	GENEVE	geneve3232252211
192.168.66.11	192.168.65.51	● Up	0 - No Diagnostic	vcfesxi3	fp-eth1	GENEVE	geneve3232252211
192.168.66.10	192.168.65.52	● Up	0 - No Diagnostic	vcfesxi1	fp-eth0	GENEVE	geneve3232252212
192.168.66.11	192.168.65.52	● Up	0 - No Diagnostic	vcfesxi1	fp-eth1	GENEVE	geneve3232252212
192.168.66.11	192.168.65.53	● Up	0 - No Diagnostic	vcfesxi1	fp-eth1	GENEVE	geneve3232252213
192.168.66.10	192.168.65.53	● Up	0 - No Diagnostic	vcfesxi1	fp-eth0	GENEVE	geneve3232252213
192.168.66.11	192.168.65.54	● Up	0 - No Diagnostic	vcfesxi4	fp-eth1	GENEVE	geneve3232252214
192.168.66.10	192.168.65.54	● Up	0 - No Diagnostic	vcfesxi4	fp-eth0	GENEVE	geneve3232252214
192.168.66.10	192.168.65.55	● Up	0 - No Diagnostic	vcfesxi4	fp-eth0	GENEVE	geneve3232252215
192.168.66.11	192.168.65.55	● Up	0 - No Diagnostic	vcfesxi4	fp-eth1	GENEVE	geneve3232252215
192.168.66.11	192.168.65.56	● Up	0 - No Diagnostic	vcfesxi2	fp-eth1	GENEVE	geneve3232252216
192.168.66.10	192.168.65.56	● Up	0 - No Diagnostic	vcfesxi2	fp-eth0	GENEVE	geneve3232252216
192.168.66.10	192.168.65.57	● Up	0 - No Diagnostic	vcfesxi2	fp-eth0	GENEVE	geneve3232252217
192.168.66.11	192.168.65.57	● Up	0 - No Diagnostic	vcfesxi2	fp-eth1	GENEVE	geneve3232252217

Figure 5-51. *Edge Node 1 GENEVE tunnels and BFD sessions list*

To obtain the similar information using the command line, issue the command *get bfd-sessions* when logged in as admin on an Edge Node. The output in Figure 5-52 is a snippet of the output from the command; this shows the BFD session over the Edge Node management interface. The rest of the command output has been omitted.

```
edge1> get bfd-session
BFD Session
Dest_port                      : 4784
Diag                           : No Diagnostic
Encap                          : null
Forwarding                     : last true (current true)
Interface                      : 00000000-0000-0000-0000-000000000000
Keep-down                      : false
Last_cp_diag                   : No Diagnostic
Last_cp_rmt_diag               : No Diagnostic
Last_cp_rmt_state              : up
Last_cp_state                  : up
Last_down_time                 : 2021-08-08 22:45:48
Last_fwd_state                 : NONE
Last_local_down_diag           : Neighbor Signaled Session Down
Last_remote_down_diag          : Control Detection Time Expired
Last_up_time                   : 2021-08-08 22:45:49
Local_address                  : 10.0.0.60
Local_discr                    : 2565556182
Min_rx_ttl                     : 1
Multiplier                     : 3
Received_remote_diag           : No Diagnostic
Received_remote_state          : up
Remote_address                 : 10.0.0.61
Remote_admin_down              : false
Remote_diag                    : No Diagnostic
Remote_discr                   : 337128270
Remote_min_rx_interval         : 100
Remote_min_tx_interval         : 1000
Remote_multiplier              : 3
Remote_state                   : up
Router_down                    : false
Rx_cfg_min                     : 1000
Rx_interval                    : 1000
Session_type                   : MGMT
State                          : up
Tx_cfg_min                     : 100
Tx_interval                    : 1000
```

Figure 5-52.   Edge Node 1 BFD sessions list using CLI

Host Transport Node BFD Sessions

Host Transport Nodes have the following BFD sessions automatically instantiated:

- Each Host Transport Node TEP interface

- Each Host Transport Node TEP interface to each Edge TEP interface

Like the Edge Nodes, BFD sessions for Host Transport Nodes can be viewed using the user interface; however, it is not possible to view the BFD sessions using the CLI. Figure 5-53 shows an example of the BFD sessions and GENEVE tunnels from a Host Transport Node.

Source IP	Remote IP	Status	BFD Diagnostic Code	Remote Transport Node	Encap Interface	Encap	Tunnel Name
192.168.65.57	192.168.65.50	● Up	0 - No Diagnostic	vcfesxi3	vmk11	GENEVE	geneve3232252...
192.168.65.56	192.168.65.50	● Up	0 - No Diagnostic	vcfesxi3	vmk10	GENEVE	geneve3232252...
192.168.65.57	192.168.65.51	● Up	0 - No Diagnostic	vcfesxi3	vmk11	GENEVE	geneve3232252...

Tunnel Status: ALL 18 UP 0 DOWN   Filter by BFD Status: ALL

Figure 5-53. *Host Transport Node GENEVE tunnels and BFD sessions*

BFD to the Physical Network Fabric

It is possible to configure BFD when configuring routing protocols and upstream neighbors. BFD is not a mandatory configuration item when configuring Tier-0 gateways; however, it is highly recommended to configure and utilize BFD for northbound peering.

BFD can be configured in the following sections of a Tier-0 gateway:

- BGP neighbor configuration
- OSPF interface configuration
- Static route BFD peer configuration

BFD to the physical network will be expanded upon in Chapter 6, which will discuss BGP, OSPF, static routing, design, and configuration, which will also include BFD configuration.

Equal Cost Multipathing (ECMP)

ECMP has been briefly referred to earlier in this chapter. This section discusses the implementation of ECMP in the NSX-T fabric.

ECMP is used at two different layers; they are:

- Tier-0 DR to the Tier-0 SR
- Tier-0 SRs to the physical network

ECMP enables the NSX-T environment to utilize multiple paths to destination prefixes. This is beneficial in two ways:

1. Provides additional paths to a destination, increasing availability

2. Allows for additional throughput to the physical network by means of additional ingress and egress points

The following sections will display ECMP behavior in NSX-T.

ECMP From the DR to SR

To understand the concepts in this section better, a summary of the logical components that will be referred to is given here:

- **Routing-backplane or backplane port:** This port links the DR and SR components across the Internal Transit Subnet. On a Host Transport Node, the port type is referred to as a "routing-backplane" port, and on the Edge Nodes, they are referred to as a backplane port.

- **Internal Transit Subnet:** The subnet range 169.254.0.0/25, which is used to logically link DR and SR components of a gateway.

Figure 5-54 represents the logical topology for a standard 2 Edge Node NSX-T deployment.

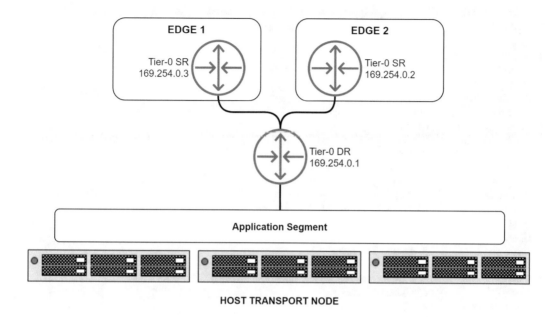

HOST TRANSPORT NODE

Figure 5-54. *Standard 2 Edge Node deployment*

The Host Transport Nodes each have the Tier-0 DR instantiated on them, configured with the same IP address (169.254.0.1) and virtual MAC address (02:50:56:56:44:52). For simplicity, the examples in this section will not cover Tier-1 gateways and the Logical Routing components between them and the Tier-0. Chapter 4 covered this process in detail.

Figure 5-55 shows the routing-backplane port on the three hosts in Figure 5-54. It demonstrates that the routing-backplane port configuration is consistent across all three hosts.

```
HOST TRANSPORT NODE 1> get logical-router 8a0762ce-e31a-4447-9379-8a0d36c3c65c interfaces
LIF UUID              : a1852c52-9305-440b-8505-54f6534f7e2c
Mode                 : [b'Routing-Backplane']
Overlay VNI          : 71698
IP/Mask              : 169.254.0.1/25;  fe80::50:56ff:fe56:4452/128(U)
Mac                  : 02:50:56:56:44:52
Connected DVS        : vds01
Control plane enable : True
Replication Mode     : 0.0.0.1
Multicast Routing    : [b'Enabled', b'Oper Down']
State                : [b'Enabled']
Flags                : 0x90308
DHCP relay           : Not enable
DAD-mode             : ['LOOSE']
RA-mode              : ['SLAAC_DNS_THROUGH_RA(M=0, O=0)']
HOST TRANSPORT NODE 2> get logical-router 8a0762ce-e31a-4447-9379-8a0d36c3c65c interfaces
LIF UUID              : a1852c52-9305-440b-8505-54f6534f7e2c
Mode                 : [b'Routing-Backplane']
Overlay VNI          : 71698
IP/Mask              : 169.254.0.1/25;  fe80::50:56ff:fe56:4452/128(U)
Mac                  : 02:50:56:56:44:52
Connected DVS        : vds01
Control plane enable : True
Replication Mode     : 0.0.0.1
Multicast Routing    : [b'Enabled', b'Oper Down']
State                : [b'Enabled']
Flags                : 0x90308
DHCP relay           : Not enable
DAD-mode             : ['LOOSE']
RA-mode              : ['SLAAC_DNS_THROUGH_RA(M=0, O=0)']
HOST TRANSPORT NODE 3> get logical-router 8a0762ce-e31a-4447-9379-8a0d36c3c65c interfaces
LIF UUID              : a1852c52-9305-440b-8505-54f6534f7e2c
Mode                 : [b'Routing-Backplane']
Overlay VNI          : 71698
IP/Mask              : 169.254.0.1/25;  fe80::50:56ff:fe56:4452/128(U)
Mac                  : 02:50:56:56:44:52
Connected DVS        : vds01
Control plane enable : True
Replication Mode     : 0.0.0.1
Multicast Routing    : [b'Enabled', b'Oper Down']
State                : [b'Enabled']
Flags                : 0x90308
DHCP relay           : Not enable
DAD-mode             : ['LOOSE']
RA-mode              : ['SLAAC_DNS_THROUGH_RA(M=0, O=0)']
```

Figure 5-55. *Host Transport Nodes backplane ports*

When a packet needs to be forwarded to the Tier-0 SR from a Host Transport Node, it is forwarded from the Tier-0 DR backplane port. A route lookup is performed, and if the prefix exists in the forwarding table, the packet is forwarded accordingly.

When the packets destination is external to NSX-T (in other words, a prefix learned from the physical network), the packet must be forwarded to a Tier-0 SR (Edge Node).

Figure 5-56 shows the forwarding table on one of the Host Transport Nodes. All prefixes not relevant to this example have been omitted.

```
HOSAT TRANSPORT NODE 1> get logical-router 8a0762ce-e31a-4447-9379-8a0d36c3c65c forwarding
                      Logical Routers Forwarding Table
-------------------------------------------------------------------------------------------
Flags Legend: [U: Up], [G: Gateway], [C: Connected], [I: Interface]
[H: Host], [R: Reject], [B: Blackhole], [F: Soft Flush], [E: ECMP]

            Network              Gateway        Type        Interface UUID
==========================================================================================
0.0.0.0/0                      169.254.0.2     UGE    a1852c52-9305-440b-8505-54f6534f7e2c
0.0.0.0/0                      169.254.0.3     UGE    a1852c52-9305-440b-8505-54f6534f7e2c
```

Figure 5-56. *Tier-0 DR forwarding table on Host Transport Node*

The forwarding table shows the two gateways listed, which are each of the Tier-0 SR on each Edge Node. These are two default routes that packets can be balanced across.

To achieve this, a two-tuple hashing algorithm is used which considers the source and destination IP address.

It is important to remember that this section refers to ECMP behavior between the Tier-0 DR and Tier-0 SR. ECMP functionality from the Tier-0 SR to the physical network will be discussed in the next section.

Each additional Edge Node added to the cluster adds an additional path. Currently, eight ECMP paths are supported, which translates to having eight active Edge Nodes in the Edge cluster. While eight paths from eight Edge Nodes are supported, an Edge cluster supports up to ten Edge Nodes.

To demonstrate this, the next example will be of a four-Edge Node deployment.

Figure 5-57 is the logical topology that will be used in this example.

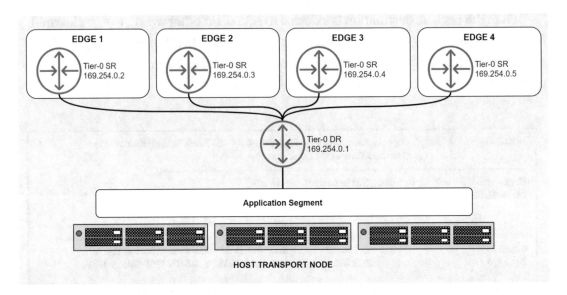

Figure 5-57. *Four-Edge Node deployment*

As the previous example displayed the backplane ports of the Host Transport Nodes, they will not be covered again.

Figure 5-58 shows two additional default routes, pointing to each additional Tier-0 SR (Edge Node).

```
HOSAT TRANSPORT NODE 1> get logical-router 8a0762ce-e31a-4447-9379-8a0d36c3c65c forwarding
                    Logical Routers Forwarding Table
-----------------------------------------------------------------------------------------------------
Flags Legend: [U: Up], [G: Gateway], [C: Connected], [I: Interface]
[H: Host], [R: Reject], [B: Blackhole], [F: Soft Flush], [E: ECMP]

          Network                Gateway       Type      Interface UUID
==================================================================================== ==============
0.0.0.0/0                     169.254.0.2      UGE    a1852c52 -9305-440b-8505-54f6534f7e2c
0.0.0.0/0                     169.254.0.3      UGE    a1852c52 -9305-440b-8505-54f6534f7e2c
0.0.0.0/0                     169.254.0. 4     UGE    a1852c52-9305-440b-8505-54f6534f7e2c
0.0.0.0/0                     169.254.0. 5     UGE    a1852c52-9305-440b-8505-54f6534f7e2c
```

Figure 5-58. *Tier-0 DR forwarding table on Host Transport Node with four Edge Nodes*

Remember, ECMP is only available to gateways in Active-Active. The moment a gateway is placed in Active-Standby, there is a single default route, which points to the active Tier-0 SR. This includes both Tier-0 and Tier-1 gateways.

ECMP from Tier-0 SR to the Physical Network

This section focuses on ECMP behavior from the Tier-0 SR (Edge Node) to the physical network.

The Tier-0 SR supports up to eight different next hops to a destination prefix. To balance traffic across these uplinks, a five-tuple hashing algorithm is used. This hashing algorithm considers the source IP, destination IP, IP protocol, layer 4 source port, and layer 4 destination port.

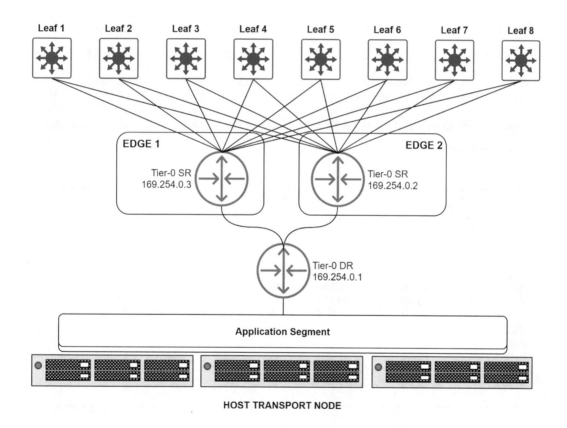

Figure 5-59. *Tier-0 SR ECMP to the physical network*

This section will demonstrate ECMP configuration across two Tier-0 SR with eight configured next hops. The diagram in Figure 5-59 does not include IP address information for the Edge Nodes and the Leaf Switches; however, those details are listed in the Table 5-1.

Table 5-1. *ECMP IP Details*

Subnet	Edge Node 1	Edge Node 2	Gateway
10.47.0.0/24	10.47.0.2	10.47.0.3	10.47.0.1
10.48.0.0/24	10.48.0.2	10.48.0.3	10.48.0.1
10.49.0.0/24	10.49.0.2	10.49.0.3	10.49.0.1
10.50.0.0/24	10.50.0.2	10.50.0.3	10.50.0.1
10.51.0.0/24	10.51.0.2	10.51.0.3	10.51.0.1
10.52.0.0/24	10.52.0.2	10.52.0.3	10.52.0.1
10.53.0.0/24	10.53.0.2	10.53.0.3	10.53.0.1
10.54.0.0/24	10.54.0.2	10.54.0.3	10.54.0.1

Figure 5-60 displays all of Edge Node 1 BGP neighbors using the get bgp **neighbor** summary command.

```
edge1(tier0_sr)> get bgp neigh sum
BFD States: NC - Not configured, DC - Disconnected
        AD - Admin down, DW - Down, IN - Init, UP - Up
BGP summary information for VRF default for address-family: ipv4Unicast
Router ID: 10.50.0.2  Local AS: 65000
Neighbor          AS      State Up/DownTime BFD       InMsgs   OutMsgs  InPfx    OutPfx
10.49.0.1         65002   Estab 00:36:49    NC        49       52       33       41
10.48.0.1         65002   Estab 0:46:50     NC        51       52       33       41
10.50.0.1         65002   Estab 00:23:58    NC        11151    9904     39       10
10.51.0.1         65002   Estab 00:23:07    NC        16042    14283    1        48
10.52.0.1         65002   Estab 00:24:51    NC        23324    23456    33       13
10.53.0.1         65002   Estab 00:18:19    NC        27       36       9        41
10.47.0.1         65002   Estab 00:36:47    NC        52       52       33       41
10.54.0.1         65002   Estab 00:18:10    NC        27       36       9        41
```

Figure 5-60. *Edge Node 1 BGP neighbors*

Figure 5-61 displays all of Edge Node 2 BGP neighbors.

```
Edge2(tier0_sr)> get bgp neigh sum
BFD States: NC - Not configured, DC - Disconnected
       AD - Admin down, DW - Down, IN - Init, UP - Up
BGP summary information for VRF default for address-family: ipv4Unicast
Router ID: 10.50.0.2  Local AS: 65000
Neighbor          AS      State Up/DownTime  BFD      InMsgs   OutMsgs   InPfx    OutPfx
10.49.0.1         65002   Estab 00:36:49     NC       49       52        33       41
10.48.0.1         65002   Estab 0:46:50      NC       51       52        33       41
10.50.0.1         65002   Estab 00:23:58     NC       11151    9904      39       10
10.51.0.1         65002   Estab 00:23:07     NC       16042    14283     1        48
10.52.0.1         65002   Estab 00:24:51     NC       23324    23456     33       13
10.53.0.1         65002   Estab 00:18:19     NC       27       36        9        41
10.47.0.1         65002   Estab 00:36:47     NC       52       52        33       41
10.54.0.1         65002   Estab 00:18:10     NC       27       36        9        41
```

Figure 5-61. *Edge Node 2 BGP neighbors*

With the diagram in Figure 5-58 and the subsequent details shown in the table and images, the BGP topology should now be clear.

Now that BGP is configured and all the neighbors are established, it is time to check how many paths are available. The prefix that will be checked is **192.168.1.0/24** from both Edge Nodes.

Figure 5-62 shows that there are eight paths available to the prefix from Edge Node 1.

```
edge1(tier0_sr)> get bgp 192.168.1.0/24
BGP routing table entry for 192.168.1.0/24
Prefix advertised to:  10.49.0.1 10.48.0.1 10.50.0.1 10.51.0.1 10.52.0.1 10.53.0.1 10.47.0.1 10.54.0.1
8 Paths available:
 Origin incomplete, Metric 2, LocalPref 100, Weight 0, best, valid
 Peer is 10.54.0.1 with router id 10.54.0.1
 Last Updated: Sum Jun 27 04:58:01 2021

 Origin incomplete, Metric 2, LocalPref 100, Weight 0, best, valid
 Peer is 10.53.0.1 with router id 10.53.0.1
 Last Updated: Sun Jun 27 04:50:01 2021

 Origin incomplete, Metric 2, LocalPref 100, Weight 0, best, valid
 Peer is 10.52.0.1 with router id 10.52.0.1
 Last Updated: Tue Aug 17 00:58:01 2021

 Origin incomplete, Metric 2, LocalPref 100, Weight 0, best, valid
 Peer is 10.47.0.1 with router id 10.47.0.1
 Last Updated: Sat Jun 26 03:54:01 2021

 Origin incomplete, Metric 2, LocalPref 100, Weight 0, best, valid
 Peer is 10.49.0.1 with router id 10.49.0.1
 Last Updated: Sat Jun 26 02:58:05 2021

 Origin incomplete, Metric 2, LocalPref 100, Weight 0, best, valid
 Peer is 10.48.0.1 with router id 10.48.0.1
 Last Updated: Tue Aug 17 00:58:01 2021

 Origin incomplete, Metric 2, LocalPref 100, Weight 0, best, valid
 Peer is 10.51.0.1 with router id 10.51.0.1
 Last Updated: Tue Aug 17 00:45:02 2021

 Origin incomplete, Metric 2, LocalPref 100, Weight 0, best, valid
 Peer is 10.50.0.1 with router id 10.50.0.1
 Last Updated: Tue Aug 17 01:58:09 2021
```

Figure 5-62. *Edge Node 1, eight paths to 192.168.1.0/24*

If Edge Node 1 (Tier-0 SR) receives any packets from workloads within the NSX-T domain that are destined for 192.168.1.0/24, it will use the five-tuple hashing algorithm to determine a path to forward the traffic to the destination.

If any more BGP peers were created, the Edge Nodes would still peer with them. However, as mentioned, the maximum supported paths are eight, and that is how many next hops would be installed into the routing table.

Figure 5-63 shows Edge Node 1, now with nine neighbors.

```
edge1(tier0_sr)> get bgp neigh sum
BFD States: NC - Not configured, DC - Disconnected
       AD - Admin down, DW - Down, IN - Init, UP - Up
BGP summary information for VRF default for address-family: ipv4Unicast
Router ID: 10.50.0.2  Local AS: 65000

Neighbor              AS     State Up/DownTime  BFD      InMsgs   OutMsgs   InPfx    OutPfx

10.49.0.1            65002   Estab 00:36:49     NC       49       52        33       41
10.48.0.1            65002   Estab 0:46:50      NC       51       52        33       41
10.50.0.1            65002   Estab 00:23:58     NC       11151    9904      39       10
10.51.0.1            65002   Estab 00:23:07     NC       16042    14283     1        48
10.52.0.1            65002   Estab 00:24:51     NC       23324    23456     33       13
10.53.0.1            65002   Estab 00:18:19     NC       27       36        9        41
10.47.0.1            65002   Estab 00:36:47     NC       52       52        33       41
10.54.0.1            65002   Estab 00:18:10     NC       27       36        9        41
10.46.0.1            65002   Estab 00:00:11     NC       10       16        34       42
```

Figure 5-63. *Edge Node 1 with 9 BGP neighbors*

Figure 5-64 shows eight paths to prefix 192.168.1.0/24.

```
edge1(tier0_sr)> get bgp 192.168.1.0/24
BGP routing table entry for 192.168.1.0/24
Prefix advertised to:  10.49.0.1 10.48.0.1 10.50.0.1 10.51.0.1 10.52.0.1 10.53.0.1 10.47.0.1 10.54.0.1
8 Paths available:
 Origin incomplete, Metric 2, LocalPref 100, Weight 0, best, valid
 Peer is 10.54.0.1 with router id 10.54.0.1
 Last Updated: Sum Jun 27 04:58:01 2021

 Origin incomplete, Metric 2, LocalPref 100, Weight 0, best, valid
 Peer is 10.53.0.1 with router id 10.53.0.1
 Last Updated: Sun Jun 27 04:50:01 2021

 Origin incomplete, Metric 2, LocalPref 100, Weight 0, best, valid
 Peer is 10.52.0.1 with router id 10.52.0.1
 Last Updated: Tue Aug 17 00:58:01 2021

 Origin incomplete, Metric 2, LocalPref 100, Weight 0, best, valid
 Peer is 10.47.0.1 with router id 10.47.0.1
 Last Updated: Sat Jun 26 03:54:01 2021

 Origin incomplete, Metric 2, LocalPref 100, Weight 0, best, valid
 Peer is 10.49.0.1 with router id 10.49.0.1
 Last Updated: Sat Jun 26 02:58:05 2021

 Origin incomplete, Metric 2, LocalPref 100, Weight 0, best, valid
 Peer is 10.48.0.1 with router id 10.48.0.1
 Last Updated: Tue Aug 17 00:58:01 2021

 Origin incomplete, Metric 2, LocalPref 100, Weight 0, best, valid
 Peer is 10.51.0.1 with router id 10.51.0.1
 Last Updated: Tue Aug 17 00:45:02 2021

 Origin incomplete, Metric 2, LocalPref 100, Weight 0, best, valid
 Peer is 10.50.0.1 with router id 10.50.0.1
 Last Updated: Tue Aug 17 01:58:09 2021
```

Figure 5-64. *Edge Node 1, eight paths to prefix 192.168.1.0/24*

Despite there being nine BGP peers, Figure 5-65 shows that only eight paths are installed into the global routing table.

```
edge1(tier0_sr)> get route 192.168.1.0/24

Flags: t0c - Tier0-Connected, t0s - Tier0-Static, b - BGP, o - OSPF
t0n - Tier0-NAT, t1s - Tier1-Static, t1c - Tier1-Connected,
t1n: Tier1-NAT, t1l: Tier1-LB VIP, t1ls: Tier1-LB SNAT,
t1d: Tier1-DNS FORWARDER, t1ipsec: Tier1-IPSec, isr: Inter-SR,
> - selected route, * - FIB route

Total number of routes: 1

b  > * 192.168.1.0/24 [20/2] via 10.50.0.1, uplink-285, 00:41:48
b  > * 192.168.1.0/24 [20/2] via 10.51.0.1, uplink-296, 00:41:48
b  > * 192.168.1.0/24 [20/2] via 10.48.0.1, uplink-369, 00:41:48
b  > * 192.168.1.0/24 [20/2] via 10.49.0.1, uplink-370, 00:41:48
b  > * 192.168.1.0/24 [20/2] via 10.47.0.1, uplink-366, 00:41:48
b  > * 192.168.1.0/24 [20/2] via 10.52.0.1, uplink-373, 00:41:48
b  > * 192.168.1.0/24 [20/2] via 10.53.0.1, uplink-374, 00:41:48
b  > * 192.168.1.0/24 [20/2] via 10.54.0.1, uplink-376, 00:41:48
```

Figure 5-65. *Edge Node 1 global routing table with eight paths*

If a peer was to be disconnected or go offline, the remaining path would be installed into the routing table and used at that point.

This example displays ECMP behavior with BGP as the configured protocol. ECMP can also be utilized with OSPF or static routing. It is also important to note that the data path a packet may take cannot be predicted. This should be considered when Edge Nodes are deployed, to avoid suboptimal routing, for example, if there are two active Edge Nodes each with an active SR. A Host Transport Node could select the path to the SR that is not closest to the workload.

Summary

This chapter has discussed some critical points to do with data plane availability. It discussed proper deployment and configuration of the Edge Nodes, Inter-SR routing, link failures, bidirectional forwarding detection, and equal cost multipathing. Readers should now be comfortable in dealing with different data plane outages within NSX-T.

Chapter 6 will look into routing within the data center and cover static and dynamic routing. It will also cover unicast reverse path forwarding mechanisms used in NSX-T.

CHAPTER 6

Datacenter Routing

Chapter Objectives

The preceding chapters of this book focused on the NSX-T data plane, including the communication and configuration of Host Transport Nodes and Edge Nodes. Readers should now be familiar with NSX-T data plane constructs, their functionality, and how they operate.

 This chapter's focus is on communication with the wider data center. By the end of this chapter, readers should be more familiar with:

- The use of Border Gateway Protocol (BGP) in NSX-T

- The addition of Open Shortest Path First (OSPF) in NSX-T

- Static routing in NSX-T

- Deterministic peering

- How unicast reverse path forwarding (uRPF) is used

This chapter will begin by introducing the need for layer 3 connectivity with the data center and then discuss the challenges that are faced in designing connectivity with the physical network.

The remainder of this chapter will focus on routing protocols, deterministic peering, and uRPF.

© Shashank Mohan 2022
S. Mohan, *NSX-T Logical Routing*, https://doi.org/10.1007/978-1-4842-7458-3_6

Communication with the Physical Network

With Logical Routing and connectivity between NSX-T components covered, it is time to cover routing with the physical network. This section will introduce routing concepts, common challenges with adoption of BGP, the addition of OSPF to overcome some of these hurdles, and finally a comparison of using a dynamic routing protocol over static routing.

When designing NSX-T, there are many considerations that must be accounted for. Often a large portion of these considerations are to do with routing with the physical network. Currently, there are three choices to achieve this: BGP, OSPF, and static routing. OSPF support has been a recent addition to accommodate data centers where BGP is not a viable option; however, many customers prefer a dynamic routing protocol over static routing.

Within NSX-T administrators can create segments with varying subnets, and if configured appropriately, they are automatically propagated to the rest of the NSX-T domain. However, with physical networks, prefixes must either be advertised using a dynamic routing protocol or devices must be told how to reach a prefix with the use of static routing.

BGP

VMware recommends the configuration and use of BGP with NSX-T. BGP allows fine-grained control over policy, which means more control over data that is ingressing and egressing the NSX-T Edge Nodes. BGP is also more scalable than both OSPF and manually created static routes. The intricacies of BGP are covered later in this chapter.

However, even though BGP is the preferred routing protocol, there are considerations that may impact implementation of the protocol in data centers.

The most common roadblocks for the adoption of BGP include:

- **Lack of knowledge:** This could be for various reasons. An example could be the compute or virtualization team that is implementing NSX-T does not have in-depth knowledge of BGP. The networking team is not engaged in all networking discussions. As a result, information relayed from the compute team to the networking may not be accurate, resulting in poor design and implementation.

- **Licensing:** Enabling BGP sometimes requires additional licensing, whereas OSPF is generally included with the base licensing of networking devices.

- **Communication:** Lack of communication between teams; teams that are siloed rarely have open discussions, which results in either technical issues or communication roadblocks. Achieving a desired end state becomes difficult in these scenarios.

- **Interoperability:** NSX-T is often being deployed into existing environments. Even for greenfield deployments, it must still interact with the rest of the data center. It is not common to find BGP as the protocol of choice within a data center.

OSPF

OSPF was introduced as a supported routing protocol in NSX-T as it is a common protocol used within data centers. Prior to its addition, it was frequently requested by NSX-T adopters. While OSPF addresses the roadblocks faced by BGP mentioned previously, administrators lose the fine-grained controls over policy. This may or may not be an issue for some; however, it must be noted during the design phase.

Why do administrators prefer OSPF?

- **Knowledge:** OSPF is more common in data centers, which means administrators are more aware of this protocol and its operation.

- **Licensing:** OSPF is generally included in base licensing for network equipment.

- **Communication:** Teams can relay requirements relating to OSPF, as it is *simpler* to adopt and already exists within the data center.

- **Interoperability:** Route redistribution and other considerations when using more than one routing protocol in a data center are no longer a concern.

Static Routing

The final option for advertising routes is to configure static routes. This option is the least preferred option, and this is because of its scalability and rigidness. Depending on the static routing design, administrators may find themselves needing to change prefixes allowed or configured. While static routing is still a valid option, NSX-T allows administrators to be more agile with network creation, and therefore, a dynamic routing protocol is preferred. There are some benefits to static routing, such as:

- **Resources:** Static routes are programmed; therefore, no compute resources are required to calculate routes and topologies.

- **Knowledge:** Simple to implement, network administrators need to create a static route pointing a prefix toward NSX-T, and the NSX-T administrators need to create a default route to their next hop.

- **Licensing:** No licensing required.

- **Communication:** Teams no longer concern themselves with in-depth discussions relating to routing protocols.

- **Interoperability:** Network administrators can control prefixes being redistributed into routing protocols within the physical network.

NSX-T and BGP

This section will begin by diving deeper into the BGP and why it is the preferred protocol to use with NSX-T.

BGP is the most used routing protocol on the Internet and is a path vector routing protocol. This means BGP maintains path information for prefixes and gets updated dynamically. The following list includes the main reasons to use BGP with NSX-T:

- **Interoperability:** Has been tested widely and used by many vendors.

- **Database:** BGP does not need to maintain a database, which makes it more stable.

- **Common:** In the most recent leaf and spine topologies, BGP is the protocol of choice.

- **Simple:** Easy-to-understand loop prevention mechanism.

- **Dual stack:** Support for IPv4 and IPv6.

- **VRF support:** VRFs can currently only be configured with BGP.

- **Advanced policy control:** Communities, route filtering, AS-PATH prepend, MED, weight, and local preference.

BGP comes in two flavors: External Border Gateway Protocol (eBGP) and Internal Border Gateway Protocol (iBGP). The flavor of BGP used is dependent on the Autonomous System Number (ASN) configuration. For example, if the ASN used to configure the Tier-0 gateway is different to that of the physical network fabric, they are configured with eBGP. If they both have the same ASN, then they are configured for iBGP.

The general recommendation and preferred option is eBGP. Both options will be discussed in this chapter, and the reasons to use eBGP over iBGP will be highlighted.

eBGP Peering with the Physical Fabric

Figure 6-1 is an example of a Tier-0 gateway that has two Edge Nodes peering with the upstream Leaf Switches. The Tier-0 gateway is configured with ASN 64513, and the Leaf Switches are configured with ASN 64512. As the Tier-0 and Leaf Switches are configured with different ASNs, this example reflects an eBGP peering between the Edge Nodes and Leaf Switches.

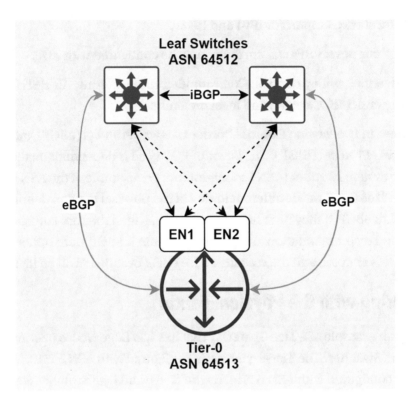

Figure 6-1. *Example Tier-0 eBGP configuration*

 The example in Figure 6-1 shows an iBGP peering between the Leaf Switches. This is not a requirement and may not be possible in every environment. Physical fabric design is out of scope for this book.

VMware recommends NSX-T adopters configure eBGP between the Tier-0 SR9s) and the physical fabric. There are numerous reasons for this recommendation, including:

- Removes the requirement of a full mesh topology

- Prefix propagation

  - eBGP automatically propagates prefixes to other eBGP peers.

  - A prefix learned from an eBGP peer will be advertised to other iBGP peers.

- Utilizes AS-PATH for loop prevention

This book will not cover the fundamentals of BGP; however, it will cover the topics relevant to an NSX-T deployment.

Typical NSX-T eBGP Topology

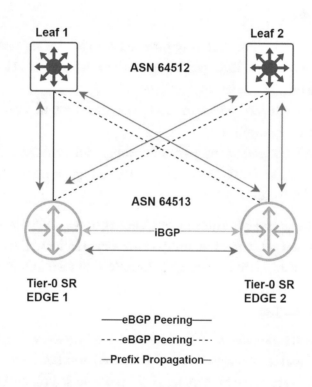

Figure 6-2. *NSX-T Edge Node eBGP topology*

Figure 6-2 is an example of NSX-T Edge Nodes configured with eBGP. The topology shown is considered a standard deployment that consists of:

- Two NSX-T Edge Nodes

- Tier-0 gateway deployed in Active-Active HA mode

- Two Leaf Switches, configured with an ASN that is different to the Tier-0 gateway

- eBGP peering between each Edge Node and Leaf Switch

An environment deployed with eBGP does not require a full mesh between each BGP speaker. This means that the Leaf Switches are not peered with each other and there is an iBGP peering between the Edge nodes in ASN 64513.

In contrast, iBGP does require a full mesh topology, route reflectors, or confederations to ensure iBGP speakers are able to learn prefixes from one another and avoid loops. iBGP will be discussed in further detail later in this chapter.

Prefix Propagation

As mentioned earlier, the default behavior for eBGP is to propagate prefixes to both eBGP and iBGP peers. The topology displayed in Figure 6-2 will be referred to throughout this section to elaborate on eBGP behavior.

The example in this section will cover prefix propagation both from the Tier-0 perspective and the Leaf Switches.

NSX-T segments (subnets) are propagated through redistribution. Segments can be attached to either a Tier-1 or Tier-0 gateway. Depending on where the segment is attached, the behavior varies slightly:

- If a segment is directly attached to a Tier-0 gateway, with the correct redistribution settings configured on the Tier-0 (refer to the following section for configuration settings), the subnet associated with the segment is added as part of a prefix list, attached to a route-map, and redistributed into BGP.

- If a segment is created and attached to a Tier-1 gateway, a static route is created and tagged with an auto-generated number. A route-map is then auto-created which matches the prefix based on the tag and is then redistributed into BGP.

The next section will cover both methods in more detail. Regardless of the gateway the segments are attached to, the prefixes are advertised to each BGP neighbor.

The method of prefix propagation on the Leaf Switches depends on how they are configured. Prefix propagation can be achieved with either redistribution or the use of the network command, either option will then advertise prefixes to both Edge nodes. Once the Edge Nodes receive the advertisement, they check the prefix and perform the required checks for BGP and finally install the prefix into the routing table if deemed appropriate to do so.

As standard eBGP behavior, prefixes learned from Leaf 1 on Edge Node 1 will be re-advertised to Leaf 2; however, Leaf 2 should not install these prefixes into its routing table. There are two possible reasons for this:

1. The prefix is locally connected and is preferred over a learned prefix.

2. eBGP loop prevention mechanism prevents Leaf 2 from installing the prefix.

eBGP loop prevention mechanism will be covered later in this chapter.

The following example will focus on the topology represented in Figure 6-2. For simplicity, it will only include output from Edge Node 1 and the Leaf Switches.

Verifying Prefix Propagation

This section will be broken up into three examples. The first two examples will display behavior when segments are attached to either a Tier-1 or Tier-0 gateway, and the third will display prefixes being advertised from the Leaf Switches into the NSX-T Edge Nodes. Understanding the behavior for prefixes advertised into NSX-T will assist with troubleshooting when required.

Segments Created in NSX-T
Segments Attached to a Tier-1

The first example displays the default behavior for segments attached to a Tier-1 gateway. To begin, the configuration of the segment and gateway is shown.

Figure 6-3 shows a segment with subnet 10.32.0.0/24 attached to a Tier-1 gateway, with all default settings configured.

Figure 6-3. *Segment attached to Tier-1*

Figure 6-4 shows the configuration of the Tier-1 gateway; outside of the settings displayed, all other configuration settings have been left as default.

Figure 6-4. *Tier-1 route advertisement settings*

Figure 6-5 displays the redistribution settings for the Tier-0 gateway, which the Tier-1 gateway in Figure 6-4 is linked to.

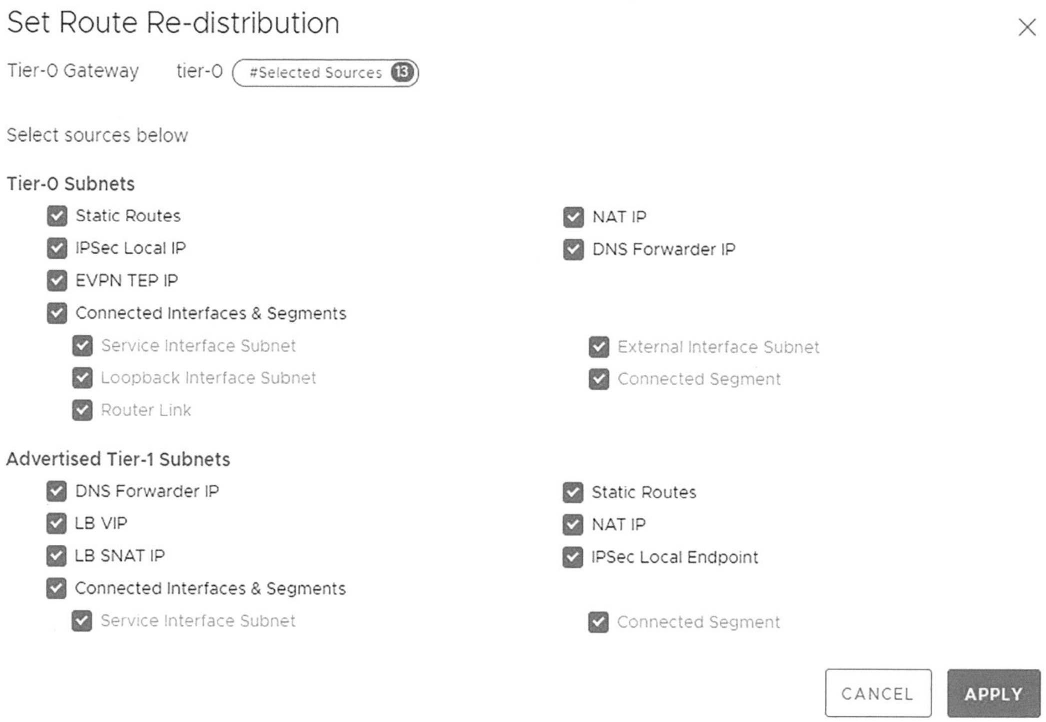

Set Route Re-distribution   ×

Tier-0 Gateway   tier-0   (#Selected Sources ⑬)

Select sources below

Tier-0 Subnets

- ☑ Static Routes   ☑ NAT IP
- ☑ IPSec Local IP   ☑ DNS Forwarder IP
- ☑ EVPN TEP IP
- ☑ Connected Interfaces & Segments
    - ☑ Service Interface Subnet   ☑ External Interface Subnet
    - ☑ Loopback Interface Subnet   ☑ Connected Segment
    - ☑ Router Link

Advertised Tier-1 Subnets

- ☑ DNS Forwarder IP   ☑ Static Routes
- ☑ LB VIP   ☑ NAT IP
- ☑ LB SNAT IP   ☑ IPSec Local Endpoint
- ☑ Connected Interfaces & Segments
    - ☑ Service Interface Subnet   ☑ Connected Segment

CANCEL   APPLY

Figure 6-5. *Tier-0 redistribution settings*

Figure 6-6 is a diagram to display the configuration that was just completed. The segment (10.32.0.0/24) is plumbed into a Tier-1 gateway, which is then plumbed into a Tier-0 gateway, which subsequently has uplink interfaces to both Leaf Switches.

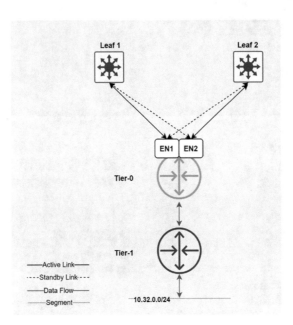

Figure 6-6. *Logical representation segment plumbed into Tier-1*

It is important to remember that any configuration that is applied in NSX-T user interface is applied to the FRRouting instance running on the Edge Nodes. Figure 6-7 displays the FRRouting configuration applied on the Edge Node.

```
root@en1:~# cat /etc/frr/frr.conf
frr version 7.0.17058858
frr defaults traditional
hostname en01
ip route 10.32.0.0/24 100.64.16.1 linked-304 tag 4016 3
router bgp 64513
 bgp router-id 10.22.0.2
 bgp log-neighbor-changes
 coalesce-time 1000
 bgp graceful-restart stalepath-time 600
 bgp graceful-restart restart-time 180
 bgp graceful-restart preserve-fw-state
 bgp bestpath as-path multipath-relax
 neighbor 10.22.0.1 remote-as 64512
 neighbor 10.22.0.1 update-source 10.22.0.2
 neighbor 10.22.0.1 timers 60 180
 neighbor 10.23.0.1 remote-as 64512
 neighbor 10.23.0.1 update-source 10.23.0.2
 neighbor 10.23.0.1 timers 60 180
 !
 address-family ipv4 unicast
  redistribute connected route-map redist_conn_to_bgp_v4
  redistribute static route-map redist_to_bgp_v4
  maximum-paths 8
  maximum-paths ibgp 8
 exit-address-family
 !
 address-family ipv6 unicast
  redistribute connected route-map redist_conn_to_bgp_v6
  redistribute static route-map redist_to_bgp_v6
  maximum-paths 8
  maximum-paths ibgp 8
 exit-address-family
 !
route-map redist_to_bgp_v4 permit 4016
 match tag 4016
```

Figure 6-7. *FRR configuration on Edge Node 1 displaying Tier-1 segments*

Pay close attention to the configuration lines from the output in bold, which include the following:

- A static route with the segment prefix (10.32.0.0/24) has been configured and tagged with 4016.

- A route-map is configured, which permits 4016 and uses the matching criteria for the tag.

- Redistribution settings into the BGP process.

 FRRouting configuration has been supplied to highlight the different methods used to propagate prefixes when segments are attached to a Tier-1 or directly to a Tier-0.

After the route-map is redistributed into BGP, the Leaf Switches 10.22.0.1 and 10.23.0.1 will receive the advertisement. Figure 6-8 shows the BGP table on Leaf 1.

```
admin@Leaf-1:~$ show ip bgp | match 10.32.0.0/24
   Network              Next Hop        Metric    LocPrf        Weight           Path
*= 10.32.0.0/24         10.22.0.2       0                       0                64513 ?
```

Figure 6-8. *Leaf 1 BGP table*

```
admin@Leaf-2:~$ show ip bgp | match 10.32.0.0/24
   Network              Next Hop        Metric    LocPrf        Weight           Path
*= 10.32.0.0/24         10.23.0.2       0                       0                64513 ?
```

Figure 6-9. *Leaf 2 BGP table*

In summary, when segments are attached to a Tier-1 gateway, the prefix they are configured with are configured as a static route in FRRouting, tagged, added to a route-map, and redistributed into BGP.

Attached to Tier-0

In this example, the segment that was attached to Tier-1 is now plumbed directly into Tier-0. This example will not cover prefix propagation to the Leaf Switches or Tier-0 gateway configuration, as this is identical to the previous example. This example is to highlight the difference between a Tier-1 connected segment and Tier-0 connected segment with regard to prefix redistribution. Figure 6-10 displays the segment created in Figure 6-3 now plumbed directly into the Tier-0 gateway.

| 10.32.0.0/24-T1 | * | tier-0 | Tier0 | ▾ | * | sm-m0-tz-overlay01 | ▾ | * | 10.32.0.1/24 | * | Set |

CIDR e.g. 10.22.12.2/23

Gateway CIDR IPv6

CIDR e.g. fc7e:f206:db42::1/48

SET DHCP CONFIG

Segment needs to have either Subnets or VPN defined, or both.

Admin State	⬤		Connectivity	⬤ ⓘ
L2 VPN	You have no L2 VPN sessions for this Gateway. For that, go to VPN Services . Note that for L2 sessions to work, you also need IP Sec session defined.		VPN Tunnel ID	
VLAN	Enter List of VLANs		Uplink Teaming Policy	Select Uplink Teaming Policy
Domain Name	Enter Fully Qualified Domain Name		IP Address Pool	Select IP Pool
Edge Bridges	Set		Metadata Proxy	Select Metadata Proxy
Multicast Routing	⬤ Enabled		Replication Mode	Hierarchical Two-Tier replication
Address Bindings	Set ⓘ		Tags	◌ Tag Scope ⊕
Description	Description			Max 30 allowed. Click (+) to add.

Figure 6-10. *Segment attached to Tier-0*

Figure 6-11 displays the logical topology for the segment that is now plumbed into the Tier-0 gateway.

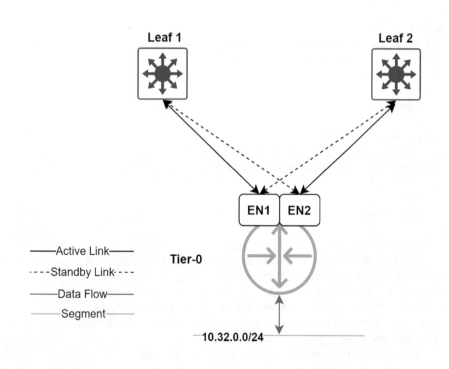

Figure 6-11. *Logical representation segment plumbed into Tier-0*

The purpose of this example is to demonstrate the differences in FRRouting configuration when segments are plumbed directly into the Tier-0 gateway. Figure 6-12 provides the FRRouting configuration output on an Edge Node with the relevant configuration changes.

```
root@en01:~# cat /etc/frr/frr.conf
hostname en01
router bgp 64513
 bgp router-id 10.22.0.2
 bgp log-neighbor-changes
 coalesce-time 1000
 bgp graceful-restart stalepath-time 600
 bgp graceful-restart restart-time 180
 bgp graceful-restart preserve-fw-state
 bgp bestpath as-path multipath-relax
 neighbor 10.22.0.1 remote-as 64512
 neighbor 10.22.0.1 update-source 10.22.0.2
 neighbor 10.22.0.1 timers 60 180
 neighbor 10.23.0.1 remote-as 64512
 neIghbor 10.23.0.1 update-source 10.23.0.2
 neighbor 10.23.0.1 timers 60 180
 !
 address-family ipv4 unicast
  redistribute connected route-map redist_conn_to_bgp_v4
  redistribute static route-map redist_to_bgp_v4
  maximum-paths 8
  maximum-paths ibgp 8
 exit-address-family
 !
 address-family ipv6 unicast
  redistribute connected route-map redist_conn_to_bgp_v6
  redistribute static route-map redist_to_bgp_v6
  maximum-paths 8
  maximum-paths ibgp 8
 exit-address-family
 !
ip prefix-list 1f4be5d9-194c-445f-8a05-f9dd9ac96c26 seq 1 permit any
ip prefix-list 3f663f18-5094-4eca-8fe0-505ac3e4fa91 seq 1 permit 100.64.0.0/16 ge 16
ip prefix-list 4948c304-3cb4-47a1-9ac1-231ed6f58c85 seq 1 permit 10.22.0.0/24
ip prefix-list 4948c304-3cb4-47a1-9ac1-231ed6f58c85 seq 2 permit 10.23.0.0/24
ip prefix-list c0b92805-cfae-4e04-b2cd-0c734b43f9b4 seq 2 permit 10.32.0.0/24
ip prefix-list e3108bf9-95f3-4ee2-b3ee-44657ca106b8 seq 1 permit 169.254.0.0/24 ge 24
route-map redist_conn_to_bgp_v4 permit 1
 match ip address prefix-list c0b92805-cfae-4e04-b2cd-0c734b43f9b4
```

Figure 6-12. *FRRouting configuration on Edge Node 1 displaying Tier-0 segments*

Notice in Figure 6-12, there is no longer a static route that is being tagged. Instead, there is:

- A prefix list permitting the prefix

- A route-map matching the address in the prefix list

- Redistribution of the *connected* prefix using a route-map into BGP

In summary, segments attached to a Tier-0 are configured as part of a prefix list and then redistributed into BGP.

Prefixes Configured on the Leaf Switches

This example displays Leaf Switch 1 advertising prefix 10.30.0.0/24 to Edge Node 1, and Edge Node 1 re-advertising it back to Leaf Switch 2. When this occurs, the Edge Nodes or NSX-T becomes a transit AS. There are different ways to avoid this, some of which will be discussed later in this chapter. In this example, Leaf Switch 2 has a directly connected interface with the same prefix. This is generally the case when a first hop redundancy protocol, such as hot standby router protocol (HSRP) for gateway redundancy, has been configured.

```
admin@Leaf-1:~$ show int
Codes: S - State, L - Link, u - Up, D - Down, A - Admin Down
Interface                           IP Address              S/L      Description
---------                           ----------              ---      -----------
eth1                                10.20.0.1/24            u/u
eth2                                -                       u/u
eth2.121                            10.21.0.1/24            u/u
eth2.122                            10.22.0.1/24            u/u
eth3                                10.30.0.1/24            u/u
admin@Leaf-1# show protocols bgp
address-family {
  ipv4-unicast {
    network 10.20.0.0/24 {
    }
    network 10.21.0.0/24 {
    }
    network 10.30.0.0/24 {
    }
  }
}
local-as 65003
neighbor 10.22.0.2 {
  remote-as 65004
}
neighbor 10.22.0.3 {
  remote-as 65004
}
```

Figure 6-13. *Leaf Switch 1 configuration*

The configuration output in Figure 6-13 shows that Leaf Switch 1 has a connected interface configured with 10.30.0.1/24 and has advertised the prefix into BGP using the network command.

Figures 6-14 and 6-15 display the behavior being discussed; the prefix 10.30.0.0/24 has been learned from Leaf Switch 1 (10.22.0.1) and is being re-advertised to Leaf Switch 2 (10.23.0.1) through Edge Node 1.

```
en01(tier0_sr)> get bgp neighbor 10.22.0.1 routes | find 10.30.0.0
Network                              Next Hop                      Metric    LocPrf
Weight  Path
 > 10.30.0.0/24                      10.22.0.1
```

Figure 6-14. *Edge Node 1, received routes from Leaf 1*

```
en01(tier0_sr)> get bgp neighbor 10.23.0.1 advertised-routes | find 10.30.0.0
Network                    Next Hop           Metric   LocPrf  Weight      Path
 > 10.30.0.0/24            0.0.0.0                 0      100     0       65003 i
```

Figure 6-15. *Edge Node 1 route, routes advertised to Leaf 2*

Figure 6-16 shows the output of two commands run on Leaf Switch 2: the first command shows the received routes from Edge Node 1, and the second command shows the global routing table. The first command shows that Leaf Switch 2 has in fact received the prefix 10.30.0.0/24 from Edge Node 1. However, the output from the global routing table displays that the locally connected prefix is preferred over the BGP learned prefix.

```
admin@Leaf-2:~$ show ip bgp neighbors 10.23.0.2 routes | match 10.30.0.0
BGP table version is 29, local router ID is 11.0.0.14, vrf id 0
Default local pref 100, local AS 65003
Status codes:  s suppressed, d damped, h history, * valid, > best, = multipath,
         i internal, r RIB-failure, S Stale, R Removed
Nexthop codes: @NNN nexthop's vrf id, < announce-nh-self
Origin codes:  i - IGP, e - EGP, ? - incomplete
   Network                          Next Hop         Metric   LocPrf   Weight   Path
 *  10.23.0.0/24                     10.23.0.2        0                 0        65004 ?
 *> 10.31.0.0/24                     10.23.0.2        0                 0        65004 ?
 *> 10.30.0.0/24                     10.23.0.2        0                 0        65004 65003 i
Displayed 3 routes and 54 total paths
admin@Leaf-2:~$ show ip route
Codes: K - kernel route, C - connected, S - static, R - RIP,
    O - OSPF, I - IS-IS, B - BGP, E - EIGRP, N - NHRP,
    T - Table, v - VNC, V - VNC-Direct, A - Babel, D - SHARP,
    F - PBR, f - OpenFabric,
    > - selected route, * - FIB route, q - queued, r - rejected, b – backup


 B  10.30.0.0/24 [20/0] via 10.23.0.2, eth1.123, weight 1, 00:03:25
 C>* 10.30.0.0/24 is directly connected, eth2, 2d20h47m
```

Figure 6-16. *Global routing table installed routes*

 Depending on the behavior of the physical device being used, the prefix may not be displayed when checking the received routes from the Edge Node. If there was no connected interface with the same prefix, then eBGP's loop prevention will stop the prefix from being installed.

Inter-SR iBGP Routing

To understand this functionality, refer to the "Inter-SR iBGP Routing" section in Chapter 5. This section will demonstrate Inter-SR iBGP functionality in conjunction with eBGP.

As mentioned earlier in this chapter, eBGP natively supports prefix propagation to both eBGP and iBGP peers. This section will focus on eBGP behavior with Inter-SR routing; iBGP will be covered later in this chapter.

Figure 6-17 is like the diagram used in Chapter 5 to demonstrate Inter-SR routing. The difference is the prefix being advertised from Leaf 1.

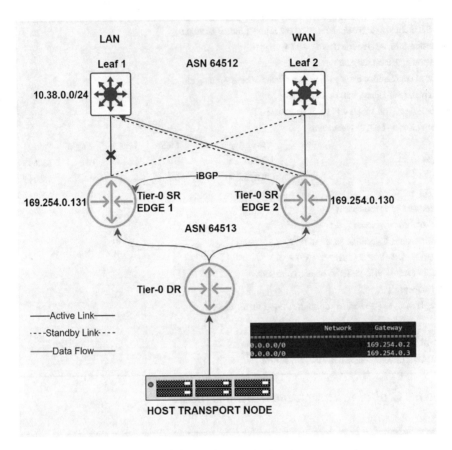

Figure 6-17. *Inter-SR routing with eBGP*

The following is a summary of this example:

- Prefix 10.38.0.0/24 advertised from Leaf Switch 1 and ASN 64512.

- Both Edge Nodes are aware of the prefix.

- Edge Node 1 suffers an uplink failure to Leaf Switch 1; however, the Edge is not in a failed state.

- Traffic is still being forwarded to Edge Node 1 destined for prefix 10.38.0.0/24.

- The routing and forwarding table entry to prefix 10.38.0.0/24 from Edge node 1 through Leaf 1 are removed.

- Edge Node 1 injects the prefix learned from its iBGP peer, Edge Node 2, into its forwarding table.

- Communication resumes to the prefix, with slight packet loss.

Therefore, when Tier-0 is peering with the Leaf Switches using eBGP, Inter-SR routing is supported and functional. The feature is also supported with iBGP; however, there are some slight changes in its behavior, which will be discussed later.

Refer to the "Inter-SR iBGP Routing" section in Chapter 5 for details on this feature.

Loop Prevention

When NSX-T and the physical fabric are configured with eBGP, the AS-Path attribute can be utilized for loop prevention. This mechanism is not limited to NSX-T and is the native loop prevention mechanism for eBGP. The AS-Path attribute is one of several others that are propagated between autonomous systems.

```
en01(tier0_sr)> get bgp
BGP IPv4 table version is 103, BGP IPv6 table version is 0
Local router ID is 10.22.0.2
Status flags: > - best, I - internal
Origin flags: i - IGP, e - EGP, ? - incomplete


EVPN type-2 prefix: [2]:[EthTag]:[MAClen]:[MAC]:[IPlen]:[IP]
EVPN type-3 prefix: [3]:[EthTag]:[IPlen]:[OrigIP]
EVPN type-4 prefix: [4]:[ESI]:[IPlen]:[OrigIP]
EVPN type-5 prefix: [5]:[EthTag]:[IPlen]:[IP]
```

Network	Next Hop	Metric	LocPrf	Weight	Path	RD
> 10.30.0.0/24	10.22.0.1	0	100	0	64512 i	
> 10.38.0.0/24	10.22.0.1	0	100	0	64512 i	

Figure 6-18. BGP table on Edge Node 1

Figure 6-18 displays the BGP table on Edge node 1, seven attributes can be seen:

- Network

- Next hop

- Metric (MED)

- LocPrf (local preference)

- Weight

- Path (AS-Path)

- RD (route distinguisher)

The eBGP loop detection mechanism is, if it receives an advertisement and sees its own ASN in the AS-Path attribute, the prefix is not installed. The logic behind this is the router assumes the prefix was advertised from itself and has somehow managed to be re-advertised to it. Rather than form a routing loop, the prefix is discarded.

There may be scenarios where this is intended behavior; if this is part of the design, then the attribute allow-as in should be configured in NSX-T; doing so will allow the prefix to be installed into the table.

iBGP Peering with the Physical Fabric

This section will be used as a comparison to between configuring NSX-T with iBGP rather than eBGP. The aim is to draw attention to the main reasons to configure eBGP over iBGP. Figure 6-19 is an example of a Tier-0 gateway, configured with two Edge Nodes peering with the upstream Leaf Switches. The Tier-0 gateway and Leaf Switches are configured with the same ASN 64512 and therefore peering using iBGP.

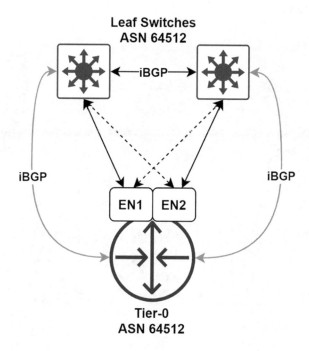

Leaf Switches
ASN 64512

iBGP

iBGP

iBGP

EN1   EN2

Tier-0
ASN 64512

Figure 6-19. *Example Tier-0 iBGP configuration*

Unlike the eBGP example, every peering represented in this diagram must exist when deploying iBGP. This forms part of the full mesh requirement.

The following sections will cover the topics listed here:

- Full Mesh Topology

- Prefix Propagation

- Inter-SR iBGP Routing

- Loop Prevention

Full Mesh Topology

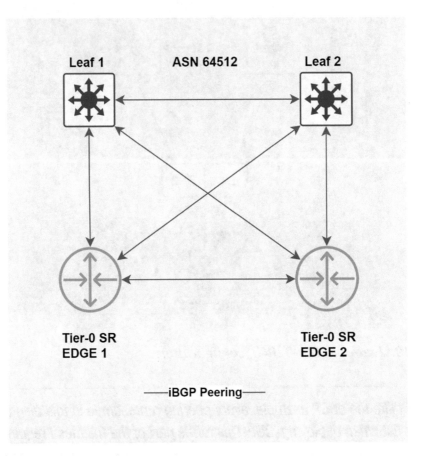

Figure 6-20. *Edge Node iBGP peering*

Figure 6-20 is an example of NSX-T Edge Nodes configured with iBGP. Notice there is a single ASN that consists of:

- Two NSX-T Edge Nodes

- Tier-0 gateway deployed in Active-Active HA mode

- Two Leaf Switches, configured with iBGP

- iBGP peering between each Edge Node and Leaf Switch

As can be seen in this example, there is a full mesh of BGP speakers within the ASN. Unlike eBGP, a prefix learned from one BGP speaker within an ASN will not be re-advertised to another neighbor, also known as the BGP split-horizon rule. For example, a prefix advertised from Leaf 1 will not be re-advertised from Edge 1 to Leaf 2. Leaf 1 must directly advertise the prefix to Leaf 2 and Edge 2.

In larger environments, this is generally not scalable, and administrators may choose to use route reflectors or confederations. However, as of version 3.1, route reflectors or confederations are not configurable in NSX-T.

Prefix Propagation

The mechanisms used to advertise prefixes in NSX-T remain the same regardless of whether eBGP or IBGP is configured. The major difference with iBGP is that the prefixes are not re-advertised through the Edge. This essentially means the Edge Nodes no longer act as a transit AS.

Once again this is standard iBGP behavior, due to the BGP split-horizon rule.

Verifying Prefix Propagation

Segments Created in NSX-T

Any segments or prefixes created in NSX-T will be propagated as normal to the Leaf Switches. Rather than walking through all the examples again, this section will display the learned prefix on the Leaf Switches. Then to finish the section, the BGP split-horizon rule will be demonstrated.

The prefix 10.32.0.0/24 is assigned to a segment that is attached to a Tier-1 gateway, which is plumbed into a Tier-0 gateway. The configuration is identical to Figures 6-3, 6-4, and 6-5, under the eBGP section.

```
en01> show ip bgp neighbors 10.22.0.1 advertised-routes
BGP table version is 11, local router ID is 10.22.0.2, vrf id 0
Default local pref 100, local AS 64512
Status codes:  s suppressed, d damped, h history, * valid, > best, = multipath,
           i internal, r RIB-failure, S Stale, R Removed
Nexthop codes: @NNN nexthop's vrf id, < announce-nh-self
Origin codes:  i - IGP, e - EGP, ? - incomplete


   Network                    Next Hop         Metric    LocPrf        Weight         Path
*> 10.32.0.0/24               0.0.0.0          0         100           32768          ?


Total number of prefixes 1
en01> show ip bgp neighbors 10.23.0.1 advertised-routes
BGP table version is 11, local router ID is 10.22.0.2, vrf id 0
Default local pref 100, local AS 64512
Status codes:  s suppressed, d damped, h history, * valid, > best, = multipath,
           i internal, r RIB-failure, S Stale, R Removed
Nexthop codes: @NNN nexthop's vrf id, < announce-nh-self
Origin codes:  i - IGP, e - EGP, ? - incomplete


   Network                    Next Hop         Metric    LocPrf        Weight         Path
*> 10.32.0.0/24               0.0.0.0          0         100           32768          ?


Total number of prefixes 1
```

Figure 6-21. *Edge Node 1 prefix advertisement*

Figure 6-21 shows Edge Node 1 propagating prefix 10.32.0.0/24 to both Leaf Switches. This behavior is identical to eBGP. This doesn't trigger the BGP split-horizon rule as the Edge and Leaf Switches are directly peered.

Prefixes Configured on the Leaf Switches: BGP Split-Horizon Rule

This example is to demonstrate the BGP split-horizon rule in effect. In this example, prefix 10.38.0.0/24 is configured on Leaf 1, which is part of a full mesh topology.

Figure 6-22 displays Leaf 1 advertising prefix 10.38.0.0/24 to Edge 1.

```
admin@Leaf-1:~$ show ip bgp neighbors 10.22.0.2 advertised-routes
BGP table version is 58, local router ID is 11.0.0.10, vrf id 0
Default local pref 100, local AS 64512
Status codes:  s suppressed, d damped, h history, * valid, > best, = multipath,  i internal, r RIB-failure, S Stale, R Removed
Nexthop codes: @NNN nexthop's vrf id, < announce-nh-self
Origin codes:  i - IGP, e - EGP, ? - incomplete
   Network              Next Hop           Metric        LocPrf          Weight       Path
*> 10.38.0.0/24         0.0.0.0            0             100             32768        i
```

Figure 6-22. *Leaf 1 advertising prefix*

Figure 6-23 shows that Edge Node 1 has received prefix 10.38.0.0/24 from Leaf 1 (10.22.0.1); however, it is not advertising back to Leaf 2 (10.23.0.1).

```
en01> vrf 1
en03(tier0_sr)> get bgp neighbor 10.22.0.1 routes
BGP IPv4 table version is 11
Local router ID is 10.22.0.2
Status flags: > - best, I - internal
Origin flags: i - IGP, e - EGP, ? - incomplete


   Network              Next Hop           Metric   LocPrf           Weight         Path
*> 10.38.0.0/24         0.0.0.0            0        100              32768          i


en01(tier0_sr)> get bgp neighbor 10.23.0.1 advertised-routes | find 10.38.0.0/24
BGP IPv4 table version is 11
Local router ID is 10.22.0.2
Status flags: > - best, I - internal
Origin flags: i - IGP, e - EGP, ? - incomplete


   Network              Next Hop           Metric   LocPrf           Weight         Path
```

Figure 6-23. *Edge Node 1 received and advertised routes with iBGP*

Figure 6-24 confirms that Leaf 2 has not received the prefix from Edge Node 1 (10.23.0.2).

```
admin@Leaf-2:~$ show ip bgp neighbors 10.23.0.2 routes | match 10.38.0.0/24
BGP table version is 56, local router ID is 11.0.0.14, vrf id 0
Default local pref 100, local AS 64512
Status codes:  s suppressed, d damped, h history, * valid, > best, = multipath,
         i internal, r RIB-failure, S Stale, R Removed
Nexthop codes: @NNN nexthop's vrf id, < announce-nh-self
Origin codes:  i - IGP, e - EGP, ? – incomplete


Network           Next Hop                    Metric          LocPrf          Weight      Path
```

Figure 6-24. *Leaf 2 received routes*

Inter-SR iBGP Routing

Like eBGP, Inter-SR iBGP routing also works with iBGP; however, there are some slight differences with the PATH attribute attached to the prefix. Figure 6-25 displays the inter-SR-VRF routing table on Edge Node 1.

```
BGP table version is 189, local router ID is 10.50.0.2, vrf id 2
Default local pref 100, local AS 64513
Status codes:  s suppressed, d damped, h history, * valid, > best, = multipath,
        i internal, r RIB-failure, S Stale, R Removed
Nexthop codes: @NNN nexthop's vrf id, < announce-nh-self
Origin codes:  i - IGP, e - EGP, ? - incomplete


Network              Next Hop              Metric      LocPrf    Weight    Path
* i10.38.0.0/24       169.254.0.131                     100       0        64512 64513 i
*>                    10.51.0.1@0                                 32765     64512 64513 i
```

Figure 6-25. *Inter-SR-VRF routing table with eBGP*

The output displays the prefix and its path when eBGP is configured from the Tier-0 to the Leaf Switches; notice it has the Leaf Switches ASN as well as the ASN configured on the Tier-0 gateway. Figure 6-26 is the output from the same command when iBGP is configured with the Leaf Switches.

```
BGP table version is 189, local router ID is 10.50.0.2, vrf id 2
Default local pref 100, local AS 64512
Status codes:  s suppressed, d damped, h history, * valid, > best, = multipath,
          i internal, r RIB-failure, S Stale, R Removed
Nexthop codes: @NNN nexthop's vrf id, < announce-nh-self
Origin codes:  i - IGP, e - EGP, ? - incomplete


   Network                 Next Hop                 Metric          LocPrf    Weight   Path
 * i10.38.0.0/24            169.254.0.131                            100       0        i
```

Figure 6-26. *Inter-SR-VRF routing table with iBGP*

Notice, the path value has changed. This is standard behavior with iBGP; also the second path is missing because the Edge Node will not re-advertise the prefix learned from Leaf Switch 1; this is due to the BGP split-horizon rule. Outside of these differences, Inter-SR iBGP routing works as intended.

The reason Inter-SR Routing works with iBGP is, rather than simply re-advertise the prefix, the default routing table is being imported into a separate VRF. Within this VRF there is another iBGP session between both Tier-0 SR internal-routing ports, and the prefix is advertised as part of that.

 This book does not endorse or recommend the use of iBGP. The purpose of this section is to highlight the differences that should be expected if iBGP was to be configured.

Loop Prevention

Unlike eBGP, iBGP cannot utilize the AS-PATH attribute for loop prevention. This is because each gateway within an AS is configured with the same ASN. Therefore, the AS-Path remains unchanged.

This behavior is the reason a prefix advertised from one iBGP peer is not re-advertised to another iBGP peer. This is an example of the BGP split-horizon rule in effect.

Figure 6-27 shows Leaf Switch 1 propagating prefix 10.38.0.0/24 to each iBGP peer. However, the prefix is not being re-advertised from any of the peers that received the advertisement. For example, Edge Node 1 receives the prefix from Leaf Switch 1, but Edge Node 1 will not re-advertise the same prefix to Leaf Switch 2.

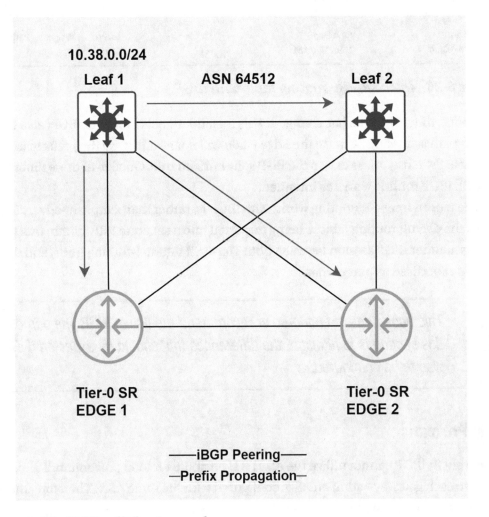

Figure 6-27. iBGP split-horizon rule

  The behavior described here should not be confused with the behavior of Inter-SR routing. This section describes default iBGP behavior in a single VRF.

Policy Control

BGP is the preferred policy for numerous reasons; this section will focus on policy control. Both OSPF and static routing do not offer fine-grained policy control the way BGP does.

What this means is that BGP offers flexibility and configuration options to control ingress and egress route advertisements.

NSX-T currently supports the following features for policy control:

- AS-PATH prepend

- Metric (MED)

- Weight

- Communities

- Local preference

Each attribute has its own use case; however, when configured, it can impact route propagation and best path selection.

 This book's focus is on NSX-T and integration with this routing protocol rather than the routing protocol itself. Therefore, each attribute's use and configuration will not be covered.

Supported Topologies

A Tier-0 gateway configured with BGP can be deployed in either Active-Active or Active-Standby mode. The AS-PATH configuration on Edge Nodes is different depending on the mode. The differences are listed as follows:

- **Active-Active:** All edges and routes are advertised as normal.

- **Active-Standby:** Routes advertised from the standby edge have the AS-PATH prepended three times.

The AS-PATH for the prefix is prepended three times on the standby edge, so the path is least preferred from the physical fabric. Traffic sent from the physical network into NSX-T will ingress using the paths through the active Edge Node, which will have a shorter AS-PATH to the prefix, therefore is selected as the preferred path.

NSX-T and OSPF

This section will focus on the OSPF implementation in NSX-T and will not cover all aspects of the routing protocol.

Currently, NSX-T supports configuration of OSPF neighbors using either broadcast or point-to-point network types. It is recommended to use point-to-point links for simplicity and faster convergence. The following section will describe both interface types.

Prefix propagation mechanisms remain the same regardless of routing protocols and therefore will not be covered again.

Network Type

Broadcast

When configuring OSPF using the broadcast network type, adjacencies are formed using hello messages. All devices on a network segment configured for OSPF that receive the message will *attempt* to form an adjacency. Consider Figure 6-28; this example displays shared network segments with OSPF configured using broadcast mode.

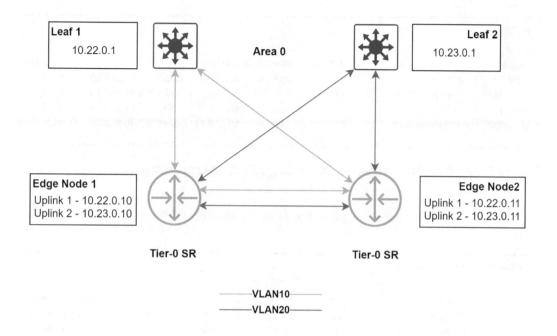

Figure 6-28. *Tier-0, OSPF, and broadcast*

In this example, the adjacencies listed in Table 6-1 will form automatically if all OSPF prerequisites are met.

Table 6-1. *Adjacencies in each VLAN*

VLAN10	VLAN20
Edge 1 and Leaf 1	Edge 2 and Leaf 1
Edge 1 and Leaf 2	Edge 2 and Leaf 2
Edge 1 and Edge 2	Edge 2 and Edge 1

The output in Figure 6-29 displays the adjacencies formed on Edge Node 1.

```
en01(tier0_sr)> get ospf neighbor


Neighbor ID   Pri State          UpTime     Dead Time  Address      Interface          RXmtL RqstL DBsmL
10.22.0.1     1 Full/DR          27.542s    32.447s    10.22.0.1    uplink-284:10.22.0.10  0   0   0
10.22.0.11    0 2-Way/DROther    33.683s    36.310s    10.22.0.11   uplink-284:10.22.0.10  0   0   0
10.23.0.1     1 Full/DR          28.642s    31.330s    10.23.0.1    uplink-287:10.23.0.10  0   0   0
10.22.0.11    0 2-Way/DROther    27.929s    32.066s    10.23.0.11   uplink-287:10.23.0.10  0   0   0
```

Figure 6-29. *Neighbor adjacencies on Edge 1 using broadcast*

The output in Figure 6-30 displays the adjacencies formed on Edge Node 2.

```
en02(tier0_sr)> get ospf neighbor


Neighbor ID   Pri State          UpTime     Dead Time  Address      Interface          RXmtL RqstL DBsmL
10.22.0.1     1 Full/DR          27.542s    32.447s    10.22.0.1    uplink-292:10.22.0.11  0   0   0
10.22.0.10    0 2-Way/DROther    33.683s    36.310s    10.22.0.10   uplink-2292:10.22.0.11 0   0   0
10.23.0.1     1 Full/DR          28.642s    31.330s    10.23.0.1    uplink-295:10.23.0.11  0   0   0
10.22.0.10    0 2-Way/DROther    27.929s    32.066s    10.23.0.11   uplink-295:10.23.0.11  0   0   0
```

Figure 6-30. *Neighbor adjacencies on Edge 2 using broadcast*

Deploying NSX-T with broadcast interfaces is not the preferred method due to:

- Requiring DR/BDR election, which impacts convergence time
- Flooding of Network LSAs (type 2) from the elected DR to devices on the same segment
- Harder to troubleshoot with more adjacencies to track

 NSX-T Edge appliances will never be elected as a DR or BDR. This is because when the uplink interfaces are configured, they are configured with a priority of 0.

Point-to-Point Link

Unlike broadcast mode, point-to-point link does not form adjacencies using hello packets on a network segment. When configuring point-to-point link, a neighbor must be defined for an adjacency to form. Figure 6-31 is the topology being referred to in this section. Notice the additional VLANs and subnets configured for the point-to-point links.

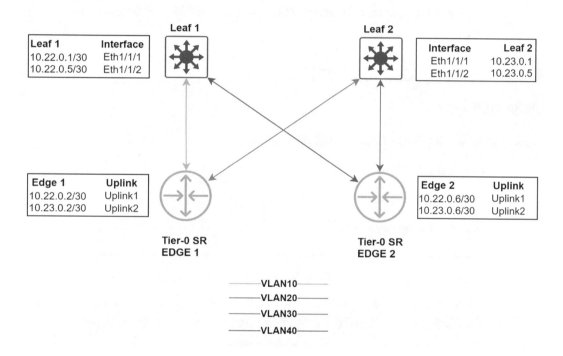

Figure 6-31. *Tier-0, OSPF, point-to-point links*

Table 6-2 lists the adjacencies that are configured in Figure 6-31.

Table 6-2. *OSPF Point-to-Point Adjacencies*

VLAN10	VLAN20	VLAN30	VLAN40
Edge 1 and Leaf 1	Edge 2 and Leaf 2	Edge 1 and Leaf 2	Edge 2 and Leaf 1

When deploying OSPF with point-to-point links, only two routers can form an adjacency over said link. Deploying OSPF in NSX-T with point-to-point links is preferred because:

- It does not require DR/BDR election, which results in quicker convergence.

- It does not require flooding of Network LSAs.

- Adjacencies are more deterministic, and there are less adjacencies to track.

Areas, Route Types, and Cost

Supported Areas

Currently NSX-T supports three OSPF area types:

- Backbone area (0)

- Non-backbone

- Not-So-Stubby Area (NSSA)

 Standard OSPF rules apply; if a gateway is configured with a non-backbone area (0), it must be connected to a gateway that is connected to the backbone area. NSX-T currently does not support virtual links.

Route Types and Cost

This section will outline the route types and metrics for backbone area, non-backbone area, and NSSA types. This section will not outline the route types and their differences.

Backbone and Non-backbone Areas

When NSX-T Tier-0 gateways configured with either a backbone or non-backbone area, they use an E2-type route. Routes that are advertised to the physical network from the Tier-0 gateway, and those redistributed and advertised into NSX-T, are E2-type routes with a cost of 20. Figure 6-32 and Figure 6-33 are outputs from Edge Node 1 and Leaf Switch 1.

```
en01(tier0_sr)> get ospf route
Codes: R - Router, N - Network, D - Discard,
    IA - Inter Area, E1 - Type1 external, E2 - Type2 external,
    N1 - Type1 NSSA external, N2 - Type2 NSSA external,
    ABR - Area Border Router, ASBR - Autonomous System Border Router
============ OSPF network routing table ============
N   10.22.0.0/24      [10] area: 0.0.0.0
                directly attached to uplink-284
N   10.23.0.0/24      [10] area: 0.0.0.0
                directly attached to uplink-287


============ OSPF router routing table ============
R   10.22.0.1        [10] area: 0.0.0.0, ASBR
                via 10.22.0.1, uplink-284
R   10.22.0.11       [10] area: 0.0.0.0, ASBR
                via 10.22.0.11, uplink-284
                via 10.23.0.11, uplink-287


============ OSPF external routing table ==========
N E2 10.0.0.0/24      [10/20] tag: 4016  - route advertised from Leaf switches
                via 10.22.0.11, uplink-284
                via 10.23.0.11, uplink-287
```

Figure 6-32. *OSPF Routes on Edge Node 1, Area 0*

```
admin@Leaf-1:~$ show ip ospf route
============ OSPF network routing table ============
N   10.22.0.0/24      [1] area: 0.0.0.0
                directly attached to eth2.122
N   10.23.0.0/24      [11] area: 0.0.0.0
                via 10.22.0.10, eth2.122
                via 10.22.0.11, eth2.122
============ OSPF router routing table ============
R   10.22.0.10       [1] area: 0.0.0.0, ASBR
                via 10.22.0.10, eth2.122
R   10.22.0.11       [1] area: 0.0.0.0, ASBR
                via 10.22.0.11, eth2.122
============ OSPF external routing table ==========
N E2 10.32.0.0/24      [1/20] tag: 4016 – route advertised from NSX-T
                via 10.22.0.10, eth2.122
                via 10.22.0.11, eth2.122
```

Figure 6-33. *Leaf Switch 1 routes, Area 0*

NSSA

NSSAs in NSX-T utilize two route types: E2 and N2. Routes that are redistributed and advertised into OSPF are N2-type routes. Routes that are advertised out of NSX-T are E2-type routes. Both the E2 and N2 routes have a cost of 20.

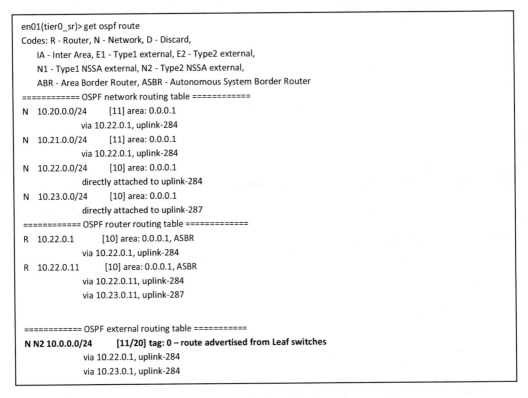

Figure 6-34. OSPF routes on Edge Node 1, NSSA

```
admin@Leaf-1:~$ show ip ospf route
=========== OSPF network routing table ============
N   10.20.0.0/24       [1] area: 0.0.0.1
                directly attached to eth1
N   10.21.0.0/24       [1] area: 0.0.0.1
                directly attached to eth2.121
N   10.22.0.0/24       [1] area: 0.0.0.1
                directly attached to eth2.122
N   10.23.0.0/24       [11] area: 0.0.0.1
                  via 10.22.0.10, eth2.122
                  via 10.22.0.11, eth2.122
============ OSPF router routing table =============
R   10.22.0.10       [1] area: 0.0.0.1, ASBR
                  via 10.22.0.10, eth2.122
R   10.22.0.11       [1] area: 0.0.0.1, ASBR
                  via 10.22.0.11, eth2.122
============ OSPF external routing table ===========
N E2 10.32.0.0/24       [11/20] tag: 4016  -- route advertised from NSX-T
                  via 10.22.0.10, eth2.122
                  via 10.22.0.11, eth2.122
```

Figure 6-35. *Leaf Switch 1 OSPF routes, NSSA*

Supported Topologies

A Tier-0 gateway configured with OSPF can be deployed in either Active-Active or Active-Standby mode. The cost configuration on Edge Nodes varies depending on the mode. The differences are listed as follows:

- **Active-Active:** Prefixes advertised from all Edge Nodes are advertised with a cost of 20.

- **Active-Standby:** Prefixes advertised from the standby Edge have a cost of 65534, whereas the active Edge Node advertises them with a cost of 20.

The cost for the route is increased on the standby Edge, so the path is not preferred. Traffic sent from the physical network into NSX-T will ingress using the paths through the active Edge Node due to the lower cost.

Recovering from Uplink Failures

Chapter 5 discussed uplink failures and recovery mechanisms using Inter-SR iBGP routing. This section will focus on uplink failure recovery with OSPF.

An NSX-T environment configured with OSPF does not require Inter-SR iBGP routing because all routers within an area are aware of all prefixes. This is a benefit of running OSPF: all routers within an area have identical link state databases (LSDBs).

This section will demonstrate an uplink failure using a broadcast network type.

 Due to their similarities, uplink failure behavior using point-to-point networks will not be demonstrated in this section.

Figure 6-36 shows the topology that will be demonstrated, prior to an uplink failure.

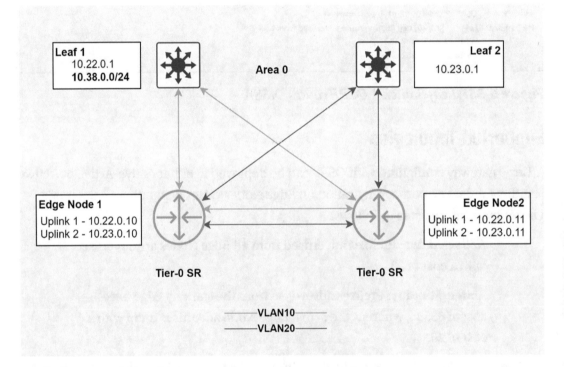

Figure 6-36. *NSX-T OSPF environment pre-uplink failure*

The prefix 10.38.0.0/24 is learned directly from Leaf 1. Figure 6-37 displays this behavior; 10.38.0.0/24 is learned via 10.22.0.1 (Leaf 1).

```
en01(tier0_sr)> get route

Flags: t0c - Tier0-Connected, t0s - Tier0-Static, b - BGP, o - OSPF
t0n - Tier0-NAT, t1s - Tier1-Static, t1c - Tier1-Connected,
t1n: Tier1-NAT, t1l: Tier1-LB VIP, t1ls: Tier1-LB SNAT,
t1d: Tier1-DNS FORWARDER, t1ipsec: Tier1-IPSec, isr: Inter-SR,
> - selected route, * - FIB route

o > * 10.38.0.0/24 [110/20] via 10.22.0.1, uplink 284, 00:59:12
```

Figure 6-37. *Prefix 10.38.0.0/24 on Edge Node 1*

To simulate an adjacency failure between Edge Node 1 and Leaf 1, the link between the two nodes is severed.

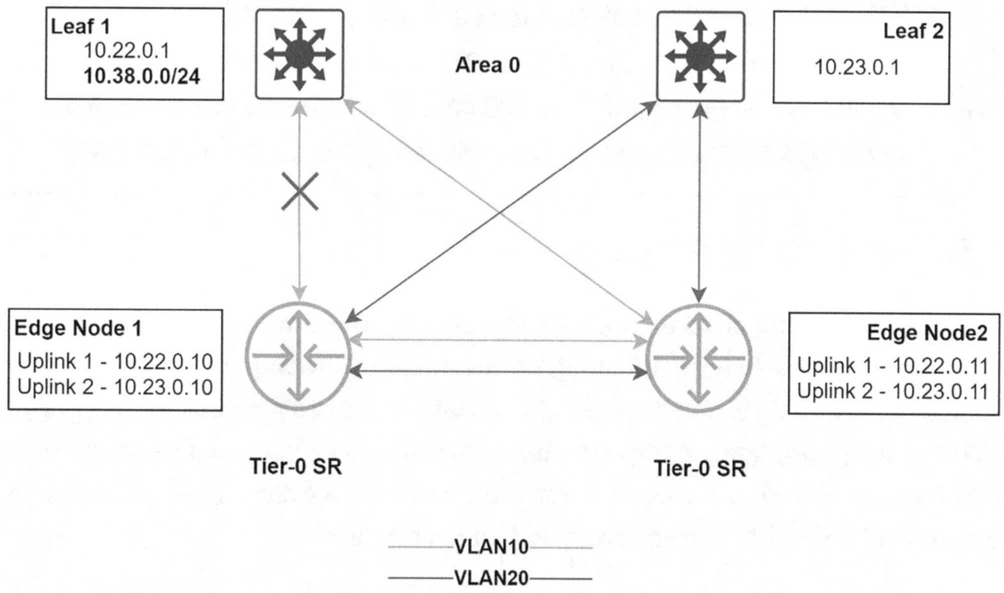

Figure 6-38. *Uplink from Edge 1 to Leaf 1 severed*

The output in Figure 6-39 is the routing table on Edge Node 1 after the connection was severed.

```
en01(tier0_sr)> get route

Flags: t0c - Tier0-Connected, t0s - Tier0-Static, b - BGP, o - OSPF
t0n - Tier0-NAT, t1s - Tier1-Static, t1c - Tier1-Connected,
t1n: Tier1-NAT, t1l: Tier1-LB VIP, t1ls: Tier1-LB SNAT,
t1d: Tier1-DNS FORWARDER, t1ipsec: Tier1-IPSec, isr: Inter-SR,
> - selected route, * - FIB route

o  > * 10.38.0.0/24 [110/20] via 10.23.0.11, uplink-287, 00:00:18
```

Figure 6-39. *Prefix 10.38.0.0/24 learned through Edge 2*

As can be seen, without Inter-SR iBGP routing, when the uplink between an Edge Node 1 and Leaf 1 failed, Edge Node 1 was still able to reach the destination prefix through the second Edge Node.

If the uplink from Edge Node 2 to Leaf 1 was to also fail, the prefix will then be removed from the routing table, as all adjacencies from Leaf 1 would have failed. Figure 6-39 depicts behavior for an OSPF broadcast topology; similar behavior will be seen with point-to-point topologies.

NSX-T and Static Routing

NSX-T supports the use of static routes for ingress and egress traffic. As a dynamic routing protocol is not being configured, static routes are also required on the Leaf Switches. Static routing is much more rigid in comparison to a dynamic routing protocol.

When configuring static routes, administrative distances can be set to prefer one static route over the other. If this is not set, the administrative distance is left as default and traffic will be load-balanced across both default routes.

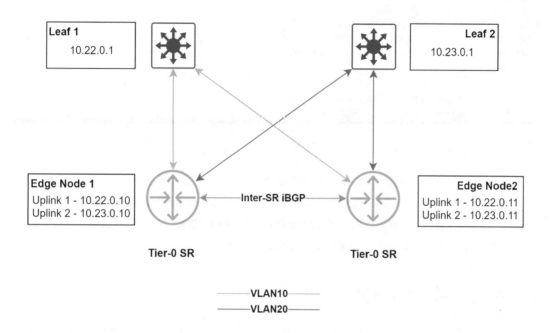

Figure 6-40. *Static routing with NSX-T*

Figure 6-40 looks very similar to the OSPF topology; however, there is an iBGP link between the two Edge Nodes, which assists with adjacency or uplink failures.

 Inter-SR iBGP routing must be enabled for the iBGP link between the Edge Nodes to be active. For details on this feature's functionality, refer to Chapter 5.

In this example, two default routes are created – one to each Leaf Switch, with equal administrative distance. Figure 6-41 displays the routing table on Edge Node 1.

```
en01(tier0_sr)> get route
Flags: t0c - Tier0-Connected, t0s - Tier0-Static, b - BGP, o - OSPF
t0n - Tier0-NAT, t1s - Tier1-Static, t1c - Tier1-Connected,
t1n: Tier1-NAT, t1l: Tier1-LB VIP, t1ls: Tier1-LB SNAT,
t1d: Tier1-DNS FORWARDER, t1ipsec: Tier1-IPSec, isr: Inter-SR,
> - selected route, * - FIB route


t0s> * 0.0.0.0/0 [1/0] via 10.22.0.1, uplink-284, 00:00:04
t0s> * 0.0.0.0/0 [1/0] via 10.23.0.1, uplink-287, 00:00:04
```

Figure 6-41. *Edge Node 1 routing table*

Figure 6-41 shows two default routes, both of equal cost and administrative distance, with each of the Leaf Switches as the next hop. This will allow outbound access to the physical network. A matching reciprocal route must exist on the Leaf Switches or elsewhere on the physical network for ingress traffic.

Deterministic Peering

Deterministic peering refers to the accurate configuration of Edge Node uplinks to the physical fabric. This means VLANs are only allowed over the uplinks they are required on, and direct mappings of Edge Node uplinks to physical NICs on the hosts. In NSX-T, it is also possible to configure **named teaming** policies to govern ingress and egress traffic to the physical network.

Designing and configuring deterministic peering is good practice, as it simplifies any troubleshooting and ensures administrators are aware of traffic flow in their environment.

It is due to this reason that any form of link aggregation protocol or vPC to the hypervisor is not recommended. If any form of link aggregation is configured, the peering cannot be deterministic, and as a result the traffic will likely be load-balanced across several links.

 If configuring any form of link aggregation protocol or vPC, bidirectional forwarding detection (BFD) to the physical fabric from the Edge Nodes is not supported.

Named teaming in NSX-T requires the configuration of:

1. Additional teamings in the uplink profile

2. Linking the additional teamings to a Transport Zone

3. Attaching segments to the Transport Zone referenced in step 2

4. Using these segments as uplink interfaces on a Tier-0 gateway

To make the preceding steps clearer, the process will be demonstrated in the following section.

Uplink Profile

To begin, either edit an existing uplink profile or create a new one. This uplink profile will be attached to the Edge Nodes. Figure 6-42 is an example of an existing uplink profile being edited.

Edit Uplink Profile - uplink-profile-66   ⑦ ✕

Name*	uplink-profile-66
Description	

LAGs

+ ADD   🗑 DELETE

☐	Name*	LACP Mode	LACP Load Balancing*	Uplinks*	LACP Time Out
			No LAGs found		

Teamings

+ ADD   ≡ CLONE   🗑 DELETE

☐	Name*	Teaming Policy*	Active Uplinks*	Standby Uplinks
☐	[Default Teaming]	Load Balance Source	uplink1,uplink2	
☐	uplink1-named-teaming-policy	Failover Order	uplink1	
☐	uplink2-named-teaming-policy	Failover Order	uplink2	

Active uplinks and Standby uplinks are user defined labels. These labels will be used to associate with the Physical NICs while adding Transport Nodes.

Transport VLAN	66	⌃⌄
MTU ❶	9000	⌃⌄

Figure 6-42. *Named teaming uplink profile*

Notice in Figure 6-42, there are two additional teamings for uplink 1 and uplink 2. Both have different active uplinks; this is specifying which uplink on the VDS the teaming policy should use.

The Edge Nodes in this example already have the uplink profile attached. This will not be covered; however, ensure the profile that was created is attached to the Edge Nodes.

The names of these teamings will be required in the next step; copying them to a text file or keeping the names handy will be beneficial.

Transport Zone

After the uplink profile has been modified, the VLAN Transport Zone that is attached to the Edge Nodes must be modified or a new one created and attached to the Edge Nodes. This allows segments that are created and attached to this Transport Zone to utilize the named teaming policies.

Figure 6-43 displays an existing Transport Zone that is used specifically for Edge uplink segments being modified.

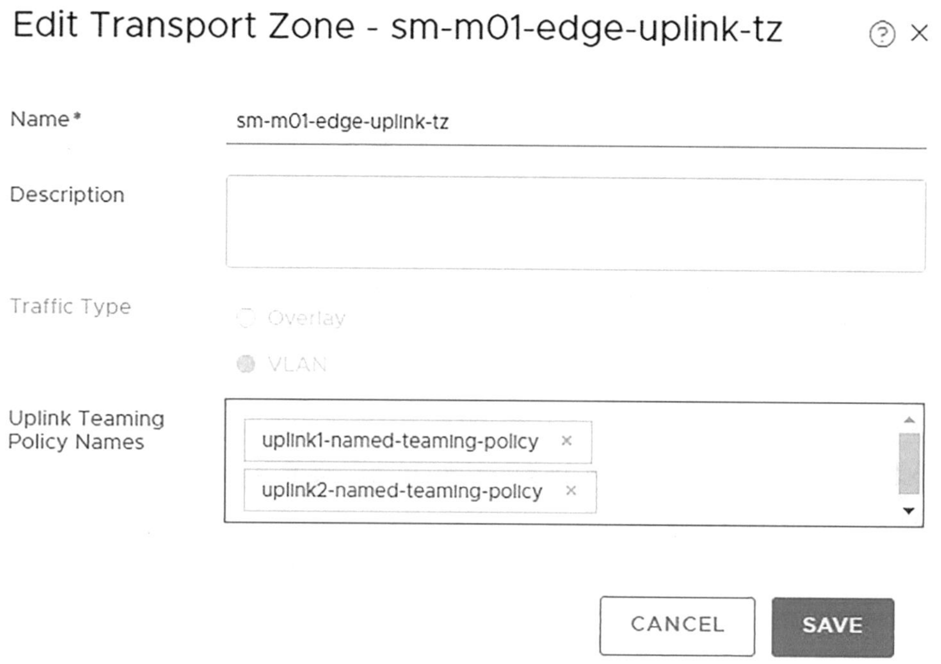

Edit Transport Zone - sm-m01-edge-uplink-tz ⑦ ×

Name *	sm-m01-edge-uplink-tz
Description	
Traffic Type	○ Overlay
	● VLAN
Uplink Teaming Policy Names	uplink1-named-teaming-policy ×
	uplink2-named-teaming-policy ×

CANCEL   SAVE

Figure 6-43. *Edge uplink Transport Zone*

Figure 6-43 shows the two teamings that were created in the previous step, now mapped to the Transport Zone.

Segments

Segments that are created and attached to the Edge uplink Transport Zone can now utilize named teaming policies. Figure 6-44 shows the configuration of a segment that will utilize a named teaming policy.

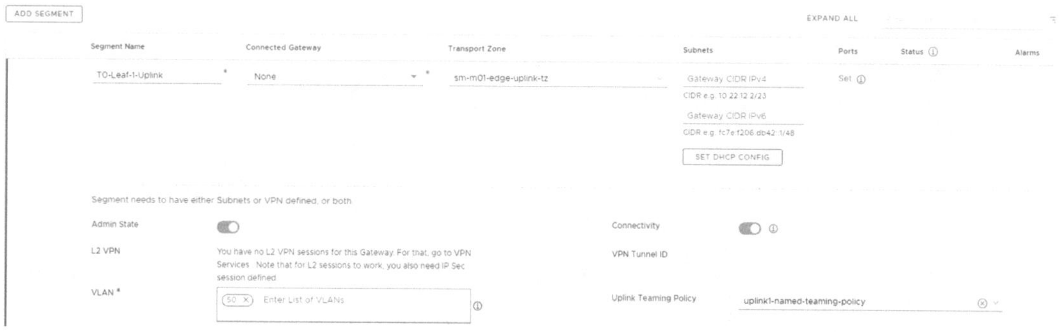

Figure 6-44. *Creating a Tier-0 uplink segment*

The following settings ensure traffic utilizing this segment will traverse uplink 1:

- **Transport Zone:** The segment is attached to the Transport Zone in Figure 6-43.

- **Uplink Teaming Policy:** One of the teamings that was created in the first step has been attached to the segment.

- **VLAN:** A specific VLAN is being tagged on this segment.

Tier-0 Interface Creation

The final step is to create an interface using the segment created in Figure 6-44. Remember, using this segment ensures that traffic leaving this Tier-0 interface egresses the Edge Node on a specific uplink.

 When an uplink profile is applied to an Edge Node, the Edge uplinks are mapped to a VDS port group if an Edge VM is deployed or a pNIC if a Bare Metal Edge is deployed.

Figure 6-45 shows an interface on the Tier-0 being created and being attached to the segment that was created in the previous step.

Figure 6-45. *Tier-0 interface creation*

Once all these configuration steps have been completed, traffic and peering from the Edge Node will be deterministic.

Bidirectional Forwarding Detection (BFD)

BFD was covered in Chapter 5, however, was specific to the NSX-T fabric. This section will focus on BFD capabilities from NSX-T to the physical network.

Currently, NSX-T supports the configuration of BFD in conjunction with BGP, OSPF, and static routes. It makes sense to configure BFD as it will allow for quicker failure detection, which means quicker reconvergence of the network. BFD sessions can be configured on each uplink interface from the Tier-0 gateway to an available next hop or peer. As an example, a Tier-0 with four uplinks can have four BFD sessions to the physical network.

Currently, NSX-T supports the following BFD timers:

- **Edge VM:** Minimum 500ms TX/RX

- **Bare Metal:** Minimum 50ms TX/RX

Unicast Reverse Path Forwarding (uRPF)

uRPF is not specific to NSX-T and is configurable on most, if not all, enterprise-grade infrastructure. uRPF is a security mechanism that is often used to assist in mitigating malicious traffic, namely, spoofed addresses on the network.

Typically, uRPF is configurable in two modes:

- Strict mode

- Loose mode

If neither of these modes are configured, then uRPF is disabled, which is the default configuration on most physical fabric. When discussing the uRPF implementation in NSX-T, currently two options are available:

- Strict Mode

- None

NSX-T currently does not have support for loose mode; however, it may be included in future versions of the product.

This topic will be broken down into two parts to display uRPF behavior:

- Active-Active topology, with and without ECMP

- Active-Standby topology, with and without ECMP

uRPF in an Active-Active Topology

A common misconception when deploying a Tier-0 gateway in Active-Active with ECMP enabled is that uRPF should be disabled. The rationale behind this thought is, as routing and return traffic will likely be asymmetric, legitimate packets may be dropped due to uRPF.

However, this is not entirely accurate; when a packet arrives on an interface, uRPF (strict) performs two checks, which are as follows:

- The prefix exists in the forwarding table.

- The prefix/destination address is reachable via the interface the packet was received on.

If both conditions are satisfied, the packet is not dropped, the remainder of the Logical Routing operation is executed, and the packet is sent to its destination. The following sections will demonstrate uRPF behavior with and without ECMP in an Active-Active topology.

ECMP Enabled

This section will have two examples: the first is a simple ECMP deployment, and the second introduces a preferred path configured in NSX-T. This is to highlight the difference in behavior when there is true asymmetric routing.

All Paths Equal

Figure 6-46 displays communication from a virtual machine that resides outside of an NSX-T environment to a virtual machine sitting on an NSX-T segment attached to a Tier-0 gateway.

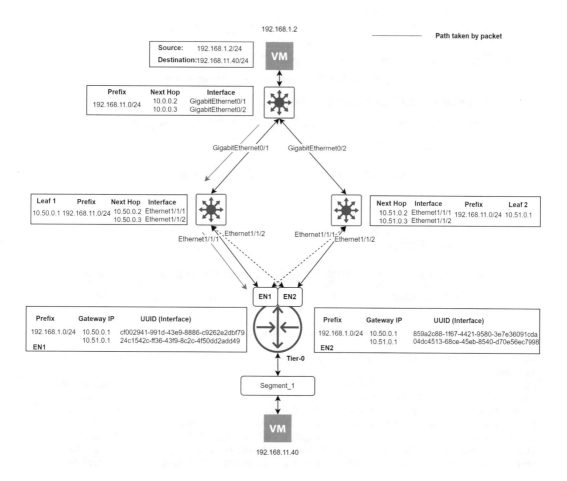

Figure 6-46. *Active-Active with ECMP and uRPF strict*

The following steps are a breakdown of the diagram in Figure 6-46:

1. VM (192.168.1.2) sends a packet to VM (192.168.11.40). The packet arrives at the switch, which determines there are two paths to the prefix, via GigabitEthernet0/1 and GigabitEthernet0/2. The switch uses a hashing algorithm to pick an egress interface and forwards the packet. In this example, the path chosen is through Leaf 1.

2. The packet arrives at the next hop, Leaf 1. The switch inspects the packet and determines there are two paths to the prefix. Ethernet1/1/1 and Ethernet1/1/2 are plumbed into EN1 and EN2, respectively. Once again, a hashing algorithm is used; the egress interface to reach the destination is selected. In this example Ethernet1/1/1, which is connected to EN 1, is selected.

3. The packet arrives on the EN1 uplink interface (cf002941-991d-43e9-8886-c9262e2dbf79), and as the packet arrives, uRPF performs its checks. It determines that the prefix is in the forwarding table, and the prefix is reachable using this uplink interface and permits the packet.

   The uRPF checks can be verified manually using the following steps:

   a. Log in to the respective edge, in this case EN1, using a SSH client such as PuTTy.

   b. Issue the command to get logical-routers to identify the Tier-0 SR vrf number.

```
en1> get logical-routers
Sun Aug 01 2021 UTC 00:36:53.390
Logical Router
UUID                                      VRF  LR-ID Name          Type                         Ports  Neighbors
736a80e3-23f6-5a2d-81d6-bbefb2786666   0    0                   TUNNEL                        4      14/5000
b4338cdd-b628-47cd-8b6f-5f293aac2927   2    1027  SR-t1-gw01    SERVICE_ROUTER_TIER1          5      2/50000
35c9127b-ceb4-469b-aef5-09f52163a693   3    4     DR-t1-gw01    DISTRIBUTED_ROUTER_TIER1      6      0/50000
8a0762ce-e31a-4447-9379-8a0d36c3c65c   4    8193  DR-t0-gw01    DISTRIBUTED_ROUTER_TIER0      6      1/50000
2ff833ab-b5ac-4840-beb6-bd873c0664a5   5    9226  SR-t0-gw01    SERVICE_ROUTER_TIER0          7      3/50000
b9ba5b04-9055-42cb-897e-0242307393c2   7    3075  DR-Tier-1-a-a DISTRIBUTED_ROUTER_TIER1      6      2/50000
```

Figure 6-47. *Identifying the Tier-0 SR*

c. Based on the output in Figure 6-47, vrf 5 is the Tier-0 SR. Now issue the command vrf 5, followed by get route 192.168.1.0/24 (source prefix of the packet).

d. Figure 6-48 shows that there is a matching entry in the global routing table for the prefix.

```
en1(tier0_sr)> get route 192.168.1.0/24
Flags: t0c - Tier0-Connected, t0s - Tier0-Static, b - BGP, o - OSPF
t0n - Tier0-NAT, t1s - Tier1-Static, t1c - Tier1-Connected,
t1n: Tier1-NAT, t1l: Tier1-LB VIP, t1ls: Tier1-LB SNAT,
t1d: Tier1-DNS FORWARDER, t1ipsec: Tier1-IPSec, isr: Inter-SR,
> - selected route, * - FIB route
Total number of routes: 1
b  > * 192.168.1.0/24 [20/0] via 10.50.0.1, uplink-290, 00:01:44
b  > * 192.168.1.0/24 [20/0] via 10.51.0.1, uplink-301, 00:01:44
```

Figure 6-48. *Checking the global routing table for the prefix*

e. Next, it needs to confirm that the prefix is reachable on interface cf002941-991d-43e9-8886-c9262e2dbf79.

f. This can be verified by issuing the command get forwarding 192.168.1.0/24. Based on the output, the prefix is reachable from EN1's uplink interface.

```
en1(tier0_sr)> get forwarding 192.168.1.0/24
Logical Router
UUID                                          VRF       LR-ID  Name                    Type
2ff833ab-b5ac-4840-beb6-bd873c0664a5    5       9226  SR-sm-edge-cl01-t0-gw01  SERVICE_ROUTER_TIER0
IPv4 Forwarding Table
IP Prefix            Gateway IP            Type   UUID                                       Gateway MAC
192.168.1.0/24       10.50.0.1            route   cf002941-991d-43e9-8886-c9262e2dbf79       cc:4e:24:b7:bd:14
                     10.51.0.1                    24c1542c-ff36-43f9-8c2c-4f50dd2add49       cc:4e:24:b7:bd:18
```

Figure 6-49. *Checking the forwarding table for the prefix and interface*

4. Once the checks are successfully completed, the packet is forwarded as normal.

The example in Figure 6-49 is the expected behavior when there are no preferred paths or any form of route steering configured in NSX-T. The next example will demonstrate the same topology with a preferred path.

Preferred Path

This example will use the same topology used in Figure 6-46; however, this time a preferred path for egressing NSX-T is defined. The goal of this example is to demonstrate the impact of a packet being received on an interface that is not preferred or expected in the routing and forwarding table. It is also worth mentioning that this is only one example of asymmetric routing. There are many other reasons for asymmetric routing, such as a prefix only being advertised from one of two Leaf Switches.

Figure 6-50 shows the preferred path to prefix 192.168.1.0/24 is through the EN1 uplink connected to Leaf 1. However, in this scenario, the physical network returns the packet to uplink 1 on EN2, which is not the preferred path.

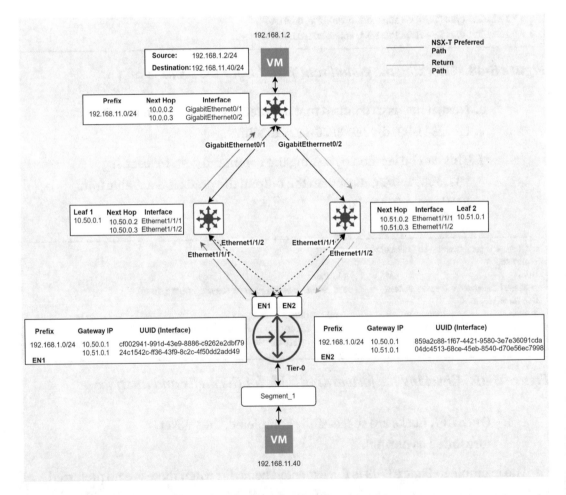

Figure 6-50. *Active-Active topology with a preferred path*

This example will not cover the steps included in the previous example; it will focus on the behavior with the introduction of preferred paths. The following summary details the scenario in Figure 6-50:

- Each Edge is configured with two uplinks:
  - Uplink 1 to Leaf 1 (10.50.0.1)
  - Uplink 2 to Leaf 2 (10.51.0.1)
- Tier-0 gateway configuration:
  - HA mode: Active-Active
  - Prefix list, any, permit (NSX-T)
  - Route-map, local preference set to 110, prefix list as match criteria on the Tier-0 gateway
  - Route-map attached to BGP neighbor 10.50.0.1 (Leaf 1)
- Physical network directing all traffic through 10.51.0.1 (Leaf 2)

Figure 6-51 demonstrates the impact of applying the route-map to BGP neighbor 10.50.0.1. Notice the second path has been removed from the forwarding table, as the path through Leaf 1 is preferred.

```
en1(tier0_sr)> get forwarding 192.168.1.0/24
Logical Router
UUID                                     VRF     LR-ID  Name                    Type
2ff833ab-b5ac-4840-beb6-bd873c0664a5     5       9226   SR-sm-edge-cl01-t0-gw01 SERVICE_ROUTER_TIER0
IPv4 Forwarding Table
IP Prefix            Gateway IP           Type    UUID                                       Gateway MAC
192.168.1.0/24       10.50.0.1            route   cf002941-991d-43e9-8886-c9262e2dbf79       cc:4e:24:b7:bd:14
```

Figure 6-51. *Single path available to the prefix in the forwarding table on EN1*

The same command run on EN2 displays identical behavior.

```
en2(tier0_sr)> get forwarding 192.168.1.0/24
Logical Router
UUID                                           VRF  LR-ID  Name                              Type
53df787a-e4f2-49fb-806f-dde086f3edf7  6   1025  SR-sm-edge-cl01-t0-gw01        SERVICE_ROUTER_TIER0
IPv4 Forwarding Table
IP Prefix          Gateway IP             Type     UUID                                          Gateway MAC
192.168.1.0/24   10.50.0.1             route    859a2c88-1f67-4421-9580-3e7e36091cda  cc:4e:24:b7:bd:14
```

Figure 6-52. *Forwarding table on EN2*

To see that the path still exists, issue the command get bgp ipv4 | find
192.168.1.0. Figure 6-53 displays that both paths still exist; however, the path through
10.50.0.1 has a higher preference; therefore, it is the preferred path and is the path
installed into both the forwarding and routing tables.

```
en1(tier0_sr)> get bgp ipv4 | find 192.168.1.0
   Network                    Next Hop            Metric  LocPrf Weight  Path
   192.168.10.0/24          10.51.0.1             0        100     0        65002 i
 > 192.168.10.0/24          10.50.0.1             0        110     0        65002 i
```

Figure 6-53. *BGP prefix table*

Now that the preferred path has been identified in NSX-T, the behavior of uRPF in
this asymmetric topology can be verified. With this current configuration, a packet being
sent from the VM at IP address 192.168.1.2 will be dropped.

```
C:\Users\>tracert 192.168.11.40
Tracing route 192.168.11.40
over a maximum of 30 hops:
  1     21 ms     21 ms     19 ms  192.168.1.1
  3     18 ms     19 ms     18 ms  11.0.0.6
  4      *         *         *      Request timed out.
  5      *         *         *      Request timed out.

*the remainder of the traceroute output has been omitted
```

Figure 6-54. *Trace route from VM with IP 192.168.1.2*

The output from the trace route command shows:

- The VM with IP address 192.168.1.2 sending the packet to its local gateway (192.168.1.1), which is the layer 3 switch in the diagram

- The switch checks its routing table and determines the packet should be forwarded to the next hop (11.0.0.6 – GigabitEthernet0/2 – Leaf 2).

- Leaf 2 receives the packet and checks its routing table and has two available equal cost paths.

  - Path 1: EN1 uplink 2

  - Path 2: EN2 uplink 2

- Leaf 2 uses a hashing algorithm to select a path and forwards the packet.

- The packet arrives at the next hop; in this example, it arrives on EN2 uplink 2. The uRPF check fails one of the conditions:

  - *The prefix/destination address is reachable via the interface the packet was received on.*

- Due to this failure, uRPF drops the packet. Therefore, the trace route command stops at 11.0.0.6.

The packet capture in Figure 6-55 is from uplink interface 04dc4513-68ce-45eb-8540-d70e56ec7998 on EN2. This can be obtained by running the following command on EN2.

```
en2> start capture interface 04dc4513-68ce-45eb-8540-d70e56ec7998 direction input file en2u2.pcap
Capture to file initiated, enter Ctrl-C to terminate
5 packets captured
5 packets received by filter
0 packets dropped by kernel
```

Figure 6-55. *Generating packet capture on EN2*

Figure 6-56 is the WireShark display of the captured output. It shows the packet arriving on EN2 uplink interface.

Source	Destination	Protocol
192.168.1.2	192.168.11.40	ICMP

Figure 6-56. *Packet capture on EN2 uplink 2*

The final check can be done on the Edge Node in a PuTTy session. The output in Figure 6-57 shows the command used and that there are dropped packets due to RPF checks.

```
en2> get logical-router interface  04dc4513-68ce-45eb-8540-d70e56ec7998 | json
{
  "access_vlan": "untagged",
  "admin": "up",
  "ifuuid": "04dc4513-68ce-45eb-8540-d70e56ec7998",
  "internal_operation": "up",
  "ipns": [
    "10.51.0.3/24"
  ],
  "mac": "00:50:56:98:ee:c7",
  "mtu": 9000,
  "name": "en02uplink2",
  "stats": {
    "rx_bytes": 11492061,
    "rx_drop_dst_unsupported": 6288,
    "rx_drop_rpf_check": 4177,
  },
*The above output is a snippet of the full output.
```

Figure 6-57. *RPF check dropping packets on EN2*

In this scenario, changing the interface from uRPF strict to none will allow traffic to pass. This configuration is only recommended if there are true asymmetric routing issues; doing so is generally considered risky in terms of security.

ECMP Disabled

This section will focus on the effects of disabling ECMP in an Active-Active topology with uRPF configured in strict mode. The issue that surfaces here is the equivalent of having a preferred path configured.

The Edge Nodes still have all their peers established, the same as in the previous example. BGP advertises the 192.168.11.0/24 prefix to both Leaf Switches. The physical network assumes the prefix is reachable through both Leaf Switches and all four Edge uplink interfaces.

Once ECMP is disabled, the Edge Nodes install a single path and next hop for prefix 192.168.1.0/24 into the routing table. Figure 6-58 displays the EN1 forwarding table. Notice there is only one entry in the forwarding table.

```
en1(tier0_sr)> get forwarding | find 192.168.1.0

192.168.1.0/24    10.50.0.1        route     6f8750f1-02ed-48ec-a502-cbf76f6fad9b   cc:4e:24:b7:bd.14
```

Figure 6-58. *RPF check dropping packets on EN2*

Figure 6-59 is routing table on EN1; only a single entry for the prefix exists. As you can see, the effects of having ECMP disabled are very similar to having a preferred path.

```
en1(tier0_sr)> get route 192.168.1.0

Flags: t0c - Tier0-Connected, t0s - Tier0-Static, b - BGP,
t0n - Tier0-NAT, t1s - Tier1-Static, t1c - Tier1-Connected,
t1n: Tier1-NAT, t1l: Tier1-LB VIP, t1ls: Tier1-LB SNAT,
t1d: Tier1-DNS FORWARDER, t1ipsec: Tier1-IPSec, isr: Inter-SR,
> - selected route, * - FIB route
Total number of routes: 1

b  > * 192.168.1.0/24 [20/2] via 10.50.0.1, uplink-331, 00:09:27
```

Figure 6-59. *EN1 routing table*

Figure 6-60 is an updated topology diagram; it highlights the potential paths the packet could take for both egress and ingress for the Edge Nodes.

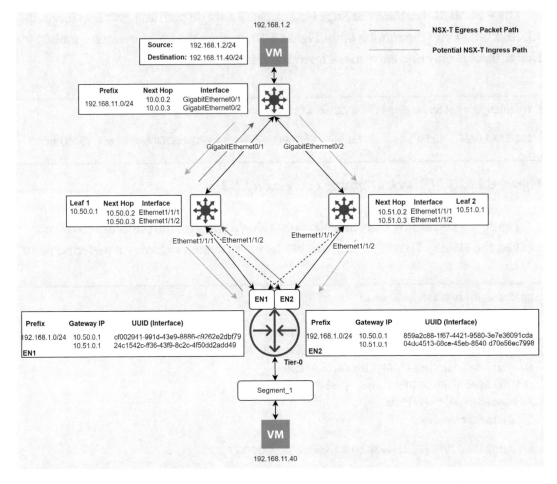

Figure 6-60. *Forwarding paths in Active-Active with ECMP disabled*

The following is a summary of Figure 6-60:

- EN1 and EN2 have a single routing and forwarding table entry to reach prefix 192.168.1.0/24, that is, via Leaf 1 (10.50.0.1).

- The physical network is still peered with all uplink interfaces of Tier-0 and thinks the prefix 192.168.11.0/24 is available through all uplinks. This is because the prefix is still being advertised across all uplinks to each peer.

- Depending on the path selected, the packet may arrive at VM with the IP address 192.168.11.40; however, it is not guaranteed.

- If the path taken is through Leaf 2, the packet will be discarded once forwarded to the EN1 or EN2 uplink interface. Once again, this is because uRPF is discarding the packets for not meeting both conditions:

  - It passes the routing table check.

  - The source prefix of 192.168.1.0/24 is not reachable via these interfaces.

To overcome this scenario, there are two options:

1. **Enable ECMP:** Enabling ECMP will install multiple paths into both the routing and forwarding tables. If all configuration is completed correctly, it will ensure the uRPF check passes, and therefore will not discard the packet.

2. **Disable uRPF on the interfaces:** With uRPF disabled, the checks are not performed, and the packets will pass.

uRPF in an Active-Standby Topology

ECMP Enabled

When configuring an Active-Standby Tier-0 gateway, all Edge Node uplinks are still active and have BGP peerings established with the physical network. To avoid packets being forwarded to the standby Edge, NSX-T automatically prepends the AS-PATH to the physical network. In doing so, the physical network prefers the path through the active edge, and no packets ingress into NSX-T through the standby Edge.

Figure 6-61 is the topology diagram that will be discussed in this section. Notice EN2 has been grayed out; this is to highlight that it is the standby Edge but still has active peerings. The available paths have been highlighted to indicate EN1 is the active Edge.

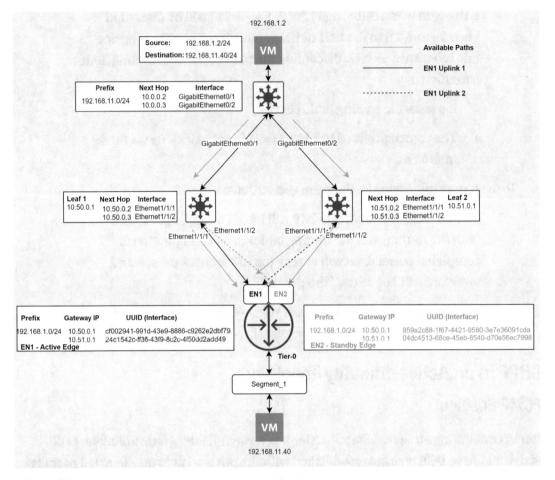

Figure 6-61. *Tier-0 Active-Standby topology*

The following is a summary of Figure 6-61:

- EN1 is the active Edge Node, with two uplinks, one to each Leaf Switch.

- EN2 is the standby Edge Node.

- The physical network has two paths into EN1, through each Leaf Switch.

- EN1 has two paths to egress to the physical network; this is with ECMP enabled.

- Local preference and AS-PATH prepend are automatically configured to steer ingress and egress traffic. Refer to the BGP section earlier in this chapter for more details.

All Paths Equal

The behavior of this scenario is identical to the "All Paths Equal" section detailed under the Active-Active topology. Administrators will need to remember that there is only a single Edge forwarding and receiving packets; outside of this, ECMP behavior is the same.

Preferred Path

Because traffic steering is done automatically when the Active-Standby Tier-0 is configured, the concerns for asymmetric traffic are like an Active-Active Tier-0 gateway. There are still two active paths through the active Edge Node; if there is asymmetric routing and a path is preferred over the other, uRPF will discard the traffic, just as it was demonstrated with an Active-Active Tier-0.

The principles highlighted in the previous sections still apply, those being:

- The prefix must exist in the routing table.

- The prefix must be reachable via the interface the packet was received on.

Failing to meet both these conditions will result in uRPF discarding the packet. There are two options to overcome this:

1. Disable uRPF on the Edge interfaces.

2. Resolve the asymmetric routing issues; however, this is not always possible.

ECMP Disabled

The behavior of an Active-Standby Tier-0 gateway with ECMP disabled is the same as an Active-Active Tier-0 gateway. The only difference is there is a single Edge Node performing routing functions. The active Edge Node installs a single entry into the routing and forwarding table. Once again, the behavior is very similar to having a preferred path. The Edge Node sends egress packets to Leaf 1, as that is the only available next hop for the prefix 192.168.1.0/24.

However, the physical network has multiple paths to reach 192.168.11.0/24. These paths are through both uplink interfaces of EN1 and EN2; however, the path through EN2 is longer. If a packet arrives through Leaf 2 on the second uplink interface of EN1, uRPF will discard the packet.

To overcome this scenario, there are two options:

1. **Enable ECMP:** Enabling ECMP will install multiple paths into both the routing and forwarding tables. If all configuration is completed correctly, it will ensure the uRPF check passes and therefore will not discard the packet.

2. **Disable uRPF on the interfaces:** With uRPF disabled, the checks are not performed, and the packets will pass.

Summary

This chapter covered datacenter routing topics such as routing protocols, deterministic peering, BFD, and uRPF. Readers should now be comfortable with NSX-T Logical Routing functionality and how the Edge Nodes communicate with the physical network. This book has covered the fundamentals of Logical Routing in NSX-T, readers should now be comfortable in identifying, configuring and demonstrating Logical Routing concepts. The knowledge gained from this book will allow readers to understand and implement various solutions within their own environments.

Index

A

Active-active portgroup
    wiring, 188
Active-active topology, 276, 280, 284, 289
Active-active uplink
    configuration, 187
Active-standby uplink configuration,
    183, 184
Active/unused uplink
    configuration, 176–178
Autonomous System
    Number (ASN), 231

B

Bare Metal edge node placement, 54,
    163, 197
Bare Metal edge node wiring
    16 DPDK Fastpath
        interfaces, 189
    FP-ETH1 down, 195
    host transport node, 194
    leaf 1 ARP entry after link
        failure, 195
    leaf switch ARP entry, 194
    multi-TEP configuration, 190, 191
    physical NIC failure, 193–196
    port mappings, 192
    TEP addresses, 193
    TEP failover, 197
    TEP interfaces, 192

uplink 1 failure testing, 196
    visual representation, 190
Bidirectional forwarding detection
    (BFD), 275
    external peers, 209
    NSX-T fabric
        edge node sessions, 210–212
        host transport nodes sessions,
            212, 213
        sessions, 211
        TEP interfaces, 210
        timers, 210
        tunnel endpoints, 210
    physical network
        fabric, 213
Border gateway protocol (BGP)
    adoption, 228, 229
    NSX-T and
        eBGP (see External border gateway
            protocol (eBGP))
        flavors, 231
        iBGP (see Internal border gateway
            protocol (iBGP))
        reasons, 230
    policy control, 257
    supported topologies, 257
Broadcast network
    type, 258–260

C

Central control plane (CCP), 10, 11

© Shashank Mohan 2022
S. Mohan, *NSX-T Logical Routing*, https://doi.org/10.1007/978-1-4842-7458-3

O

Printed in the United States
by Baker & Taylor Publisher Services